Jo Cox
More in Common

Foreword by Kim Leadbeater

Brendan Cox

THE **JO COX** FOUNDATION

TWO ROADS

First published in Great Britain in 2017 by Two Roads
An Imprint of John Murray Press
An Hachette UK company

This paperback edition published in 2021

1

A CIP catalogue record for this title is available from the British Library

Paperback ISBN 978 1 473 65920 9
eBook ISBN 978 1 473 65921 6
Audio Digital Download 978 1 473 66068 7

Typeset in Celeste by Palimpsest Book Production Ltd, Falkirk, Stirlingshire

Printed and bound by Clays Ltd, Elcograf S.p.A.

John Murray policy is to use papers that are natural, renewable and
recyclable products and made from wood grown in sustainable forests.
The logging and manufacturing processes are expected to conform to the
environmental regulations of the country of origin.

Two Roads
Carmelite House
50 Victoria Embankment
London EC4Y 0DZ

www.tworoadsbooks.com

For Lejla and Cuillin

Contents

Foreword

It's difficult for me for me to read this book. Even though it's five years since my sister was murdered, I still can't believe it. I'm not in denial – I know what happened – but I just can't process the horror of the events of 16th June 2016 or what has happened to my life since that day.

But I know that it is important for Jo's story to be told – so it can inspire as many people as possible to be the change that they want to see in the world and to feel empowered to take action to make a difference in the same way she did.

I always knew how great Jo was (although I was also very aware of how annoying she could be) but I didn't fully appreciate the inspirational effect and profound impact she had on the lives of so many people. Whether it was convincing young children in Batley and Spen that they could be anything they want to be and do anything they want to do with their lives, passionately encouraging women locally and nationally to stand for public office, or fighting for the rights of people around the world who were unable to do so for themselves, Jo touched many lives in many ways.

When she was killed, she was an MP, but she was first and foremost a humanitarian who fought for justice, equality and for the rights of those less fortunate than herself. After working in the voluntary sector for over 15 years, Jo moved into politics in the UK, but her main objective remained the same – to make a difference to the lives of those around her – and from Bosnia to Batley and Syria to the Spen Valley, this is what she did. She knew how lucky we had been in life to have two wonderful parents who loved us unconditionally, and to have each other, along with a wide network of friends and family, enough food to fill our bellies and a safe environment in which to live. Sadly, through her humanitarian work, she saw many people who were not so fortunate.

Jo and I were really lucky to have a brilliant childhood. We were the best of friends and were brought up in a loving home with a Mum and Dad who always made us feel loved and valued and instilled in us a core set of values and beliefs. Our parents taught us to treat *everyone* with respect, compassion and kindness, and to try and empathise with the lives of others.

We learned simple principles based around hard work, respect, equality, sometimes agreeing to disagree, compromising and treating other people how you would wish to be treated, and focusing on inner happiness, not just material success and money. But these things weren't drilled into us – more inherently included as part of everyday life, and they stayed with us both through our adult lives. It was no surprise, then, that Jo went on to pursue a career and a life based on these principles.

These values live on through the work of The Jo Cox Foundation and I am hugely proud to be a part of this. Indeed, I view it as my most important role, second only to that of being the best Auntie I can possibly be to Jo's amazing children, Cuillin and Lejla. They were Jo's world and are her greatest and most important legacy. They have her spark, her energy and her compassion, along with her beautiful smile. And I will do everything I can to keep their lives full of fun, love and adventures in the way that I know Jo would want me to.

I hope this book gives you a feeling for the kind of person Jo was and, in a world which sadly still faces many challenges, may even inspire you to do something good in your community or to find out more about the work of The Jo Cox Foundation. I think about Jo every single day and I can't see that ever changing. I work hard to channel the anger and despair I sometimes feel into my work at The Jo Cox Foundation and by remembering the principle she gave us of having 'more in common than that which divides us.'

Kim Leadbeater MBE
Ambassador and Director of More in Common
Batley and Spen

A Note from Brendan Cox

I started writing within days of Jo's murder and have continued ever since. I began after Julia Samuel, the child psychologist I was drawing advice from like a sponge, advised me to write things down. She said that in years to come the kids will want to know the details of what happened – how they responded, how they felt, what we did.

I didn't set out to write a book and there are things in my diary that will remain for ever between the kids and me. But in writing things down, I have also found it has helped me process what has happened. As Jo would vouch, I often find it hard to talk about how I feel, but I know how important it is not just to carry on as if nothing has happened. So I wrote more and more as a way of forcing myself to confront reality.

A few months after Jo's murder various people started suggesting I write a book about Jo; some were friends who wanted her story told, others were strangers who wanted to learn more about her – people who felt she stood for something.

At the same time I was reading through Jo's diaries. It helped me to hear her in her own voice. She was a sporadic diary-keeper and tended to write either when she was travelling or when she was feeling down and needed to try and straighten out her head. As a result Jo's writing varies between frenetic and introspective, life-affirming and slightly unsettling. I knew her diaries were a treasure trove of insight that would help me fill the gaps and really give Jo her voice, if only I could bring myself to put pen to paper.

In the end I decided to write for four reasons. Firstly, to help me process my own emotions. I knew an external deadline would force me to take the time I should over this, otherwise the pain it involved would mean I would constantly find excuses to push it down my 'To Do' list and, as a result, that pain would sit there unprocessed.

Secondly to capture a set of stories for the kids about their mum. When they read this book, I hope it will help bring alive the mum who now resides in their heads and hearts.

Thirdly, I want to tell Jo's story. In doing so, I don't want to pretend that she was perfect, a modern-day saint; she wasn't. When I spoke at her funeral I said – to knowing nods from friends, former flatmates and family – that she could be the most annoying person in the world to live with. But even with all of her human imperfections, her story is hugely important. A woman from a working-class family who fulfilled her dreams; a woman who was proud of where she came from and used that confidence in her roots to embrace the world; a woman who struggled with self-doubt but, despite this, drove herself and others forward. Above all, Jo's life is a story of supreme and unyielding empathy. No matter how long I live, I know I will never come close to Jo's kindness and compassion, but her example will always make me better. I hope it will inspire others to be their best selves, to step forward when all you want to do is step back, to live life with a passion.

Finally, I wrote this book because I want to continue Jo's fight. For decency, tolerance, fair play, the best of British values. Her killing was meant to set back this fight. It has already failed, but there is a wider struggle at hand. It's not about party politics, it's between those who want to bring communities together to take on the challenges that face society and those who seek to turn us against each other to distract from them. Trump, Le Pen and others epitomise this, but no country is immune.

I would have been unable to write this book without my friend and collaborator Don McRae. Don couldn't have been a better writing partner, combining Jo-like levels of empathy with dedication and professionalism. He helped me find the shape and structure for many of the thoughts and memories it contains; he also helped me research the gaps in my memory, talking in detail to Jo's family and friends. Don is a brilliant writer and it was an honour to work with him. My kids already miss his regular visits to the boat.

* * *

When I spoke in court, I said that Jo's killing was intended to silence a voice and what an irony it was that, instead, it had allowed millions of others to hear it. This book is part of that mission. Thank you for reading it.

Brendan Cox
May 2017

Jo Cox
More in Common

1

Happiness

Four days before we lost Jo to hatred and savagery, she had looked happier and more alive than ever. The river below us glinted in the pale sunshine as we relaxed over the weekend at our cottage on the borders between England and Wales.

It was a serene Sunday morning and I was stretched out in the hammock. I had damaged my foot two days earlier, and it was propped up for comfort. Jo kept zipping up from working in the garden she loved, to see me or the kids. Whenever she nudged my foot by mistake it felt like a hammer hitting my swollen ankle.

'Sorry, Coxy,' Jo said, every time. 'I keep forgetting.'

The Friday before, back in London, I'd spent the day looking after Lejla and we'd gone to pick up Cuillin from his reception class. On the way back to our boat on the Thames, where we had lived for five years, I was mucking around as usual with the kids. We were playing monsters. I was the monster and they screamed gleefully while I chased them.

They were so used to Jo and me climbing mountains, caving, cycling, swimming and canoeing that Cuillin and Lejla were startled suddenly to see their dad lying on the ground. Mid-chase I had turned my ankle and fallen. I thought I might have broken it as I felt something snap.

Cuillin and Lejla helped me lift my bike which I had left against the railing. At least I could lean on the handlebars. The kids, amused by my hopping, laughed again.

Jo was about to get home after a night away in Yorkshire. As the Labour MP for Batley and Spen – where she had grown up – she had been busy with a mixture of campaigning for the UK to remain within the EU and the work she loved above all: helping her constituents with their problems. She always returned tired but full of stories and ideas for what else she could do to make a difference.

When she saw me stretched out on the sofa she took one look at my ankle and said, 'I should take you to hospital.' I hadn't looked under my sock but now noticed that my foot had ballooned and darkened.

'I'll be fine,' I protested, wanting to avoid a Friday evening in A&E. A weekend at our cottage would be the best treatment.

Jo, as always, drove us down that night; through a combination of living in London and laziness, I had yet to pass my driving test. We arrived at the cottage just before midnight and, using a big branch as a crutch, I limped down the steep hillside to the cottage while Jo

2

carried Lejla. Poor Cuillin had to be woken up to walk down by himself as I could barely carry myself, let alone him. Jo and I often used to wonder when the kids would realise that being carried down a hillside through a forest in the middle of the night every weekend wasn't normal, but luckily that night they took it in their stride.

By Sunday I felt much better – at least until Jo banged my foot for the umpteenth time. I actually laughed as she apologised yet again. She could be maddening and wonderful both at the same time.

Jo and I had been together more than ten years. She was the most incredible person I had ever met.

I remember her smiling face as she bent to kiss me was flecked with mud and sticky smudges, evidence of the gooseberry jam she and the kids had made that morning, followed by some gardening. Jo went to stand in the centre of our newly completed open-walled barn, dubbed 'Beater Barn', which she had designed and got built. I had been a sceptic on the project but now it was finished, we all agreed that it was magnificent, a lovely spot from which to savour the view. After all Jo's work it seemed fitting we should name it after her. I often used her old nickname of Beater (before our marriage she was Jo Leadbeater) just as she still sometimes called me Coxy, in her distinctive Yorkshire accent.

The cottage was a long way from Yorkshire but it was our hinterland, our retreat from the world. Our son Cuillin, named after a great mountain range on the Isle of Skye that Jo and I had climbed when she was pregnant in 2010, was still only five. Our daughter Lejla, whose name came from friends of ours in Bosnia, was just three years old.

It was the first weekend after the barn had been completed and Jo was very pleased with it and with herself.

'So, what do you think, Coxy?' she said with a smile, sinking back into a chair next to my hammock.

'Okay, you were right,' I admitted.

Jo had been sold on the idea of the cottage from the moment she saw the photo I texted her. My best friend Will Paxton and I had spotted it, and a hand-painted For Sale sign, while canoeing down the river in 2012. We'd had to back-paddle desperately while we tried to remember the estate agent's details.

Jo and I hadn't been looking for anywhere to buy – but this place just caught our imagination.

The next day we spoke to an estate agent who did his best to put us off. It was a mile from the nearest track and he was clearly sick of getting his smart shoes muddied on site visits with people who were never going to buy it.

'You do realise it's in a wood with no road access? And no electric? And no running water? And no heating?'

We reassured him that that was precisely why we were interested.

The first time we went to look at it, my mum drove us down from Reading. She was our adviser-in-chief on all projects. She has an awesome level of energy and sense of adventure fused with great practicality. Having looked around Jo and I were giddy with excitement, but on the drive back we anxiously asked my mum what she thought.

4

'It's ridiculous. No one should buy it,' she said. 'Apart from you. You should definitely buy it.'

Jo and I grinned at each other. Our decision was made.

It was pretty cheap for a house (the upside of being off-grid) but we couldn't convince a single bank or building society to give us a mortgage. We only managed to buy it because the previous owners, a retired couple, offered us an incredibly generous deal where we paid them back on a monthly basis. They could tell how much we had fallen for it, even in its wild state, and they wanted it to be in good hands.

The cottage became our latest life adventure and a shared family project. The damp was so bad that water ran down the walls, and the garden had been reclaimed by the forest. We spent every weekend we could chopping wood, carrying out old generators and agricultural machinery from a hundred years ago, painting and planting. It was the centre of our family life, the place our kids adored beyond anywhere else. Gradually, with a lot of hard work, we made it more like a home.

We still loved living on our boat on the Thames during the week, while Jo commuted between London and Batley, but our cottage gave us space to get away from it all.

'I love everything about this place – and us,' Jo said. Her life-affirming smile was even wider than normal.

Late that Sunday afternoon, on our last day at the cottage, Jo and I sat close together on a bench overlooking the garden. We watched Cuillin and Lejla climb higher and higher into the air on the death swing – the name we had given the rope from which the kids flew like birds.

Only Clare, partner of Jo's sister Kim, had fallen from it. A month before she had slipped off the rope and crashed into the nettles below. It was worrying for a while but half a bottle of whisky numbed the pain of Clare's cuts and bruises.

We had taught the kids to treat the swing with respect even when they were whooping high in the air. Naturally there was a chance they could fall, but we wanted them to learn to make their own judgements about risk. We allowed Cuillin and Lejla to play freely. In return they were sensible most of the time, even if Lejla's fearlessness sometimes terrified us.

'Look, Daddy,' she yelled as she spread her arms wide in the familiar crucifix pose.

I called it the 'Jesus swing' and Lejla liked doing it. 'Looking good, Ledgie,' I shouted.

It was then Cuillin's turn for a swing. Jo squeezed my hand. After a tough and sometimes challenging year, we knew how lucky we were to share an extraordinary life. The kids were incredible, we were more in love than ever and Jo and I felt we had clear ways to make a difference in the world through our work. Everything else felt complete and in harmony. The Beater Barn had been built. Jo had made her jam and champagne; and that fizz matched her growing confidence as an MP.

This personal contentment clashed with our increasing worries about the state of the world. With the growth in hate crimes across Europe, the rise of the far right and the emergence of Trump, Jo and I increasingly feared for the direction politics was going. For the first time in our lives we felt that our fiercely held belief in progress might be sorely tested. We regularly discussed how best we might resist those trends and articulate our belief in the sanctity of a tolerant and inclusive society – while living our lives to the full and giving our kids the best start.

Jo told me how liberated and happy she felt just sitting here, watching the kids laughing on the swing at the end of another special weekend.

'You know,' Jo mused, as we sat on our sun-dappled bench, 'we'll look back on these days . . .' – she gestured to the kids and the cottage, then turned back to me, paused, and finished her sentence – 'as the happiest days of our lives.'

Jo's final diary entry had been written two weeks earlier. We had gone to the cottage for a week and were joined by my parents, my sister Stacia, her husband Andrew and their three children:

So . . . we had a glorious week and we:

- *Made a wigwam. Put up a flag. Kids loved it. Looks awesome.*

- *Cuillin, Lejla, H & L [Henry and Lucas – Stacia's sons] and BC [Brendan Cox] all slept in the wigwam. Not much sleep for BC! What an adventure.*

7

- *I made elderflower cordial and champagne. 5 bottles of cordial [though 2 smashed] & 20 litres of champagne – not sure it's fermenting.*

- *Glorious game of football and elderflower cordial drink at half time.*

- *Put up a new arch for the roses – the other one fell down (my fault!).*

- *B put in decking. Looks fab.*

- *Long walk. I carried Lejla. C walked. Ice cream at the top and played monkeys.*

- *Cycled through the buttercup fields, back to play on the beach. I had a little snooze in the sun.*

- *Home for roast lamb. Magnificent.*

- *Woke up to a truly glorious day. Cuillin currently making a sword on his workbench with B. I've just made jelly with Lejla and read to her on the patio.*

- *What an amazing holiday.*

Those four words were the last Jo ever wrote in her diary. The next words were written by me.

Jo was killed on the 16th June.

2

The Last Time

We were on the water the last time we saw Jo. She wore a bright red dress as she watched us skim and bounce along the river. On a day of broken sunshine and gathering cloud, a typical English summer's day along the Thames, Jo smiled and waved at us. She took a photo on her phone and shouted encouragement to the kids who were stationed on lookout duty.

A few minutes earlier we had been frantically getting ready. Mornings on the boat were normally a little fraught as we tried to cram food into the children at the same time as getting dressed, dealing with work crises and listening to the *Today* programme. We also hoped we wouldn't run out of water or sewage space as those downsides of boat life blighted our mornings about once a month.

That Wednesday was different. There were just eight days left before the referendum on exiting the European Union. The previous night Jo had hosted a party and invited the other fifty-two new Labour MPs to our mooring as a way of celebrating their first year in Parliament. It had been a testing twelve months but around forty people arrived and had fun in the community pier house while I looked after the kids on the boat. The next morning Jo brought across groups of MPs to see our small home. She introduced Cuillin and Lejla to the MPs they had never met, and the children cuddled old friends who already knew them.

Jo was about to return to Batley for two days of constituency work. Cuillin was off school and recovering from chickenpox which still dimpled his skin. I was going to take him and Lejla out on the speedboat – it was actually a motorised rubber dinghy but, on a day of surging exhilaration, it seemed right to call it our speedboat. Jo chatted to the kids as she helped them into their bright yellow life jackets.

A few days earlier a friend who lived on a boat further up the Thames had called to tell us that Nigel Farage would be sailing down the river to protest against the EU. Our friend was planning a counter protest, and asked if I could help.

'Okay,' I said, 'let's put something together.'

Many calls and texts later we'd got a big group together, enough to fill eight small boats, and I spent much of the next twenty-four hours arranging for our posters, banners and flags to be made up and delivered.

Jo loved the idea. Not because she was obsessively pro-Europe – having spent several years challenging the EU over its trade policy on behalf of Oxfam, she knew its failings better than most. She was pro-European, but no fanatic. Her enthusiasm for our plan stemmed from her antipathy to the extremism of Farage and his attempts to divide the country. In our view, Farage didn't care about the fishing fleet he was commandeering. He had been on the European Parliament's Fisheries Committee and skipped forty-one of the forty-two meetings he was meant to attend. His arrival on the Thames was yet more self-promotion. We hoped to deflate his arrival.

Yet, in terms of the larger debate, Jo was starting to feel that the Leave campaign would win. She supported the Remain side because she believed that staying within Europe was in the UK's best interests. But she knew from Batley that a government- and elite-backed Remain campaign would struggle to win the vote.

Jo also realised that, for many, the referendum had become a proxy vote on immigration. While she was a dedicated advocate of the benefits of immigration to Britain, and argued staunchly for our country to take its fair share of refugees, she also understood how immigration had impacted on her constituency in difficult ways. Many good people in her home town worried about losing a sense of community or the increasing pressure on housing and public services. They weren't racists and Jo felt their concerns had not been taken seriously enough. As with most issues, Jo could understand the sentiment on both sides.

She obviously stood in direct opposition to Farage and his ilk, for they pandered to racism and xenophobia. But Jo was also dismayed that the Labour Party's leadership had failed to acknowledge the downsides to immigration and sometimes sounded as if it advocated open borders. Jo believed that Britain, at its best, was inclusive, tolerant and outward looking, but that those attributes could only be maintained if migration and integration were well managed.

I shared Jo's concern that the vote was drifting towards leaving the EU; but we were not defeatist. We still hoped that, in the last week of campaigning, people would think more practically about the risks of leaving, the impact it might have on the British Union, the trade and economic implications. And so even a zany idea – sending out a fleet of zippy little speedboats to ambush Farage – appealed to Jo's sense of fun and defiance.

She helped get Cuillin and Lejla into position on the boat while I cranked the motor into spluttering life. Jessie, their nanny, climbed aboard, holding the big flag we were about to brandish along the Thames. The word IN was encased in a black square which stood out against the pristine white background. I heard a shout from the lookout I had posted on the east end of our mooring so that we could spot the arrival of Nigel Farage and his flotilla. As we looked downriver we could see the approaching police escort. Jo wondered whether she should join us, but we decided it probably wasn't very becoming for an MP. Instead, she helped the kids on board and waved furiously as we headed for open water.

As she always did when saying goodbye, Jo shouted that she loved us. I waved and saw that, back on the pontoon,

Jo was full of excitement. Now, all these blurring months later, I can't remember what might have been the last word I said to her. In my head I can just see us racing away to join seven other little speedboats aiming for Farage's flotilla.

The kids found this far more thrilling than their usual Wednesday morning routine. They were ready to concentrate, fiercely and earnestly, with Cuillin scanning the port side while Lejla looked starboard to make sure we didn't bump into anything. Their faces glowed with anticipation as they kneeled at the front of the boat, primed for action.

I wanted Jo to see Cuillin and Lejla fly past so I sped alongside the mooring and called out to the kids, pointing at Jo, saying, 'Look, it's Mummy!' Cuillin and Lejla swivelled starboard and locked on to the beautiful sight of their tiny but tenacious mother, in her red dress.

'Mummy!' they shouted, waving at Jo who, in my scrambled mind now, smiles even more deeply.

Instead of lingering on Jo we were distracted by the need to avoid the cluster of boats that turned the Thames into churning froth.

Later that day, Jo retweeted a picture on Twitter:

So proud of @MrBrendanCox & my kids for getting out on the Thames to protest against @Nigel_ Farage #Flotilla #Remain

I am at the back of the red and black speedboat, my left hand on the tiller, looking astern at the flotilla coming towards us. Jessie is in the middle, holding the IN flag. Up front, Cuillin and Lejla remain studiously focused.

As we came under Tower Bridge, Farage's boat was met by Bob Geldof on another vessel. It felt as if we were caught in a riverside cartoon between a megaphone-wielding Bob and the braying Nigel. Geldof might have made some salient points about the truth of fishing in British waters, but the combination of a loudhailer and Farage's roaring Leavers was not conducive to rational thought. I wondered if there had ever been a more surreal day in British politics.

We zigzagged between the anti-EU boats. It was fun and good-natured – we even gave a few Leave fishermen a lift to the shore. By the time we got to Westminster Bridge, however, the atmosphere had soured as more and more alcohol was consumed on the surrounding boats. We drifted past one fishing boat which turned a high-pressure hose on us.

I shouted up at one of the men holding the hose. 'Mate, I've got kids on board.'

'We don't bloody care!' he yelled.

Cuillin ducked down and I pulled Lejla on to my knee and out of the way. I decided we should get back to the mooring. It was time to steer the kids far beyond the farce on the Thames.

'Who was that nasty man?' Lejla asked.

They had loved the day until then and so I replied with some soothing words as we sped away.

By the time we reached the mooring Jo had long since

gone. She was heading back to her childhood home near Batley, to continue the constituency work she loved.

We talked on the phone late that afternoon, catching up on news and sharing stories about the absurd battle of the Thames. Jo spoke one last time to Cuillin and to Lejla as they excitedly told her about their day. She might have been weary but the usual vibrant life force poured out from her.

Later, as darkness spread, I sat at our table on the boat. The kids were in bed, safe in the depths of sleep, and everything was quiet. The rest of the night, and our ordinary lives until then, melted into oblivion.

3

A New Life

On a bitterly cold winter afternoon in late November 2010, I waited for Jo at Brentford Station. She was late, as usual. I laughed as soon as I saw her. She was wearing a balaclava and a huge Buffalo mountain jacket designed to withstand ice storms and howling blizzards. She looked as if she were heading for the highest mountain in Scotland rather than moving into our new home on the River Thames. Jo was seven months pregnant and underneath the huge coat she was wearing old clothes several sizes too small for her swollen belly.

She stood on tip-toe and hugged me. Jo was only five foot one so I had to lean down to kiss her, feeling the bump between us. Even in her balaclava and mountain jacket, and heavily pregnant, Jo looked gorgeous.

'So, Beater,' I said, 'you ready?'

'I am, Coxy. Let's do this.'

The plan – and Jo and I were always keen on detailed plans – had been clear. We would settle our newly rebuilt houseboat into a permanent mooring in time to get organised for the birth of our first baby. It was meant to be simple but, being real life, everything became complicated. The boatyard had taken months longer than agreed to do the restoration work. But, finally, our new home was ready.

Ederlezi, named after a Romani song from the Balkans and a festival marking the coming of spring, still looked stark. She had been stripped back to the bare steel and her new brass portholes only softened the appearance slightly. There was even less on the inside – no furniture, no frills, no insulation – but she had looked magnificent when we went to pick her up from the Uxbridge boatyard. We had then cruised to a berth at Bulls Bridge Junction on the Grand Union Canal near Brentford, where we left her while I went away for a short work trip.

That day, after meeting at the station, we were planning to steer *Ederlezi* east through London along the Regent's Canal, then moor again at Limehouse before venturing out on to the open waters of the Thames.

I swore angrily when we reached the canal. It was frozen. Our steel boat encased in thick sheets of ice might have looked pretty, but it filled us with worry.

'What are we going to do?' Jo asked, running a hand across her bulging tummy as if she might soothe our homeless baby.

I started the engine and drove at the ice. There was a bit of splintering but no real progress so I grabbed the barge pole. It was heavy, about four metres in length, and felt like the ice-smashing weapon we needed.

'Go on, Coxy,' Jo said.

I went to the bow and brought the barge pole down with a thwack against the cold white surface sealing us in. The ice split with a satisfying creak. We could see the rolling glimmer of dark water beneath the fissures. I raised the pole up and brought it hammering down again. A wider crack emerged. The boat nudged forward and Jo cheered.

Solid ice still lay ahead of us so, while I steered *Ederlezi* down the narrow canal, Jo stood at the bow and used the pole to smash open the ice.

We made slow progress. Jo began to tire because she found the weight of the pole hard to hold above her. She was determined, though, and devised a different method: she lay down on her side and used the barge pole to prod the ice apart.

Mist rose from the frozen surface and the canal looked ghostly. The only sounds were the eerie thud of Jo's pole, the straining engine and the groaning crack of ice. Sometimes I would call out to her, telling her how well she was doing. Behind us we left a channel of ice-free water.

And then, with Jo stretched out at the front, it began to snow. Soft, fat flakes drifted down. The snow fell harder but as we got closer to central London, the ice thinned and with a final fierce belt of the barge pole, the canal opened up completely.

We were out of the ice and into clear water.

Jo looked like a small snow-woman. She was shivering and I urged her inside. It was still only about one degree in the hull but we had a sleeping bag on the floor. Jo slipped inside and curled up in the depths of the bag. She was asleep within minutes.

I steered down the snowy canal. We coasted through central London, passing Little Venice and heading towards Camden and Islington through the dark tunnels that stretch under London and had always fired our imagination. The snow eased as we reached the Limehouse Basin which marks the end of the canal. It's always an anxious moment when you leave the canal for the tidal river and we needed to arrive at our new permanent mooring just as the tide was going out, so we had no choice but to moor up on the canal for the night and wait. We would make an early start the next day.

The following morning we were up just after five, ready for the next stage of our grand journey, moving our boat to its new permanent mooring near Tower Bridge. We'd assembled a small crew of friends to help us handle the boat on the more tumultuous waters of the tidal Thames and by the time we got going, it had begun to snow again. I steered out of the lock on to the river. Jo and I had recently got our radio licences and Jo spoke into the radio: 'London VTS this is Dutch barge *Ederlezi* – departing Limehouse Basin inward bound. Over.'

The answer crackled back: 'Message received.'

We were excited and a little apprehensive. The tidal Thames is a very different body of water to the serene canals, and we knew we had to be careful. We headed past Wappingness and as the tide began to ebb just before

7 a.m. we were ready to moor. Our new neighbour Maria, who still lives alongside our boat today, was there to catch the rope and make us fast. We were welcomed on to the mooring for a breakfast of scrambled eggs, toast and steaming mugs of tea.

Jo and I were elated. We were home.

Our new life had begun to unfold seven months earlier – in the mountains of Scotland. A week in Skye was our opportunity to recover from the Labour Party's defeat in the May 2010 general election and the formation of a new coalition government of the Conservatives and Liberal Democrats. Labour had been in power for thirteen years before that, ever since Tony Blair swept into office in 1997. All that youthful hope felt like a long time ago – and Blair had never recovered from the catastrophe of Iraq. I had spent the previous eighteen months working as an adviser on overseas development to Gordon Brown, who had replaced Blair as Prime Minister. Jo, in a weird twist of fate, worked with Sarah Brown, Gordon's wife, at the Maternal Mortality campaign. We liked the Browns and admired their values but knew that defeat at the polls was highly likely.

From a personal viewpoint I was philosophical about losing my job at Number 10. A break from political life would be healthy. Not long after the election, therefore, with David Cameron and Nick Clegg on their fleeting honeymoon as coalition partners, Jo and I decided to climb the Cuillin Mountains in Scotland. The Cuillin range is the most impressive and difficult mountain ridge in the UK and features twelve of the 282 Munros – those Scottish mountains higher than 3,000 feet. When we first met, Jo and I had decided that, before we died, we would climb every single Munro. We had just passed our half-century together – fifty peaks climbed. I liked the fact that we were not even a fifth of the way to fulfilling that momentous challenge; it meant so many more mountains awaited us.

On Skye we hiked just over six miles to a beautiful bay called Camasunary. The Cuillin Mountains are all around, majestic and ominous, but it is an easy walk over a rough track that leads to the deserted beach where I knew there was a bothy. Bothies are old shepherds' huts in remote areas and most were abandoned years ago – but they are maintained now by the Mountain Bothy Association so that walkers and climbers can rest or sleep in them. They generally have earth surfaces although some have stone floors and a wooden sleeping platform. There is usually a stove or a fireplace but no running water or electricity. Out in the wild, and up in the Munros when the winds are cruel and the rain sheets down, a bothy is a sanctuary.

Sometimes we shared a bothy with a stranger, or a whole group we had never met before. Jo loved the way the harsh isolation of our climbing would be broken by warm companionship. A spontaneous joint meal would be made even better by handing round some wine or whisky.

In the late afternoon we gathered mussels on the Camasunary beach and cooked them in wine over a fire in the bothy – which we had to ourselves. I added a little trout I had caught in the ice-cold waters. It was a delicious supper but, for once, Jo didn't eat as much as me. She was feeling sick.

She seemed fine the next morning and we set out to Loch Coruisk via the Bad Step, the steep and exposed ledge that you have to cross to get there. Loch Coruisk is dark and brooding. It is also suitably humbling, and purifying. The wind blew down the valley and we stood on the loch's edge, feeling cleansed of the electoral detritus.

The next few days were more ambitious. We crossed to the other side of the mountains and climbed the first part of the Cuillin Ridge. We had already scaled a couple of the easier Munros on Skye before we attempted the Inaccessible Pinnacle of Sgurr Dearg – the hardest mountain to climb in the UK. We did this on our fourth day with a guide because you need ropes and Jo wanted to be careful (not quite trusting my rope work). Right from the start of the climb she was hanging behind. 'What's wrong?' I asked.

'Nothing,' she replied.

But I knew something was amiss. Jo was always a ball of energy on the mountains (I called her a mountain goat) and the only time she had ever struggled before was when we later found out she was battling a series of tropical diseases. As we approached the Inaccessible Pinnacle I stayed close to her. 'Are you okay?' I asked. She nodded and on we walked.

The Inaccessible Pinnacle of Sgurr Dearg is well named. When he faced that imposing climb, Robert Macfarlane wrote in *The Wild Places* of, 'The shark's fin of black rock that jags hundreds of feet out of the ridge above Coruisk, and which had long been, to my mind, one of the wildest points in the world.'

The jagged peak jutting out at the summit of Sgurr Dearg can be frightening. I could imagine how terrifying it must look if you're feeling ill. But as Jo still wanted to climb it, we scaled the dizzying edge and discovered that it was not, technically, a difficult climb. The real test is that you are so exposed. The drop plunges down thousands of feet.

Jubilant that we had made the top of the Inaccessible Pinnacle, all that was left was to abseil off the other side. Jo was by now feeling really nauseous but, with a bit of help, she got down and when we reached the bottom of the mountain she felt better. I thought it was strange: Jo was not usually queasy with nerves.

The sky was a brilliant blue and we felt proud of our feat. We walked down the mountain quickly, with the warmth of the sun gently reddening our skin, and when we reached the campsite we had some whisky to celebrate. It then felt like time for some relaxation, and the following day we went to a friend's house in southern Scotland where we enjoyed the perfect end to an exhilarating break.

I felt sleepy but satisfied as we caught the train on the long journey back to London. I closed my eyes as the train gathered speed and raced along the tracks.

Jo was awake, and restless.

I'd decided I was going to get a pregnancy test when we passed through Glasgow train station. I didn't tell B. After a little while I popped off to the loo to do the test. Not the most salubrious of settings but I needed to know. Even then I don't think I really believed it and I did a few checks on the instructions and results before taking a moment to look in the mirror and accept it was possible. It felt like a dream. I gathered myself together, grabbed the test result and went back to B.

I was shocked but very happy. Jo grinned back at me and, as the train hurtled south, we started talking excitedly about our new baby. Our world would never be the same again.

In an exercise book covered in images of New York and the Statue of Liberty, Jo began to chart her new life. She gave the book a simple title: *Jo's Pregnancy Diary*.

May 2010

Today has not been a good pregnancy day!! After 1½ weeks of constant nausea I struggled to keep positive – and then had a weeping fit when an inflexible, rude doctor's receptionist told me I couldn't register as I was 'of no fixed abode'. I'm now on the boat feeling a bit sorry for myself, very sick, emotional and drained with very sore boobs and a bloated tummy. It's hard to focus on anything

other than the constant feeling I'm going to throw
up. Clearly, I'm not going to be one of those
endlessly positive, 'glowing' pregnant women who
love the whole affair. At the same time I'm trying to
come to terms with the whole thing. I think *I'm*
happy about it but don't feel *happy yet. I also don't*
want to think too much about the future just in case
I miscarry (which at my age is a serious risk). So I
feel a little trapped in this weird state of semi-
reality – all the signs of pregnancy are there but I
haven't yet allowed myself to think about the fact
I have a baby growing inside me – and that B and I
could this year be parents. An absolutely terrifying
prospect at this stage.

In early June Jo flew to Washington, DC, for work and
described telling my parents the news before she left.

B's family came down to help cruise from Brentford
to Teddington. We decided not to tell them – but, as
soon as Sheila and Gordon arrived, B blurted out
that I was preggers! I started crying and we all
hugged. He said it was because I was such a bad
actor! We told Stacia and Andrew too but not the
boys. All very lovely and a great day – a picnic,
loads of herons and an eel.

Early the next morning, having woken in DC, Jo added a
more sombre entry.

Terrible news from [our friends] last night. They lost
their baby. They sound devastated. A real wake-up
call for us too not to get carried away. Life can
throw some harsh punches.

Jo continued to work for Sarah Brown but she was planning to scale down in preparation for maternity leave. I
was working part time on a nine-month study, trying to
understand some of the issues affecting the world's poorest
countries, which meant I could be flexible with my
schedule and spend lots of time with Jo. She was about
to have her first scan.

Suddenly it all felt very real, especially when we
both looked up at the screen to see a tiny little baby
jumping around. I'd been convinced the whole thing
was a phantom pregnancy. Then, suddenly, there it
was – a real-life baby in my tummy! B looked
elated/in shock/amazed! The whole visit was incred-
ibly reassuring. I was low risk, healthy and the baby
was fine. The dating scan showed that we were 11
weeks and one day – amazingly accurate. Relief all
round. We texted everyone to say all was well, got
copies of the photos and left the hospital all smiles.

Jo suffered badly from morning sickness. But, when it
finally eased, we decided to make the most of our relatively
relaxed work schedules and the last months before the
baby was born. We had moved on to *Ederlezi* a few months

previously, and decided to take her out of London. We lived for a while between Kingston and Hampton Court – where we moored the boat and took long walks and cycles across Bushy Park and around the trout lakes. Most languid summer evenings we sat on the roof of the boat and gazed at the picturesque Thames.

For a change of scene we settled in Windsor and, as a joint wedding anniversary gift to each other, we bought a Canadian canoe. Soon, we moved on to Maidenhead and discovered the Cliveden Reach where it seems as if you are entering Joseph Conrad territory. With a bit (or perhaps a lot) of imagination it feels like the river in *Heart of Darkness*. The Thames becomes dark and the overgrown riverbanks are steep. A forest hangs over the water, silent and baleful, and we liked mooring the boat on the secluded islands around Cliveden. We went on little canoe expeditions down the back-streams where you slip around fallen trees in primeval, swamp-like water.

Towards the end of that summer we moved west again, living near Marlow and then at Sonning. We were lucky to be able to work from the boat with only occasional trips back into London for meetings. During those leisurely months, Jo and I truly began to appreciate why we loved living on boats. It's an unfolding adventure as you cruise along the river, not really knowing where you are on the map. You then step out into the English countryside, jump on to your bike and ride until you find the local pub. It's a good way to see the country at a slow pace.

We continued on to Reading, where my parents live,

and spent a couple of months just upstream in Pangbourne, a pretty little village. Pangbourne Meadow, where we moored the boat, is a perfect English meadowscape.

Every evening, at dusk, a phalanx of Canada geese flew down the river in a perfect 'V'. Jo and I started gathering wild mushrooms and we would fry them fresh from the meadow just as the birds staged their flypast. We watched the geese skim across the water before they climbed into the sky, crying in a haunting echo before wheeling over our boat as if leaving Pangbourne at the end of summer. But they kept coming back. Perhaps they were just training every evening because, one night, they were gone.

Suddenly, with a distinct chill in the air as the light faded, we knew the geese had left us. Summer was over in Pangbourne Meadow and all along the Thames. It was a reminder that soon, in the heart of winter, our world was about to be turned inside out by a new life.

By December we had smashed our way through the ice of the frozen canal to move *Ederlezi* to our permanent mooring at Tower Bridge, but there was still a lot of work to be done. I had to get our refitted but totally gutted boat insulated with spray-foam before the carpenters could begin work on the interior. Even on an unbelievably cold Thames, I could feel the heat of the deadline: Jo was only weeks from her due date. For the foam to stick to the steel it needed to be at least five degrees – a temperature hard to maintain in a savage winter. I stayed up all night, with two heaters and a big stove, jamming it full of logs and coal, to raise enough heat. It felt boiling, twenty-five degrees in the bowels of the boat. In the morning I sprayed on the insulating foam, tired but excited finally to be getting the job done that would mean we could finish the boat before our baby was born. As I turned to start the next panel I heard a sound like a wet flannel hitting the ground. Despite my best efforts the steel was too cold and the insulation was peeling off the frozen walls.

Having spent the night at my parents' house in Reading, Jo turned up early to find me exhausted and desolate. She took me to a café for a mixed grill to cheer me up.

She told me not to worry, suggesting that we should have the boat insulated by professionals and go back and live with my parents while all the work was done. It would be an imposition on them, but my mum and dad loved having Jo around.

'Right, Coxy,' Jo said. 'We'll have this baby in Reading. We'll be happy wherever we are . . .'

On New Year's Eve, we cut quite a picture as we went to my sister's house for a curry. Jo felt hugely pregnant and weary. I was more of a comic figure. I had taken my nephews rock-climbing the day before and, in a misguided attempt to look like a cool uncle, I had pushed myself too far on an overhang. I cricked my neck so badly I was forced to wear a neck-brace. We ordered the spiciest curries on the takeaway menu and I washed them down with enough beer and red wine to make me forget my neck-collar. When we got home to my parents' house, after saying one last Happy New Year to a sober Jo, I soon fell asleep.

But 2011 began with a jolt. Jo shook me awake. 'It's starting.'

I looked blearily at her. 'Really?'

'I think so,' she said, holding her giant tummy.

I rolled out of bed, strapped a TENS machine (a method of pain relief using mild electrical current) to Jo and complimented her on being so calm. It was all going according to plan.

Jo wanted a very natural birth, without any drugs or intervention. She hoped to float around the birthing pool and have our baby in the most natural way possible.

I phoned the midwife and she reminded me to start monitoring the frequency and intensity of the contractions. 'Go for a walk first,' the midwife said. 'It sounds like you've got a little while to wait.'

We went for a walk around the grounds of the University of Reading and tried to relax. But, every five minutes or so, Jo would crouch down as a contraction gripped her. Once we got home, and her pain increased, we decided to walk down to the hospital. I picked up the bag we had already packed and, waving goodbye to my anxious parents, we set off. I was still wearing the neck-brace.

It felt easier in hospital. We were shown to a room where we would wait for a bed and, to pass the time, we made a couple of lists – a very Beater-and-Coxy thing to do. We started with our highlights of 2010 and moved on to everything we planned to do with our baby in the New Year. It was lovely and uplifting.

But Jo's discomfort soon became intense. We were left pretty much on our own because, on New Year's Day, there was only a skeleton staff.

The hours passed in a slow blur. Jo's pain seemed unbearable but her cervix had only dilated slightly – nowhere near the required ten centimetres. We were being looked after by a lone midwife who said, soon after she met us, that she hadn't delivered a baby in hospital for years: she was a community midwife. I felt she was getting flustered and I started to grow nervous.

The midwife knew enough to tell us Jo's pain was probably caused by the baby's back rubbing against hers. 'Back-to-back births are quite tricky,' she said, 'but we'll do our best.'

All thoughts of a Zen-like birth were ruined. Jo was in agony. 'I need an epidural,' she cried.

'What about the birth plan?' I queried helpfully.

'Forget the birth plan,' Jo gasped. 'I need an epidural – *now!*'

The midwife called in a doctor who took one look at Jo and reached for the trolley. Jo was about to get an immediate epidural but the midwife seemed at a loss as the doctor prepared the spinal injection. I remember when the doctor asked for a particular instrument the midwife became stressed. 'I'm sorry,' she said. 'I've forgotten what that is.'

Jo stared at me and made unspeakable sounds.

Eventually the epidural was in place and the overstretched doctor raced to the next problem. We were left with the stressed midwife. She was a lovely woman and it felt unfair that she was put in the position of working alone on what was fast becoming a complicated birth. I had to point out that Jo's drip had not been connected properly.

The midwife apologised as she fumbled with the connection.

We soon faced another worrying issue. The baby's heart rate had begun to fluctuate. It needed to be monitored closely and the midwife grew even more agitated. Jo hardly knew what was happening so, silently, I left the room.

I walked quickly to the main desk and asked to speak to the person in charge. The nurses were dealing with various crises but I was determined – and frightened. We needed help. As calmly as I could, I told them what was happening and that we needed an experienced midwife or a doctor to help us. One of the nurses said, 'All right, go back to your wife and I'll send someone.'

An extraordinary woman soon followed me into Jo's room. Originally from India, she had vast experience. The first midwife smiled at the reprieve as the new woman took charge and told us what we were going to do after she had examined Jo. She calmed us all down. I listened to her as she politely told me to stay out of the way. Then she settled Jo and explained that we did not have long to go. The baby would soon be with us, healthy and safe.

The sense of relief that we were in such good hands made me giddy. I couldn't stop myself babbling and now that the potential disaster seemed to have been averted and Jo's pain was more under control, I began to ask the midwife where in India she came from and how life was unfolding economically and politically in her home city.

Jo shot me a withering glance as if I had gone completely mad. I think she would have said, 'Shut up, Coxy!' had she not had a lot more important things to worry about.

The last ten minutes were terrible for Jo – and there was dread. The baby's heartbeat dipped again as the umbilical cord was wrapped around the neck. The midwife was now working alongside a team of doctors. Reaching for the forceps, they told Jo they needed to get her baby out quickly.

Suddenly, it was over. The baby was out and the cord was unwrapped and cut. Cuillin went straight into his mum's arms.

'You did it, Jo!' I exclaimed.

Jo gazed at me in disbelief.

The baby looked beautiful.

'Is it a boy?' Jo asked. 'It looks like a boy?'

'Yes, it's a boy,' the midwife said, patting her arm admiringly. 'You did really well, Jo.'

The midwife looked at me – the babbling idiot in the neck-brace. 'Congratulations, Mr Cox.'

'Thank you for everything,' I said.

'I think he's hungry already,' the midwife commented as our baby nestled even closer to Jo. It did not take long for Jo to start breast-feeding. Love spread across her face as she watched.

Jo then turned to look at me. 'Cuillin?' she asked.

Neither of us had any preference as to whether our firstborn was a boy or a girl. We just wanted the baby to be healthy. But we did want our children's names to mean something to us and, eventually, to them. We had already decided that, if the baby was a boy, we would name him after the mountains we had climbed when Jo was pregnant. It would always be a reminder that his mum, who had scaled the summit and abseiled down the back of the Inaccessible Pinnacle with him inside her, was special.

'Cuillin,' I said and nodded, smiling at my wife and our baby, at Jo and Cuillin.

On 7 January 2011 Jo stuck into her diary the pink hospital wristband she had worn before, during and after the birth. Jo's full name was Helen Joanne – which the tag reflected.

COX, Helen
DOB: 22-Jun-1974

She also pasted the hospital's printed record of Cuillin's birth on to the next page:

COX
Baby Boy
02-Jan-2011, 08:13

Between those precious mementos, Jo remembered the birth and its immediate aftermath.

I pushed again, not really sure where I got the energy – and then he was there. I had a little baby in my arms. I actually didn't know what to do and remember looking to B for reassurance/guidance. He just looked so unbelievably happy. It all felt quite dreamlike, and I was so, so tired. The next few minutes passed in a haze. He was ok, then Cuillin was put on top of me for some skin-to-skin contact. I remember feeling suddenly very calm, content and still.

Since that night I've felt surrounded by a snug wall of love, care and support. Parenthood feels very, very natural and I'm already so in love with Cuillin – and even more in love than ever with B. The two most important people in my world.

What an amazing journey it's been – from reluctant pregnant woman to elated, content mum. This has been the most wondrous thing and, right now, I feel like the luckiest woman alive.

4

16 June 2016

I spent the morning working with my colleague Tim Dixon. We had collaborated for the previous seven months on a project studying rising xenophobia and hatred in Europe. We all saw the warning signs – rising hate crimes, growing support for the far right – but it felt like the political centre was too emasculated to respond effectively.

It was another normal Thursday as Tim and I walked down to a local restaurant. We were about to sit down for lunch when my phone rang.

It was Ruth Price, Jo's parliamentary researcher. Her voice sounded strange.

Jo had been attacked. I needed to get a train to Leeds as fast as possible.

Attacked?

I held on to the back of the chair and asked Ruth to slow down. Was Jo all right?

Ruth was upset and she didn't really know much more than the bare facts. Jo had been attacked in Birstall and they needed me to get there as quickly as I could.

Birstall is a village just two miles from Batley and six

miles south-west of Leeds. It is part of Jo's constituency and I knew she had a surgery at Birstall Library around lunchtime.

I told Tim I had to leave immediately, and raced back to the boat to get my wallet and laptop. I called Jessie, slowing to a walk when she answered. I told her what I knew and stressed that she should not say anything to Cuillin and Lejla. Could she take them to my parents in Reading? Jessie was great, as always, and said she would keep in touch.

As I arrived at the boat I called Dan Howard who worked for Jo up in Batley. I could hear his distress. He told me Jo had been shot and stabbed. He didn't know any more.

Dread seeped through me. This was the first time I knew it was serious. Jo really was in grave danger. The shock made me feel ill.

All Dan knew was that Jo had been with Fazila Aswat, her main aide and office manager, and Sandra Major, who led local casework.

I called Fazila as I rushed to the station. Was Jo going to be okay?

Fazila was calm but sounded helpless. She didn't know – the paramedics were with Jo.

I snapped off my phone and ran harder to the station. Everything else is lost but I can remember what I was thinking then. It felt as if I were talking directly to Jo.

'Just be okay,' I said in my head. 'It doesn't matter how badly hurt you are. We'll get you through this. I'll look after you and we'll build you back up.'

At the station I jumped the barriers and got on a train to Leeds. I started calling people, numbed and frantic at the same time. I began with Kim, Jo's sister, who hadn't heard anything. It was hard, but I had to tell her what I knew. Kim was near Batley and she promised to find out exactly what had happened. I tried to call Jo's mum and dad but couldn't get through. I learned later that they had already been told of the attack on Jo and were on their way to Birstall.

I tracked down some of Jo's friends and heard that news of the attack had seeped out on social media. My phone began to hum and buzz. I answered a few calls but shut them down quickly. I needed to keep my phone free for Jo. I called my mum and dad and told them what I knew. I could hear their shock and disbelief.

The train had picked up speed and the carriage was quiet. I looked out of the window. The countryside rushed past in a hazy green blur.

My phone lit up again. I looked at the screen. Kim.

'Kim, what's happened?' I asked, my voice lost in my throat.

There was a pause, small but deadly, before Kim spoke softly. 'I'm sorry, Brendan. She's not made it . . .'

I was in a daze of disbelief. 'Do you mean Jo's died?'

Kim paused again. 'I don't know what to say . . . but yes.'

I began to cry. The tears ran down my face and on to my shirt and even the plastic-topped table where I sat. We were still moving; but I was at a standstill.

The man across the aisle, who I had barely noticed before, touched my arm. 'Let me get you some tissues.'

I kept my head down. The man returned. He had brought tissues and a glass of water. I looked at him, this total stranger. I could feel his kindness. I managed to thank him. I wiped my eyes and blew my nose. I was not thirsty but I sipped the water he had given me.

Is this what you are meant to do when your wife has just been murdered?

'If there's anything I can do . . .' the man said, his voice trailing away. I knew there was no point stopping the train. I needed to keep hurtling towards the place where Jo now lay dead.

'Thank you,' I said.

My parents had loved Jo very much, and she had loved them. Cuillin and Lejla would be with them soon because Jessie was only a short distance from Reading. They were now all I cared about in the world. I tried to be calm as I called my mum and dad. I told them that Jo had died. It felt unreal to say the words. I asked them not to say anything to the kids. I would get back that night and, somehow, we would find a way to tell the children in the morning.

'Just be normal with them if you can, Mum,' I said. I knew I was asking something all but impossible but my mum agreed, shakily, that she would. We didn't talk for long. We couldn't find any words.

I called my sister Stacia next, and then some of my closest friends. I told them what had happened and asked for help. Could they find a child psychologist who might help me work out how best to explain to Cuillin and Lejla that their mum, with whom they were besotted, was dead?

This felt more important than anything else I might ever do again.

My friends bolstered me. They would help.

I was at a loss. What should I do now? There was still an hour to go before I'd arrive at the station. I called some of Jo's closest friends to tell them – I wanted them to hear it from me. They were impossible conversations: some of them had heard about the attack, others had heard nothing and I knew my call would change their lives. In between calls I sobbed uncontrollably. I felt awful for the people in the carriage who had to witness my pain. To try to compose myself I tried channelling that pain into words, to write down how I felt about Jo.

The words came easily. They began to fill the previously blank laptop screen. Later they became the basis of what I would say publicly.

The train slowed as we approached Leeds.

I packed up everything as if an ordinary train journey had just ended. I am not sure if I shook the kind stranger's hand. I was reeling.

Kim and Rachel Reeves, the Labour MP for Leeds West and a long-time friend of ours, were waiting for me at the station. They were with the police. Kim and Rachel both hugged me but I felt stunned, as if I had been struck dumb. Jo's cousin, Richard, who worked for the murder squad, was also with them. They led me to the police car. I walked silently.

I broke down in the car. I sobbed in a raw way. It was different to my silent tears on the train.

Beater was gone. She was never coming back. Jo was dead.

There would be no changing the past. There was nothing I could do.

Jo is dead.

The previous day she was alive, waving and smiling at me and the kids as we flew along the river. Not now. Everything has changed for ever.

The police drove Kim and me to the family home. Jo's mum and dad, Jean and Gordon, were waiting. We cried and hugged.

Dredging up some words, I said, 'We'll get through this. We'll help each other for Jo . . .'

The police told us what they knew. That the man who killed Jo had shouted 'Britain first' as he shot and stabbed her repeatedly. That they had found extremist literature at his house. My first thought was that she might have been targeted by an ISIS-linked extremist – either as a random assault on a British MP or because she had been outspoken over western failure in Syria. The 'Britain first' slogan was the first indication that this was home-grown hate.

I knew instinctively what Jo would want me to say in reaction. I knew she would want me to urge people to fight hatred and, even more importantly, to bathe Cuillin and Lejla in love. This has been my axiom ever since Jo's death.

I finished writing my brief statement and called my friend Patrick Wintour at the *Guardian*, intending to ask him to share my words. I didn't want our families or Jo's friends to be bothered by journalists and I knew that he would help me get my statement out, thereby giving us some privacy. I realised Patrick hadn't heard the news and was watching a game of football with his son. I couldn't bring myself to tell him and ruin that moment. It was too hard to form the words so I said I would ring him back. Ten minutes later he phoned me. By then he'd seen the news and could hardly speak. But he was able to tell me that he would do what I asked. He also gave his love before posting these words from me:

Today is the beginning of a new chapter in our lives. More difficult, more painful, less joyful, less full of love. I and Jo's friends and family are going to work every moment of our lives to love and nurture our kids and to fight against the hate that killed Jo.

Jo believed in a better world and she fought for it every day of her life with an energy, and a zest for life, that would exhaust most people.

She would have wanted two things above all else to happen now. One . . . that our precious children are bathed in love and two . . . that we all unite to fight against the hatred that killed her. Hate doesn't have a creed, race or religion, it is poisonous.

Jo would have no regrets about her life, she lived every day of it to the full.

I decided to tweet a picture of Jo. It was a lovely photograph of her, standing outside our boat. She wore a grey jumper and jeans, with one hand in her pocket, smiling as always. Silver sandals were on her bare feet. I didn't want people to think of her as a grand MP who just inhabited the House of Commons. I wanted everyone to understand she was an ordinary person.

But here's the thing. Jo was not ordinary. She was incredible. I had never met anyone like her, and I never will again, no matter how much longer I live than her. We climbed mountains together. We saw the world together. We worked and danced together. We lived on boats together. And, most of all, we brought Cuillin and Lejla into the world together.

I knew I had to go on for Jo, and for the two children we loved so much. I needed to be strong, no matter how broken I felt on the inside. I had to honour Jo and bring up Cuillin and Lejla just how she would have wanted. That would be my new way to love and to remember her.

5

Cuillin's Song

I was driven through the dark that night. The blackness of country roads eventually gave way to the yellowy hue of the motorway as we made the journey from Batley to Reading. The real darkness was buried beneath a shattering truth.

Jo had still been alive just before lunchtime that day. And now she was gone, her life destroyed in a frenzy.

The Labour Party had arranged a car to take me to my parents' home. We had decided that Cuillin and Lejla should sleep at Stacia's house. They had spent the early evening playing with their three cousins and there was no point waking them at midnight. It also gave me time to work out how best I could tell them. I hated the idea that this was the last night that they would ever sleep without a searing knowledge of how cruel the world can be – their last night of innocence.

I was strangely focused on the long journey home. Jo was in my head but my immediate concern centred on the kids. I would have found it impossible to get through the day and night but for that consuming priority. There was no good way to break such news to small children – but there were many damaging ways of doing it badly. Some of my friends had spent time that evening researching the subject. The best route led from the sister of a friend, a doctor, to a man called Dominic who worked for Winston's Wish, a charity dedicated to helping bereaved children.

I spoke to Dom for a long time as we drove south. By the time we stopped at a service station for a break, I knew how I would approach the coming morning. His advice was very clear.

It's important to let the truth out and never lock it away. Allow the kids to know that it's okay to be sad. I should always feel able to be sad with them. But it is just as important for them also to feel normal and do the stuff kids do in ordinary life. It would be wrong for me, even in the next few weeks, to expect them to be sad all the time. They need to laugh and feel more loved than ever. A key part of that love means me explaining to them what has happened to Jo and understanding how this will shape our lives ahead. I need to talk in simple language while explaining the permanence of death. They need to process the fact that their mum is never coming back. I must not soften that truth, or dress it up in a mystical way, because this will confuse them later on. The truth is horrible but, eventually, it can strengthen us.

As I walked through the service station, my raw emotions jarring with other people's continuing normality, I felt resolved. I climbed back into the car with my now silent suffering.

We arrived at my parents' home after 11 p.m. I spoke to my mum and dad for a while and then I went to bed. I did not sleep until the very early hours of the morning when, exhausted and cried out, I closed my eyes.

I soon woke up. The nightmare resumed.

– 17 June 2016 –

I told Cuillin and Lejla about Jo at my parents' house. It was almost unbearable to end the charmed innocence of their lives. I hated what I had to do; I hated myself for having to do it. They absorbed the truth in different ways. I felt heartbroken for my children – but also determined to keep these shattering moments to ourselves as much as possible.

A couple of hours later Stacia, who is the kindest, most thoughtful person I know, and a trained teacher, came up with an idea we all liked. Each of us would write down some of our favourite memories of Jo – of Mummy – on small pieces of coloured paper. We would then hang these memories on the apple tree in Mum and Dad's garden. In this way Cuillin and Lejla and I, my parents, my sister and brother-in-law and their three sons, shared our most cherished snapshots of Jo. We wrote the words on to the tiny paper sheets and, before we hung each one on a branch, we read our memories out loud.

The kids liked doing it. The apple tree looked beautiful decorated with all our words. It seemed to have taken on fresh life. It was full of Jo, with even more paper memories of her than there were apples to be picked on that summer afternoon. The kids made fun of my awful drawings.

We made it through supper and bath time, and then the crash came. The children could no longer hold anything more inside their little hearts. Cuillin and Lejla cried bitter, painful tears. They were distressed, wanting to see Jo, calling for her, needing her more than ever. I tried everything I could think of but, in my exhausted grief, nothing seemed to work. When I began to sing they became even more upset. They wanted Mummy to sing to them, not me.

Then, something extraordinary happened.

Cuillin likes to make up songs. For the last couple of years, ever since he was three, he has loved making up songs with his own words. It's a gift he gets from Jo who had a vivid imagination and always created new worlds for Cuillin and Lejla at bedtime. She wove together long stories she dreamed up about her imaginary hero, Finley the Fieldmouse, and enchanted the kids with his fantastical new adventures every night. Finley would be engaged in wild boar hunts in the woods in between dancing with moles and fighting off marauding monsters. Cuillin and Lejla absorbed everything and loved it, especially, when their mum acted out the roles while entrancing them with her rattling yarns.

That night, not much more than twenty-four hours after

her death, Cuillin asked me if he could sing a song. 'It's my new song about Mummy,' he said.

I told Cuillin that I would love to hear his song. Lejla, her chest still heaving, nodded. She would also like to hear Cuillin sing about Mummy.

Cuillin asked if I would sing with him. I hugged him. 'Of course.'

Would I record us singing together? I reached for my phone which had been switched off all day. It came blazing back to life with beeps and buzzes, texts and voicemail messages. I could tell that there were hundreds but I didn't want to look at any of them or listen to a single message. I just wanted to be with the kids and hear Cuillin sing about Jo.

We had talked all day and I'd tried to answer their questions honestly. I had to say, no, I couldn't dream up a way to bring Mummy back to us. I explained to Cuillin that his good idea that scientists might be able to inject life into her wouldn't work. We also couldn't make a new version of Mummy out of wood, as Lejla had suggested, and we weren't going to see her in another world. I told them that Jo was gone but that she lived on in our hearts and heads. We would never forget her because we would always talk about her and we would always love her.

There were times when I wasn't sure if any of my well-meaning words were sinking in — such was our torment — but I would soon see that they had understood. That gift came from Cuillin.

'Are we ready?' he asked, sitting up in bed.

'Yes, we're ready,' I said softly.

Lejla looked up at Cuillin, her face suddenly expectant.

Like an instinctive musician, Cuillin counted out the start: 'One, two . . .' And then he started.

'I really love my mum,' he sang in a husky little croak before he looked anxiously at me. 'Can you sing it with me?'

We slipped into an echoing call-and-answer routine. Cuillin's voice was soft but clear, high but strong. My own voice was a much lower burr, thick with tears and love, as I repeated his words in a husky half-spoken sing-song.

Cuillin: I love my mumma.
Me: I love my mumma.
Cuillin: But now she's dead.
Me: But now she's dead.

I took in a sharp breath at the use of 'dead' in a small child's song, but Cuillin concentrated with such purity. He lifted up his head and sang louder:

Cuillin: She used to be so kind.
Me: She used to be so kind.
Cuillin: But now she's dead.
Me: Now she's dead.
Cuillin: But she will still be with us.
Me: But she will still be with us.
Cuillin: We'll carry her in our hearts.

Lejla smiled her sweetest sleepy smile. Cuillin kept going:

Cuillin: I love my mummy.
Me: I love my mummy.
Cuillin: I will not leave her behind.
Me: I will not leave her behind.

Hope and belief were now surging through Cuillin. He looked me straight in the eye and sang:

Cuillin: That's a very big promise to you.
Me: That's a very big promise to you.
Cuillin: But I really, really promise it.

By now I was so impressed and uplifted that I added my own lines to his as we often did:

Me: Promise it, da do do do.
Cuillin: So we will not leave her behind, will we?
Me: We'll never leave her behind – she's in our
  hearts.
Cuillin: Oh, what a time it was.
Me: Every day, in every way.
Cuillin: We'll talk about her. We'll sing about her. All
  times.
Me: We'll love her every day of our lives.
Cuillin: So that is a promise. We just love our
  mumma but now she's dead.

'That was a beautiful song. Did you just make it up?'

'Yeah,' Cuillin said, sounding shy.

'That was the most beautiful song,' I said again.

'Can we listen to it?' Cuillin asked.

'You want to listen to it now?'

'Yeah,' Cuillin said.

Lejla was slipping away into sleep and, after we had tucked her in and given her a kiss, Cuillin and I settled down. I pulled him close to me and we listened again to his song of truth. Like I am doing now, we both cried as we heard him sing his song for Jo.

6

From Batley to Cambridge

Although she spent a lot of her life living away from her childhood home, Jo regarded herself as very much 'a proud Yorkshire lass'. Jo and Kim grew up in the small town of Heckmondwike, West Yorkshire, with their parents Jean and Gordon. The house backed on to open fields and the girls spent long afternoons playing outside. There was a wild horse, an old bull and, hanging from the big oak tree in the middle of the rolling barley fields, a Tarzan swing. They loved the horse and the swing, and ran away and laughed whenever the bull roused himself to make a rare mock charge, but the girls' favourite activity was rolling down the hill in an old wooden barrel they had found abandoned in the field.

Their friends Dawn and Neil, who lived opposite them, would push the barrel up to the top of the hill and then all four of them would squeeze inside. They could just fit in if they pressed themselves flat against the slatted sides. And then, all leaning together in the same direction, the little kids would tilt the barrel over. It would crash to the ground and they'd cry out in excitement, and a little fear, at the madness that awaited. Yelling and leaning hard to one side, they would start the descent. Screams echoed from inside the dark and spinning chamber, but the crash they were waiting for never came. Somehow, as if they were spared from a splintering smash by a miraculous life force, the barrel eventually slowed and their yelping hysteria turned to hilarity.

Jo and Kim always believed their high-speed roll would end safely. They were smart girls and made a calculated gamble. The barrel would hold together; and they could climb out after a ride far more thrilling than any fairground adventure.

The Leadbeaters – Jean and Gordon and Jo and Kim – lived in Berwick Avenue, in a semi-detached three-bedroom house in Heckmondwike, nine miles south-west of Leeds, two miles from Batley and just over a mile from Birstall Library. The suburban life of Heckmondwike in the early 1980s was a safe haven – at least outside a hurtling barrel.

Jo had got to know the streets and people of her home-town from a very young age. Her lovely old grandad Arthur, her dad's dad, had pushed her around in a pram from when Jo was two years old. Arthur had been a postman in the 1930s, before the Second World War, and he used to deliver letters door to door, from Heckmondwike to White Lee to Liversedge and sometimes even up into Batley and Birstall. After the war, once he was in his thirties, Arthur moved from the streets into the post office counters, and so he still knew exactly where most people lived.

Two years after Jo was born in the summer of 1974,

Arthur was forced to take early retirement. He was still only sixty-two in 1976 and so, being fit and well, his granddaughter gave Arthur Leadbeater a new lease of life. Joanne, as everyone then called her (or 'Jwan' as it was pronounced), became Arthur's sidekick. He used to turn up on the doorstep at Berwick Avenue to take Joanne out for a stroll. They would visit Jessie (Arthur's wife) or Mary and Jack (her other grandparents). Jo loved to play in their gardens and enjoyed the cooking of both her grandmothers.

Kim was born at the start of the blisteringly hot summer of 1976, and she never seemed to settle as a baby. Her big sister had been different. Jean and Gordon thought Joanne was pretty much the perfect baby. She would sleep for four hours, wake up for a feed, and then burp and smile and nod off again. But Kim kept her mum up most nights so Jean was always relieved when Arthur took Joanne out in her pram, to give her some respite.

Arthur and his little granddaughter would be out for hours on the streets he had once walked as a postman. As she got older Joanne, or Jo as she started to call herself, loved those Wednesday mornings with Grandad. The highlight was always their stop for an Eccles cake but, as the years passed, Jo enjoyed the way in which everyone seemed to adore Arthur. He was always keen to stop for a chat; and it didn't matter if it was a nattering old dear, a beefy builder or a young mum pushing her own pram in the opposite direction. Grandad was interested in everyone he met and, asking them questions and listening closely to their answers, he made each person feel special. It was a gift, of empathy and compassion, he would pass down to his granddaughter.

Jo's family weren't political, but they were caring and considerate, and Jo's values were shaped by this. She also inherited how crucial it was to be part of a close community. That appreciation drove her work as an MP and gave her a sense of the importance of traditions and textures of communities in and around towns like Batley. Jo eventually developed a desire to travel the world, and worked in Brussels, New York and London, but she never lost her love of home and always valued the solid grounding she had been given in Yorkshire. She felt there was no contradiction in being proud of coming from Yorkshire, and England and Britain while also being interested in the world.

The Leadbeater girls, aged five and three, went to ballet classes for a while, until their mum was asked, politely, to keep Kim out of a tutu because she kept disrupting all the other little ballerinas. Jo and Kim took up swimming instead and were much happier at the Tiger Sharks club at Spenborough Swimming Baths. They loved acting out *The A-Team* television series, with Jo taking the part of Hannibal and Kim being the smooth-talking Face. They were inseparable, as they had been since their earliest days of playing in the back garden of Berwick Avenue during long summer afternoons that often involved water-fights which ended in squealing delight.

'Who are you going to get?' Gordon would shout to Jean.

'I'll get you, little Kim,' their mum would say as she scampered after her younger daughter.

'Right, Joanne,' her dad would call, laughing, as he started to run after Jo. 'I'm catching you!'

They ran round and round the garden before bath time having delirious fun – just as they did when it was time to step into fancy dress. There are many photos of the sisters in strange costumes, but the most infamous is probably from late July 1981 when Jo was seven and Kim was five. Jo looks very serious, all dressed up as Prince Charles, while Kim steals the show looking like Princess Diana holding a very realistic Prince William doll.

As the years passed their interests changed. For a while they went often with their dad and grandad to watch Huddersfield Town play football. Arthur, in particular, was fanatical about the Terriers but Jo and Kim were more casual in supporting a club that lost more often than it won. By the time they were teenagers they preferred to catch the bus into Dewsbury so that they could shop at Dorothy Perkins. It was then, having given up watching football and rolling down the hill in a barrel, that the sisters became even closer.

Jo and Kim were fourteen and twelve when the family moved nearer to Batley and to a detached house in White Lee Road, with four bedrooms. There was a lovely garden and a conservatory at the back.

The girls were given good values and a strong moral sense by their parents, and taught to accept people without

56

judging them. Their dad worked at a factory in Seacroft, just outside Leeds, with a 1,200-strong workforce from diverse backgrounds. There was a large contingent of Jewish workers, whose German families had fled the Nazis and settled in Leeds, as well as many people from the West Indies and the Indian sub-continent. Gordon was used to mixing with different kinds of people as he worked his way up to being a production manager at a factory that manufactured deodorants and toothpaste.

Jean had also started working again, as a secretary at a junior school. The new house was within walking distance of Heckmondwike Grammar and Jo and Kim ambled together to and from school every day. They were soon part of a large friendship group but formed a close-knit gang of four with Heidi Toulson and Louise Woollard.

Jo never found it hard to make friends with people of her own age, but she was shy around adults. Kim was much more confident and outgoing. There was such a distinction between the sisters in terms of social confidence that Heidi and Louise hardly noticed after a while when Kim did plenty of talking for Jo. Whether they were going into a shop, or Jo needed to phone British Rail to check on train times, she urged Kim to step in for her. Kim was happy to help. Meanwhile Jo was the family peacemaker, getting Kim out of difficulties that her fiery temperament could create, and calming her down.

When I met her, years later, I found it hard to believe that Jo, so supremely confident and competent, had ever suffered from shyness or self-doubt. But she was just as insecure as the rest of us. Her teenage diaries show that she was worried about her weight and whether the boy she fancied liked her back. Despite her popularity and her achievements, she fretted that she was not, in some way, good enough. Her eighteenth birthday party had her in fits of nerves.

> I was dieting and doing loads of exercise so that I looked good for my birthday party. I got down to 8½ stone – what an idiot putting it back on. The party was on the Friday night (18th June). God, I was so nervous about Jem and Jay [Jo and Kim's potential new boyfriends] coming and I really wanted everything to be perfect. I was really nervous about whether people would turn up or not. As it was everyone came and everything went absolutely ace. I still can't believe how many cards I got – something like 60! – and how many people bought me presents and stuff. It just felt really good that people 'cared enough' to go to the trouble of buying stuff. I suppose I was really proud of myself.

Jo worked hard at school, and both she and Kim excelled academically. Jo was polite and respectful, and widely liked, and it was not much of a surprise when she became head girl at Heckmondwike Grammar. But she was an unconventional head girl and she often got Louise to sign her in at registration. Rather than bunking off school, however, Jo would go home to work in the quiet of her bedroom.

She only got busted twice, when Jo and Kim went to see gigs by Erasure and Michael Jackson, but their parents had already given them permission to miss school. Gordon and Jean knew how well the girls were doing and were relaxed enough to cut them some slack.

Despite her shyness with adults, Jo didn't have any problems meeting boys. She was pretty and, with Kim at her side, the Leadbeater sisters became very popular. But Kim and Jo were happiest going out with Heidi and Louise down the Bradford Road. On Friday and Saturday nights they would all sneak into the Batley Nash, a working men's club, where they sold cheap booze and allowed polite kids to order a half of cider. From there they would saunter down Batley's golden mile, going on a pub crawl, before ending up dancing at Legends or, more often, the Frontier. A covers band usually played at the Frontier where they also had a laser show which, at the time, seemed incredibly cool.

The Leadbeater sisters had part-time jobs – Jo was behind the till at a local Texaco garage while Kim worked at a pizza takeaway. And they were ambitious. Jo didn't say it to anyone else but, over a snakebite or vodka, she would sometimes talk to Kim, Heidi and Louise. 'Wouldn't it be a laugh if I came back one day as the MP for Batley?'

She said it in a jokey way and it didn't take them long to switch back to talking about boys again but, for a while, on dreamy, light-headed nights, a small flame of hope and drive was lit inside Jo Leadbeater. She might have been shy but she was determined and intelligent. Jo wished, even then, that one day she might do something special for her community.

At the age of eighteen, in 1992, Jo passed her A-level exams with a set of glittering results that ensured her entry to study Archaeology and Anthropology at Pembroke College, Cambridge, that October. Jo would be the first member of her family to graduate from university.

After sharing a glass of sherry with her college tutor Michael Kuczynski and five other new students reading either Archaeology and Anthropology or Social and Political Sciences (SPS) at Pembroke College, Jo felt mildly freaked out. She had never drunk sherry down the Bradford Road; but the formality of the Cambridge setting, the cut-glass accents and the formal black gowns were far more alienating.

Earlier that afternoon there had been moments when she felt dispirited and intimidated because everyone appeared so posh and so educated. Most of the boys had gone to schools such as St Paul's or Westminster and spoke quite pompously while Jo had never sounded more Yorkshire, at least in her own head, when people kept saying 'Pardon?' as they struggled to understand her.

Many of the other students had stared at her in incomprehension when, having asked her where she had gone to school, Jo said, 'Heckmondwike Grammar'. No one had even heard of Heckmondwike. 'It's near Leeds,' Jo explained helpfully. She could see their eyes glazing over. A state school near Leeds? Yorkshire? The north? They drifted away to find people of a similar background to their own.

It was much more welcoming in Kuczynski's lounge. Jo liked him because he seemed gentle and quirky. She smiled nervously at two of the SPS students, Sarah and Steve who, reassuringly for her, also appeared to be out of their comfort zones.

They were led into the grand hall for dinner. It was very elegant, but strange too, with long tables covered with shiny cutlery and sparkling glasses. The candles flickered and waiters in bow ties stood poised to begin the silver service.

Jo sat down and gazed at the menu.

Matriculation Dinner
Tuesday, 6th October 1992
Melon Dr Caius
* * *

Poulet sauté Chasseur
Petits Pois
Pommes de terre Parisiennes
* * *

Charlotte Royale
* * *

Café
* * *

Quincy Clos des Victoires 1988
Bourgueil Domaine des Raguenières 1987
Quarles Harris Late Bottled 1984

Jo could not understand why they had to print a student menu in French – unless everyone at Cambridge was determined to ram their superiority down her throat. Earlier that summer, her diary echoes with praise for the 'gorgeous nosh' on offer at her local Pizza Hut. She found the culture clash overwhelming.

Grace was said in Latin, bells were tolled. It all seemed very serious.

Jo was insulted by a pompous Fellow of Pembroke who looked her up and down and said that if he had his way, she would not be in their company because he had voted against admitting women to the college. Pembroke had been founded in 1347, making it one of the oldest colleges at Cambridge, but women had only been allowed to attend since 1984.

Jo had arrived just two days earlier, on Sunday, 4 October 1992, after her parents had driven her down from Yorkshire. She had said a tearful farewell despite having been irritable with her mum and dad all day. That night Jo had opened her garish new diary. On the cover, flecked with images of lipstick, earrings, pencils and flowers, it read: *AN ILLUSTRATED GIRL'S NOTEBOOK: A personal journal.*

Her first entry as a Cambridge University student captured her uncertainty:

I can't believe that I'm actually here and, in truth, I don't really know what the hell I'm thinking. It's like nothing I've ever experienced before so I just don't know exactly how to act. I can see me quelling my sarcastic nature somewhat if I want to make friends because it would be so easy to simply 'Take the Piss' . . .

Twenty-four hours later Jo was not in the mood to mock anyone. She felt desolate.

I want to go home and be with people who actually like me for me – with people who aren't so pretentious and posh and totally above me. I want my mum and Kim. God, I'm so upset. What am I doing here? I don't fit in. God, I can't actually believe how much I had to fight back the tears just then. OK they probably didn't mean it but, shit, they just ripped up my roots, my memories, my life. I don't want to stay.

Jo also wrote a letter to Kim.

R8
Pembroke College
Cambridge

Dear Kim,
    Kim, God, I'm missing you so much. I just feel so lonely. No, I haven't yet met anyone like me and, yes, they are all posh, pretentious bastards who I just can't get on with. It is actually now 3 a.m. and I'm crying my eyes out, writing this letter which

*probably won't even reach you because in the
morning I'll realise how stupid I was and that I
don't want to upset you Kim. But I am so upset.
I just want to come home. I want a big hug from
my little baby Sis. I can't stand Cambridge if it's
like this. I don't like it. I want to come home.*

    Jo

Kim never received that letter because Jo pasted it down
into her diary instead. It always reminded her how she
had felt at the start of her Cambridge years.

Jo was tenacious even then. She did not quit and she
resisted her dad's urgings for her to come home for the
weekend when she called her parents to explain how
miserable she felt. She kept smiling and going out and,
very slowly, life improved.

Jo and Sarah Hamilton, the SPS student who had also
drunk sherry with their tutor, met each other properly
later that Freshers' Week, when a pub crawl ended with
them on the dance floor of Cinderella Rockerfellas, a club
in Cambridge. They both thought it was pretty terrible
but, still, they danced a lot because there had been an
instant connection. Sarah's family were from Bradford and
she had gone to an ordinary school too.

Sarah had given Jo hope and she introduced her to Liz
Weston, another northern state-school girl. Liz, who came
from Crewe, was immediately likeable. Jo resolved to overcome her misery.

Sunday 9th November

*I suppose I'm never gonna fit in here. Cambridge is
a place for Public School types. But that doesn't
mean I can't offer this place anything. I know deep
down that I can. In fact, I can probably give more
than most here. I've got feelings, I can get upset – I
love and hate and can get hurt. Many people here
carry on the pretence that everything's perfect,
keeping up the false conversations and superficial
chatting. WHY? Don't they have emotions?*

*I'm gonna do this. I really, really, am gonna give
Cambridge ALL I can to it. As for happiness? There
is never 'forever' – only the moment. Be satisfied
NOW – don't live for tomorrow. OK, so it's corny but
it's so true. I should just relax and enjoy it. Let's face
it there is a lot here to enjoy. There are a lot of
opportunities, a lot of beauty and knowledge. I
mean, God, this is*

THE CAMBRIDGE UNIVERSITY

*So, Jo, don't just sit there. Make the most of being
alive.*

The seeds of Jo's politicisation at Cambridge are already
evident. A dozen years later, when our relationship blossomed, Jo explained to me how marked she felt by those
bruising personal encounters with class, prejudice and
inequality. Before she went to Pembroke she had not

travelled much beyond the odd beach holiday, and she was naïve and unworldly. But the innocence of her Batley life also meant that Cambridge shocked her. The sneering reaction of some privileged students when she arrived, and the way other people mocked her accent or lack of sophistication made her feel insecure and alienated.

It wasn't that she immediately got into politics in a big way, but her political journey began in Cambridge. She was infuriated by the blatant inequities she saw and her realisation of how divided British society remained. Class and wealth still dominated Cambridge University in a way they hadn't in Batley, where social differences were less obvious. From then on, Jo understood the power of privilege and she vowed to fight for equality in the worlds she occupied.

There was also family pain. Jo and Kim's relationship became more distant. Having always been very close, the separation hurt them both. Kim sat on the window ledge of her bedroom in White Lee and wrote poetry about how lonely she felt without Jo.

At first they spoke virtually every night. In those pre-mobile times Jo would go to the pay phone in Ivy Court and call home, reversing the charges. After chatting to her parents the phone was handed to her sister. It was difficult. Kim had always been more confident but, without her big sister, she felt a bit unmoored. Rather than having Jo lean on her, Kim was now feeling leaned on by others who would like her to follow the same path.

One morning at Heckmondwike Grammar, Kim was walking across the playground when the headteacher stopped her. 'How are you Kim?' he asked. And before Kim could answer, and perhaps even say she felt a little lost without her sisterly role, he pressed on: 'Don't forget we're expecting great things from you – just like Jo. We're expecting another set of A-level results that also take you to Cambridge. Or maybe Oxford?'

Kim was her own person. She wasn't Jo and she didn't want to be.

There were long, emotional conversations and tears. Kim spoke out. If Jo was so bloody miserable at Cambridge, why didn't she just leave? Why didn't she come home?

Jo loved Batley but she also wanted to see the world beyond Yorkshire. Cambridge made her uncertain and uncomfortable, but she resolved to see it through. To stand up to its prejudice rather than be cowed by it. Going back home too soon, before she had made a mark, would scar her. She kept going. She kept trying.

Jo began to broaden her social group including meeting Nisha Jani who would become a lifelong friend, as would Steve Morris. She'd met him on the first evening at Pembroke and Steve, who came from Gloucester, was also studying SPS. He instantly admired Jo's feisty spirit. All the southerners liked to soften her surname, and make it sound more dainty and refined by calling her Jo *Leadbetter*. She could have let them get away with it, as a way of feeling more welcome in their circle, but Jo refused.

'It's actually pronounced *LeadBEATer*,' Jo would point out. 'That's the proper Yorkshire way of saying my name.'

She was nurtured by her sympathetic tutors and

lecturers. Barbara Bodenhorn, her Director of Studies, had recognised the potential of Jo's intelligence and clarity of thinking at their first interview and she constantly encouraged her. Bodenhorn was an interesting woman, an American, and very different from everyone else Jo had met so far who came from London or the Home Counties, and seemed to have been born for this kind of life.

Dr Bodenhorn had chosen a diverse group to study Archaeology and Anthropology and SPS at Pembroke that year. The five British students were from very different backgrounds, while the sixth was from Japan. Much to Jo, Sarah and Steve's surprise, Josh had gone to the prestigious private school, Harrow, but once they got to know him, and realised that he overcame every prejudice they harboured against public school toffs, they all became close friends. Jo's confidence was renewed. She always found Cambridge intimidating and alienating, yet she was also stimulated by it. She began to truly believe in herself.

One romantic liaison followed another. It seemed to Steve and Sarah as if the boys were shattered once their whirlwind romance with Jo had run its course. She was so overpowering that they took ages to recover. Steve got used to rolling his eyes whenever Jo told him that the latest boyfriend was 'incredible' and the potential love of her life.

Kim came to visit Jo a few times, as the sisters tried to patch up things, and they usually ended up in a drunken sing-song in Steve's room, where he squirmed with embarrassment as the sisters belted out their version of 'I Know Him So Well' from the musical *Chess*.

Jo's second and third years at Cambridge contrasted sharply with her testing arrival at Pembroke. She switched to reading Social and Political Sciences. Her new course offered an eclectic but unified grounding in sociology, politics, psychology, history and anthropology. It showed Jo how she could understand the world in a way that blended a mix of disciplines with humanity at its core. SPS gave Jo the groundwork from which, in subsequent years, she would shine in international development, aid work and as an MP.

She became the Welfare Representative at Pembroke's Junior Parlour (the student union), so she could offer comfort to first-year students who felt as lost as she had done. Jo also rowed, ran, partied hard and sailed through her degree, gaining a comfortable 2:1.

Towards the end of their university days, Steve remembers a group of SPS students discussing what they would do with their lives. Jo was ready when it was her turn. 'I dunno . . . Boutros Boutros-Ghali Jo?' she quipped. Her friends laughed at the thought of a girl from Batley having the impact of the head of the United Nations.

Even then, amid the ups and downs of student life, Jo already knew what she wanted. She might have arrived in Cambridge as a shy and sensitive outsider but, three years on, she had regained the conviction and exhilaration of that little girl who rolled down the hill in a barrel with her sister back in Heckmondwike. One day, she would make her mark. She would make a difference in an unfair world.

7
The Call

Every time I switched my phone on the deluge of messages and texts was overwhelming. I read some of the texts, and they were all heartfelt, but I didn't check my voicemail. Jo's murder dominated the news – on television and radio, in the press and on social media. I changed my voicemail greeting to explain I would not be checking messages and that, if it was urgent, I should be emailed. I sounded empty.

There would need to be an autopsy; it would be weeks before the funeral. Jo's body was in a morgue. I could have snapped apart if I thought about it too closely; I turned to Cuillin and Lejla.

What would Jo and I have done if we had still been together amid a grotesque tragedy? We would have gone outside and shown Cuillin and Lejla that life continued. Immersed them in an adventure and tried to remind them of the wonder of the world, not just the pain that it can inflict.

I needed them to be surrounded by people. We needed

our friends. And so on the third night after we lost Jo, we went camping less than an hour's drive from my parents' home, near the Uffington White Horse – that ancient figure, etched in chalk in Oxfordshire, on a hill I remember rolling down with my sister when we were children. We met around twenty of our friends, most of them from the folk band I played with, and their children. We had already planned to meet up that weekend for our annual party, celebrating Jo's forthcoming birthday, at our cottage. The party turned into a camping wake for Jo.

It was the right place to be but, like every other moment, it was extremely difficult. I tried hard but I was like a robot. I spoke, I joined in and I carried out tasks. But I could not engage much with anyone. Shock had taken hold of me. The kids did better. They enjoyed the games we played and they seemed to have a good time in small patches. But they were also understandably withdrawn at times, tetchy and sullen. They were sleep-deprived but, far worse, they were Jo-deprived. They needed her so very badly.

It was traumatic trying to get them to sleep that night in the tent. They were crying and then sobbing: 'I want my mumma.' We went round in tearful circles, with Cuillin and Lejla becoming more and more upset. Finally, exhaustion won out. They grew quieter. We sang Cuillin's song and then they surrendered to sleep.

I staggered out of the tent to find my friends around the fire, tears streaming down their faces as they listened to the rawness of my children's pain. It was midsummer but the night was very cold and an icy wind blew across the open fields. I lay down next to the fire. My front soon felt hot from the flames; my back was cold in the wind. I shook and sobbed. I felt hands holding my shoulders, rubbing my back. But I couldn't stop crying. I was surrounded by friends yet I felt more alone than I had ever been.

Gradually I calmed myself down and, after a while, I sat up.

Around the fire, drawing closer to feel its warmth, we started telling each other stories about Jo. We all laughed as we remembered her funny quirks and the extraordinary passion and kindness that ran through her like a mighty river. She came alive again in the stories we told which gave me great solace that night.

I slept a little and, in the morning, it was lovely and sunny. My friends played music around the dying fire and the kids danced. Cuillin and Lejla looked more like themselves and we went for a short walk up to the White Horse. Some part of me could appreciate its beauty, even though I felt hollow as I stood there.

Later that day we met up with old friends from my scouting days in Reading. We had a picnic next door to the boat house by the Thames that used to be our scout hut. The new group of kids got Cuillin and Lejla playing football and running around. I didn't join in much, but it helped mask the pain for the kids. These were some of my oldest friends, and it was good to be with them, even if we all found it hard to talk.

Brajda, my closest Croatian friend, was there too. She had arrived in the UK to attend our party. I had met Brajda when she was only fifteen and I was doing voluntary work with kids who had survived the siege of Sarajevo. Brajda was on the camp as well. Often these kids were completely alone in the world, the only ones of their families to make it through the war. I went back to Croatia and Bosnia a couple of times a year for nearly a decade, and once I got together with Jo, she came with me. She had always loved Brajda.

The messages I received from other friends in Croatia and Bosnia were a particular comfort in the days following Jo's death. A child I had known since a toddler sent me a short message that simply read: 'You came to us when we needed help. Now we are here for you.'

– 20 June 2016 –

A couple of days later I felt strong enough to turn on my phone again and be able to talk to people. One of the friends I spoke to was Gordon Brown, my former boss at 10 Downing Street. Gordon was kind and compassionate, and he said all the right things. Just as we were saying goodbye he told me that Barack Obama had called him and asked for my contact details.

'Would that be okay?' Gordon asked. 'May I pass them on?'

I couldn't really imagine the President of the United

States wanting to get in touch, so I offered a casual response: 'Yes, that would be fine.'

We all focused on getting through the day as best we could, and looking after the kids. Hour after hour we tried hard to keep them occupied and in good spirits.

Early that evening, sitting downstairs with everyone, my phone rang again. It was a withheld number. I almost didn't answer but, because dinner was nearly over and there was a lull before we gave the kids a treat for dessert, I picked it up.

'Hello, Mr Cox. This is the White House Situation Room,' a very deep and very American voice boomed. 'We would like to transfer you to *Air Force One*.'

I nearly said, 'Yeah, right, which one of you is taking the piss?' I was convinced it was one of my friends winding me up. But no one I cared about would be in the mood to play a prank on me. I also remembered what Gordon had said.

'That's fine,' I said, rising like a zombie, heading upstairs like one of the Walking Dead. It felt so extraordinary I didn't really know what I was doing.

I had reached the top of the stairs when a new voice echoed. 'Hello. This is the control room of *Air Force One*. We would like to connect you with the President of the United States.'

I wanted to say 'Really?' But, instead, I just muttered, 'Okay.'

There was a long pause and, suddenly grasping that this really was about to happen, I fiddled with my phone and managed to hit the record button. I thought Cuillin and Lejla might want to hear this conversation about their beloved mum one day, when they were old enough to understand that her life and death had touched so many people around the world that even the President of the United States felt moved to call.

I heard the familiar voice of Barack Obama. There was a delay on the line, and I was still reeling. I was more awkward than I would have liked. But I can hear Obama's warmth now when I re-listen to that conversation.

I mentioned to Obama that Jo had admired him greatly. Only a few weeks before, she and I had snuggled up on our sofa to watch a documentary about him, which she had loved. It had prompted a lot of conversations about leadership and courage. I also told him how, in 2008, when we were living in the States, Jo and I had volunteered on his campaign team in North Carolina – in one of the areas where, in a tight contest, he won the vote that sealed his presidency.

I wondered if I should say the only area that had disappointed her was his administration's reaction to the crisis in Syria. Two things stopped me. First, I felt too torn up to know what I really wanted to say about Jo and Syria and, second, I didn't want to be ungracious during such a generous call. It was the right decision. And his kindness did not end there.

'Come and see me,' Obama said. 'Bring the kids and come out to DC . . .'

'Okay,' I said, as if one of my mates from the band had

just invited the kids and me over to an impromptu gig at Simon or Rob's house. 'We'll do that.'

When the call finished I walked downstairs in a daze. 'Who was on the phone?' my dad asked.

'Barack Obama . . .' I said. 'He's asked me and the kids to go see him in the White House.'

My parents and my sister looked at me as if I'd gone mad. And then, for the first time since Jo died, we laughed. We could imagine Jo laughing with us, in delight and incomprehension.

8

The Making of Jo

'I want to live, I really want to live,' Jo wrote in her diary at midnight on 8 November 1995. She was twenty-one years old and in Bangkok, on the first night of a three-month trip around South-east Asia and Australia with her best friend Sarah Hamilton. Jo and Sarah had graduated from Cambridge that summer. They had then worked hard for three months as typists at a building society in Bradford, in order to pay for their Asian adventure. Jo had never been out of Europe before, and the jolting adjustment to her first experience of the developing world led to her reflective mood.

Who am I? (Midnight self-assessment) . . .
*   I'm very idealistic – yet at times cynical. I'm passionate yet far too often scared. Fear holds me back too much. I believe in people, causes, experiences. I want to live. I really want to live.*

Jo had such an appetite for experience, for a visceral immersion in life, that I find it unbearably moving to read now.

Jo and Sarah were on a journey of discovery – of South-east Asia and themselves. They had a lot of fun and loved meeting local people and fellow travellers as they sampled Thai life on the road. In later years they both told me that they remembered most vividly a feeling that they never stopped talking – unless they were eating, drinking, dancing or sleeping. But, amid the casual chatter and deeper conversations, they were working their way towards clarity about what they wanted to do with their lives.

The most illuminating moment occurred on a crammed bus journey through a remote corner of Thailand. As the young women talked earnestly, it was as if a path opened up in front of each of them. Sarah became certain she wanted to become a documentary film-maker and make films about life in different parts of the world. Jo shared that global perspective. She wanted to work on aid and development, doing what she could to extend the opportunities she enjoyed to others who were less fortunate, simply because of the country of their birth.

Throughout the next twenty years, whenever Jo or Sarah achieved a breakthrough, they conjured up that memory. 'I'm having a Thailand bus moment,' one of them would say, and instantly they would be transported back to that dusty scene of youthful certainty.

They also began to appreciate fully just how lucky they were. Jo and Sarah were ordinary state-school girls from the north of England, but they had still had relatively privileged lives, and the benefit of Cambridge degrees. Whatever they decided to do in the future, they were heading for well-paid work that stimulated and rewarded them. It was different in many parts of the world, the UK included, but it was eye-wateringly different in South-east Asia.

They met an Indonesian man in a café in Ubud in the mountainous region of Bali, and were impressed by his immaculate English. He was in his early twenties too and, like them, seemed full of potential. They told him about all the places they had visited in Thailand and Indonesia and, after listening enthusiastically, he grew wistful. 'I would also love to travel one day,' he said. Jo was just about to suggest that he could look them up when he made it to London, but the young man shook his head. He would never earn enough money to leave Bali. He spoke so simply, without any attempt to engender pity, that Jo and Sarah were deeply affected. Jo had already compiled a list of her future holidays; she had stopped after twenty-eighty global destinations. The man in the Ubud café would not be able to draw up a similar list despite seeming to be just as bright and as interested in the world. He was already working far harder than they were but, no matter how long he strived, the disparity between their lives was bound to continue. He remained cheerful and interesting and their conversation moved on; but Jo never forgot that understated encounter.

Both Jo and Sarah did voluntary work the following year. In 1996 Sarah went to Tanzania while Jo headed into the jungles of Borneo as a member of Operation Raleigh. She spent three months there helping local people and working on conservation projects, with a group of fourteen young British men and women, and two expedition leaders. Jo worked hard.

They built a stilt house in a small fishing village on the north-east coast of Borneo. When the house was complete the villagers held a party as a thank you to their visitors. They also taught them indigenous-dances while Jo and her new friends showed the kids how to do the Hokey-Cokey.

In later years Jo loved to retell and embellish her adventures for our kids. She told them how she had avoided the stampede of wild elephants and escaped from pirates, a story that remains one of their favourites even now. According to Jo, the young Brits had been told that the South China Sea was teeming with cut-throat pirates who, in the dead of night, would come ashore to raid villages, pillaging and killing as they went. They were warned to listen out for the dogs whose barks filled the village soundscape at night. If the barking stopped it was because the pirates had killed them and were on their way. One night Jo was woken by one of her friends whispering in her ear: 'The pirates are coming.' Jo quietly put on her boots. The dogs were silent. All eighteen Raleigh volunteers, plus their two security guards, climbed into or on top of a Land-Rover in the dark. The engine struggled to start but eventually, with the headlights off, they got it going and sped away to a school further inland for safety. The next morning they returned to find the pirates had hit the village just up the coast.

* * *

There were no pirates in London but it felt challenging in other ways. Jo had never spent more than a couple of days at a time in the capital; she didn't know the city. She was looking for a job and trying to establish herself socially and professionally. Luckily for her, the rest of her SPS gang from Cambridge were already there and she reconnected with them. Jo and Sarah shared a flat and noticed how Steve and Josh had forged ahead in work. While Jo and Sarah had been seeing the world Steve had become a civil servant and Josh was now chief researcher to Philip Gould, one of Neil Kinnock's former advisers who had become a key architect of New Labour.

Jo decided she too wanted to work in Parliament, for the Labour Party. She wrote to dozens of Labour MPs on the off-chance someone might have a role available. Her persistence paid off and she secured a job as research assistant to Joan Walley, the Labour MP for Stoke-on-Trent North. During this first encounter with Westminster politics, Jo came to understand both its limitations and how it could still be used as a platform for change. She loved working for a female MP.

In 1998 Jo went to work for Britain in Europe, a new organisation set up to prepare for a possible referendum on the single currency. Josh was already working there and Jo made friends with Lucy Powell, who would later become MP for Manchester Central. It was soon clear to everyone that there would be no referendum and the organisation folded pretty quickly, but in the interim Jo, Josh and Lucy ended up playing a lot of pool in pubs around Horseferry Road. Josh and Jo became a couple and they lived together for a time on a houseboat on the Thames in Little Venice. I used to joke with her about whether it was me or the boat that most interested her.

Jo's first significant career break came when she applied for, and got, the job of parliamentary assistant to Glenys Kinnock, who was by then a high-profile Member of the European Parliament. Steve was already working out in Brussels and he showed Jo around when she arrived in early 2000.

Jo was thrilled with her new job and fell in love with Brussels. Her job was hard work but focused exactly on the issues she cared about. Glenys was demanding but it was just the challenge Jo needed. Glenys's high standards helped Jo to new heights and they soon became close friends as well as colleagues.

But it wasn't just the work Jo found stimulating. She developed a close group of friends and a much wider social circle. She moved in with Steve's girlfriend Tara and her friend Lucy Barker in a top-floor flat on Rue de Dublin, which Jo thought was great. It exuded a classic European style and was slap bang above a Congolese restaurant. Most nights the smell of cooked goat wafted up to their apartment. Jo was a hopeless cook and, when they were not out for the night, she would say to Tara and Lucy: 'What are you eating? Oh . . . I'd love some of that.' Tara, Lucy and Jo took French lessons together and bonded during evening chats, always over a couple of bottles of wine, about work and their love lives.

Jo was virtually adopted by the Kinnocks, as if she had become their surrogate daughter, and they opened up the European Parliament to her. They were an influential couple: Glenys was one of the most prominent MEPs in Brussels and Neil had become Vice-President of the European Commission for Administrative Reform. They held dinners in Strasbourg and Brussels and Jo, Steve, Tara and Lucy would sit around a table with thirty other people from all over the world and all walks of life. The evenings usually ended with Neil singing songs from the Welsh valleys.

Steve and Jo often found themselves sitting in the back of a car with Neil and Glenys upfront and giggling at their amazing lives. When they were kids they had both watched *Spitting Image* at a time when the Kinnocks were two of the star puppets. They sometimes felt as if they had ended up in a European Parliamentary version of the show, as they listened to the Kinnocks nattering away.

Glenys was instrumental to Jo's political development. Glenys is a political person deep down in her very bones. Jo was different. Until she left Cambridge, she was not especially political. She was driven by empathy and community, fairness and justice rather than party politics. But working with Glenys helped her to think about the intersection of her values with politics. Jo never became as tribal as the Kinnocks but she started to understand better how politics shapes almost everything we do in life. Glenys encouraged her to participate actively in her briefings, while immersing Jo in the political hurly-burly.

Her impact as an MEP meant that Jo's own work as an assistant assumed greater weight and her politicisation intensified.

Jo and Glenys visited South Africa in 2001, as part of an EU trade delegation. They went to Khayelitsha, a raw and impoverished township on the outskirts of Cape Town and learned that it had emerged in the dying days of apartheid in the early 1980s. P.W. Botha, the draconian President, sanctioned the forced removal of thousands of black people from squatter camps outside Cape Town into the new township of Khayelitsha – which, in Xhosa, means 'New Home'.

Khayelitsha was soon a dark and dirty ghetto without electricity or sanitation. Its sprawling mass of tiny houses and shacks, stacked in haphazard rows along the main N2 highway into Cape Town, became overcrowded and violent.

When Jo arrived, around 350,000 people lived there. The average family income was R20,000 (the equivalent of £1,000) a year and, while apartheid had been wiped away from official legislation, the divide between black and white South Africa remained vast.

Jo was stunned by the beauty of the country but appalled by the disparity between white and black South Africa. The majesty of Table Mountain was clearly visible from the dirt streets and corrugated shacks of the township, but it belonged to a different world, a white world of plush, high-walled suburbs and beachside beauty spots. Khayelitsha defined the lack of opportunity and hope in much of black South Africa.

Most of the people Jo met remained defiantly good-natured and surprisingly cheerful. Even if they lamented the crime and squalor, the residents of Khayelitsha inspired her with their warmth. But she felt the crushing inequality of their lives.

This was brought home to her most vividly when she visited a township clinic. Jo went to see one of the doctors and he looked desolate as he showed her his near empty dispensary. 'We have practically nothing,' he said. Jo was carrying a first aid bag and she opened it up. The doctor smiled wryly and said that it looked as if she were better equipped than his clinic. Jo felt like crying but the doctor cracked a joke and everyone laughed.

That visit was a seminal moment for Jo. It crystallised the injustice and inequality that had always motivated her. When she returned to Brussels, she vowed to do all she could to change the world, if only in her own small way. Until the day she died, Jo used Khayelitsha as the password to her phone. It was a call to action every time she turned it on.

Jo was still only in her mid-twenties and she thrived in Brussels. Rather than being a staid city, a bureaucracy full of faceless administrators and anonymous politicians, the Brussels she loved was fluid and diverse. Nearly 40 per cent of its inhabitants were non-Belgian, and Jo warmed to the contrasting cultures in a sociable atmosphere. She and her girlfriends went out a couple of nights a week. They were such regulars at their favourite bar, Coasters, that, as soon as she and her English friend Joanna Maycock walked in, the DJ would play one of their favourite tracks. Jo and Joanna were committed to making the world a better place but, rightly, they saw no contradiction between the fight for social justice and a hectic social life. Jo would always remember fondly that when she left work of an evening she could send a few texts and end up with twenty friends in a bar within twenty minutes, unlike London where you have to plan to meet up with people months in advance.

Jo's knowledge of development policies and trade issues expanded and she began to work closely with the Pacific, African and Caribbean (PAC) delegations at the EU, trying to help them compete with the dominant European economies. As much as she loved partying, she was far more committed to understanding the complex dossiers she had to present to Glenys and identifying the best strategy with which to boost the PAC trade delegations. Jo often missed a big night out to work instead. She was intellectually curious and hungry to learn.

Yet Jo was neither worthy nor po-faced. Eloise Todd, another MEP assistant who became a great friend, remembered the first time she saw Jo's plain speaking in action. A new assistant had just started work for another MEP. Jo invited her in for a chat and a coffee. 'How's it going?' Jo asked.

'Well,' the new assistant said, 'I don't quite understand some of the positions that are being taken by my MEP. It's a bit random, but I'm trying.'

Jo nodded and then, after a thoughtful pause, leaned

forward. 'To be honest,' she said seriously, 'you are working for a bit of a dick.'

Laughter broke out and, from then on, Jo, Eloise and the assistant were friends.

Eloise loved the way Jo switched seamlessly from irreverence to serious conversation. When Jo's career soared, she instilled a belief in Eloise that anything was possible.

In 2002 Jo had the breakthrough that she had been working for ever since that moment of life-defining certainty on the bus in Thailand. She was asked by Oxfam's head office to set up Oxfam International in Brussels. Jo was ecstatic and couldn't wait to get started, but she faced an uphill task. Her budget extended to just one employee, her assistant Sonia Vila-Hopkins, who had worked previously for Oxfam in Spain. They did not even have an office until Jo's friend Suzy Sumner came to the rescue. Suzy, who was working for the trade union charity Solidar, said that there was a small room, not much larger than a cubicle, in their office. The two young women – Jo was only twenty-eight and Sonia twenty-five – met for the first time just before they opened their office. Sonia had heard senior Oxfam officials asking, in disbelief, 'Who is this young woman? How can she set up an international office with no experience?' But Jo's enthusiasm was contagious and infected Sonia from the moment they shook hands. Sonia found Jo buoyant but grounded, honest and open. Early on in their friendship Jo told Sonia that she loved her job at Oxfam, it was what she had always wanted to do, but she also confided that one day she might like to go back home to try to become the MP for her community.

It wasn't long before Jo and Sonia won over the naysayers. Oxfam's executives were so impressed they agreed to fund a proper office on Rue du Commerce. Oxfam was intent on increasing its global campaigning work, therefore it was important for Jo and Sonia to operate from the centre of Brussels rather than on the fringes in Molenbeek. Jo became its international spokesperson as well as helping with the coordination of various internal policy discussions in Oxfam's five European offices.

She was instrumental in one of Oxfam's flagship campaigns, Make Trade Fair, the aim of which was to help developing countries trade their way out of poverty, by getting rid of unfair tariffs that kept their goods locked out of European markets. She soon showed her gift for speaking plainly while forging alliances with trade commissioners as well as Pacific, African and Caribbean ambassadors. She fought to rebalance the inequality in power relations between PAC producers and the EU negotiators and against the rigged double standards and basic unfairness of most trade deals. She often clashed with Peter Mandelson, the EU's Commissioner for Trade, and his team, as she encouraged countries within Europe, as well as the United States, to side with Oxfam's goals. It was this work that established her reputation as a kick-ass dynamo. That reputation never left her.

On 22 June 2004, Jo turned thirty. She had a huge party

and all her friends in Brussels were joined by her mum and dad and Kim, as well as Sarah and Heidi and Louise from Batley. When I look at the photos now I see the love for Jo shining from everyone's faces. It's also clear that they all had a riotous time, drinking and dancing into the night.

Sonia was at the party and she remembers looking at Jo and thinking how she had blossomed. When they first began working together Jo had seemed impossibly young, even wide-eyed, but she had become respected. The Brussels adventure was nearly over: Jo had confided to Sonia that she was moving back to England, to take the job she had wanted for several years, as Head of Policy for Oxfam. Sonia felt her loss. She knew she would never work again with Jo, the most genuine person she had ever met.

Jo's time in Brussels transformed her into a dogged and effective advocate for the causes she believed in. When she arrived she was still a novice, burning with desire to make the world a better place. By the time she left, that passion had been refined through years of hard work into a formidable set of skills and experience. At only thirty years of age, she was ready to step up in her fight for justice.

9
Seeing Jo, Remembering Jo

The aftershock of Jo's death continued to reverberate across the country and around the world. Parliament had been recalled that morning and all campaigning around the referendum had been suspended since the murder. Both sides of the Leave and Remain divide had been in touch with me to establish if they could resume their battle once a fitting tribute had been paid to Jo. Frankly I was too numb to care what they did.

First, however, all MPs headed to Westminster in honour of their fallen colleague – my wife and the mother of Cuillin and Lejla. The three of us, with my and Jo's immediate families, were invited to attend that extraordinary session of Parliament. I had been advised again by the child psychologists that I should include the children.

A Labour Party car took us to Westminster. Passing Buckingham Palace, I pointed out to Cuillin and Lejla that the flag had been lowered to half-mast in mourning for Jo. It was touching but they teased me that their mum had always liked the royal family much more than I did. I had to smile – they were as sharp as ever.

We arrived at the Houses of Parliament and were taken down the long corridors to a reception room. Glenys and Neil Kinnock welcomed us and the kids played while we waited. I was phoned by David Cameron who was about to leave Downing Street for the Commons. The Prime Minister was locked in a struggle for political survival, but he spoke kindly and said he would be thinking of us all day.

It was soon time to enter the packed chamber. The sight that met us was striking. Every MP wore the white rose of Yorkshire, for Jo. An empty seat, where Jo would have sat, featured two roses. One was white for Yorkshire, the other was red for Labour.

We felt the collective gaze of the House as Cuillin, Lejla and I were shown to the front row of the gallery. I avoided eye contact with anyone. I feared falling apart if I saw my own pain reflected in their faces.

As John Bercow, the Speaker, took charge I hoisted Lejla on to my knee. Cuillin reached for his colouring book and crayons. The tributes began and, after listening for a while, the kids waved to Stephen Kinnock. He was our friend and had shared a parliamentary office with Jo.

Their concentration dipped but I noticed that Cuillin kept pulling himself back. He listened to snippets and then bowed his head again, colouring in his book. Sitting with his grandma Jean, Cuillin began to draw pictures of cars and trains. I passed Lejla over to Stacia and, quietly, my sister taught my daughter how to peel grapes.

I was moved by all the tributes, especially those from people who knew Jo personally, like Stephen or Rachel Reeves. I thought the Prime Minister's speech was particularly well considered. But Jo's empty seat could not be avoided.

Afterwards, when the House was engulfed with applause for Jo, everyone looked up at us in the gallery. I was grateful for their empathy, but I just needed to get home with the kids.

The sombre handshakes and the journey drifted past. The kids and I were quiet. We got out of the car, thanked the driver and walked to the gate.

Our friends and neighbours from the river mooring had been waiting. Some came up to walk back down the bridge with us to the boat. We hugged and then, with the kids leading, we headed for *Ederlezi* for the first time since Jo's death.

Suddenly, Lejla shouted with glee: 'Look! Daddy, it's beautiful!' We stared at the boat in wonder. It had been draped in a thousand flowers. Returning home without Jo felt terribly raw. I had been dreading the impact it might have on the kids, but suddenly they were transfixed and enchanted. Living in a close community had been central to Jo's life. It also lay at the heart of her politics. The flowers turned *Ederlezi* into a tribute from all those who lived alongside us on our stretch of the river, and Jo would have been moved by their compassion.

Once we climbed down the rickety wooden staircase

into the hull everything looked the same. Wherever we looked we saw reminders of Jo.

This was a new pain. But at least we were back where we belonged, at home, on our boat.

– 22 June 2016 –

On the day we were meant to celebrate Jo's forty-second birthday, just six days after her murder, we took to the river again. Cuillin, Lejla and I sailed up the Thames in a friend's Dutch barge. All of the mooring had been hard at work sewing red and white roses and converting an old dinghy into the newly named *Yorkshire Rose*. It was like watching the Amish at work, minus the beards, and the dinghy had been freshly painted and filled with rose bushes. Cuillin and Lejla had drawn pictures of Jo and placed them on board. We tied the *Yorkshire Rose* behind us as we chugged up the Thames.

Cruising under Westminster Bridge we reached the Houses of Parliament. Our friend Tom unhitched the *Yorkshire Rose* and attached her to a mooring in front of Parliament. She looked magnificent as, around us, fire boats shot jets of water high into the air in tribute to Jo. A haze of river water filled the air as Cuillin and Lejla squealed excitedly.

We left the boat and when we reached Trafalgar Square we saw it had been transformed. Thousands of people had gathered to celebrate Jo. They held up banners and flags humanised with Jo's smiling face. The *#MoreInCommon* slogan, which seemed to have taken over Twitter, stretched across the stage.

Similar images were held up in Yorkshire, Brussels, Dublin, Edinburgh, Nairobi, New York and Sydney; it was incredibly moving.

In the market square in Batley over 2,000 people heard Kim bravely and eloquently express our family's gratitude for the 'outpouring of comfort and support' that followed Jo's death. Kim urged everyone to integrate 'tolerance, peace and understanding' in their everyday lives. Watched by her and Jo's parents, Gordon and Jean, Kim said: 'From Batley to Burma and the Spen Valley to Syria, Jo's life was centred around helping people and standing up for the causes she felt so passionately about. My sister would want her murder to mobilise people, to get on with things, to try to make a positive difference in whatever way we can, to come together and unite against hate and division and to fight instead for inclusion, love and unity. In Jo's honour, and on behalf of her grieving family, I urge you to please do so.'

Near the United Nations in New York, Samantha Power, the US ambassador to the UN, read a statement from Barack Obama to hundreds of people who had gathered to remember Jo on her birthday. 'We must never doubt how much things can change,' President Obama said. 'Jo knew that our politics at its best still works. If we recognise our humanity in each other we can advance social justice, human dignity and the peace we seek in the world.'

Jo would have loved the fact that Lily Allen came on stage in Trafalgar Square and sang what we regarded as our family's song about the cottage, 'Somewhere Only We Know'. I also thought how Jo would have been stunned by the fact that everyone there not only heard 'Do You Hear the People Sing?', but that it was sung by the cast of *Les Misérables*. We had seen the musical many times together, and the idea that all the actors would give up a free afternoon to perform in honour of Jo touched me.

It was poignant to see how my friends in our band, Diddley Dee, were consumed with nerves and adrenalin. For the last couple of days they had been exchanging increasingly desperate emails as they realised that they were about to share a bill with Lily Allen and the *Les Mis* ensemble in front of 10,000 people. Our previous biggest gig had been in front of a few hundred. Simon called me up and said something along the lines of, 'The problem is we're a bit shit.' I told him Jo would have wanted them to play. Simon and Diddley Dee had little choice.

As they came off-stage, having played brilliantly, they were thanked as 'Jo's favourite band'. I fear she will never forgive me for that slice of poetic licence.

Cuillin smiled. His teacher Kirsty, whom he adored, had brought the school choir with her. They went up and sang one of Cuillin's special songs which he and his mum always hollered out in tandem: Pete Seeger's 'If I Had a Hammer'. It was one of our most cherished moments as the crowd rose to cheer the children.

Numerous people appeared on stage – and there were

speeches, including one from Malala Yousafzai who spoke about surviving an assassination attempt by the Taliban. Jo was also honoured by the Syrian White Helmets, a heroic group of volunteers who rescue survivors from the rubble of bombings and artillery strikes. Knowing how much they had to endure made their desire to honour Jo particularly moving; we were hugely appreciative of the messages of thanks we received from across the war zone in the days following Jo's murder. They came from people living in the midst of inhumanity yet who were still able to feel others' pain. At some point though, it was my turn to walk on stage.

I had told my closest friends I didn't think I'd be able to get through my brief speech. I had lined up our friend Nick Grono to step in if I couldn't finish. To make it easier, some friends had gone to work trying to get the pictures of Jo lowered while I spoke. They were fearful that her image would push me over the edge.

'Thank you for coming together today to honour the memory of Jo,' I began, 'not just here in London, and in Batley, but around the world. Thank you also for the love that you have poured on all our family since our world collapsed on Thursday.'

My voice cracked when I said the word 'love'. I had to take a deep breath before continuing.

'Thank you to Jo's amazing friends, and friends of friends, and even complete strangers who have managed, despite your own grief, to organise all of this in less than a week. And thanks to all of you who are helping make sure that Jo's death leads to some good in this world.'

I looked up. 'Extraordinary and deeply touching as all of this is, I wish I wasn't here today. Not because I'm ungrateful to the organisers and to you for all coming, but because, of course, I'd rather be . . .'

I had to choke back the emotion ripping through me. I swallowed and took comfort from the fact that I could concentrate on reading my words. If I had spoken off the cuff, without writing down my thoughts, I would have been utterly lost. I kept going.

'I'd rather be with Jo. But I wanted to come and show my gratitude, and that of all my family, because your support and love have helped us all. I also wanted my children to see what their mum meant to all of you – and I know that they will always remember today.'

I made a brief plea for our privacy to look after the kids, and then I offered a few more personal and political points. 'Today would have been Jo's forty-second birthday. She would have spent it dashing around the streets of her home town, trying to convince people that Britain is stronger in Europe. She feared the consequences of Europe dividing again and hated the idea of building walls between us – and worried about the dynamics that could unleash. But today is not about that. It's about Jo and the much wider battle against hatred that she was engaged in.'

The applause started then, cutting me off and sweeping across Trafalgar Square.

My concern was consumed by Cuillin and Lejla and I spoke next of the fact that 'Jo was the best mum that any child could wish for. And wish we do – to have her back in our lives.'

I finished by saying: 'Jo's killing was political – it was an act of terror designed to advance an agenda of hatred towards others. What a beautiful irony it is that an act designed to advance hatred has instead generated such an outpouring of love. Jo lived for her beliefs and she died for them. And for the rest of our lives we will fight for them in her name.'

I focused on getting through my speech and, when I did, it was gratifying to see another set of words being held up by thousands of people: *#LoveLikeJo.*

At least for that day, in remembrance of Jo, we seemed immersed in unified support and love.

Early the next morning, on Thursday, 23 June 2016, voters began to enter the electoral booths. I had already cast my vote weeks before, by post. Cuillin, Lejla and I travelled to Reading to stay with my parents, and the children went to the local polling station with their aunt and uncle, Stacia and Andrew.

It was a long, slow day.

Four hours after the polls closed, and just eight days since Jo's death, I went to bed in my old room at my parents' home. The Leave campaign looked to be steaming ahead.

My thoughts, however, were only of Jo as I lay in the dark.

When I woke, I reached for my phone. I stared at the

screen for a while. Jo would have been as disappointed as me. Britain had voted to leave the EU.

I thought hard about how Jo would have responded. I knew that she would have picked herself up and, rather than being desolate, summoned new energy to say something. I tweeted:

Today Jo would have remained optimistic and focused on what she could do to bring our country back together around our best values.

*

David Cameron had stood down as Prime Minister even before the last votes had been counted: 16,141,241 people, or 48 per cent of those who had voted, supported the decision to remain within Europe – but they lost to the 17,410,742 Britons who wanted to leave the Union. I had obviously not been a political supporter of Cameron but I felt some sympathy for the implosion of his career.

While the Conservative Party worked out who would replace him, and Michael Gove prepared to double-cross Boris Johnson and leave the way open for Theresa May, I was more preoccupied by a tangled and graphic personal decision that would affect our children.

Should I take the kids to see Jo's body?

All my instincts screamed no at even the thought of them being brought into the same room as their mum's body. I had not wanted to see Jo's body myself because

I did not want that image to become the abiding picture of her in my head. I wanted Jo to remain a vibrant memory, resonating with life and laughter, with joy and love. I had been so against the idea of seeing Jo, I even asked Kim if she would identify her body. And so, in a gesture of great compassion, Kim visited the police mortuary to identify her sister.

I spoke to two child psychologists most days as I knew how important it was to be guided in the way I dealt with the kids – and provide opportunities for them to express their own feelings and understand all they had suffered. The question of whether or not they should see Jo kept featuring in our conversations. The psychologists were careful to stress that there was no unequivocally right or wrong answer. But they also explained that most children who had seen the body of their dead mother or father said, later, that the experience had helped them accept the reality. Conversely, many children who hadn't seen the body regretted it immensely.

To make the judgement, I decided I had to see Jo's body first.

I found it brutally hard. But I also realised, a day later, I couldn't really remember how Jo had looked in the mortuary. Whenever I thought of her in subsequent days, it was of my wife looking full of life. That snapshot of her lying dead could not challenge the lifetime of images we had built together.

I spent much of the train journey back to London talking to Julia Samuel, the child psychologist I spoke to most.

She is probably the leader in her field in the UK and I quizzed her thoroughly on the nature and strength of the evidence. She was clear about the weight of opinion and, despite my instincts, I decided to follow her advice.

Julia's conviction overcame my half-formed worries that it would be brutal and cruel to expose Cuillin and Lejla to death. The psychologist agreed that I should ask the kids if they wanted to see their mum – after explaining to them how different she would look and feel. They needed to understand that the mum they remembered would not be there.

The children were extraordinarily calm. Kids have none of the squeamishness of adults. They both said they wanted to come with me to see Mummy. They wanted to say goodbye to her.

On the Friday before Jo's cremation, Cuillin, Lejla and I went up to Yorkshire on the train. They had brought lots of drawings they wanted to put in the coffin. On the train we admired how lovely they were all over again. That morning someone had sent us an envelope filled with shiny love hearts. They looked like confetti and so I slipped a packet in my pocket after Lejla said we should share them with Mummy.

Kim and Clare drove us to the undertakers where we were taken to a special room. I told the children again what to expect. We went in and had to arrange chairs so that Cuillin and Lejla could stand on them to see into the coffin. We were with Jo for not much more than a few minutes but it was long enough for our children to reach out and hold their mum's hand one last time. They touched her hair and spoke to her.

'We love you Mummy,' they both said, as they sprinkled love hearts over Jo.

I didn't want them to stay long and I persuaded them, gently, that we needed to leave.

They were upset outside the room. I felt unsure whether I had done the right thing after all. But we held each other and went to spend time with Jo's parents and Kim and Clare. The tears eased. By the time we were back on the train to Reading, they were composed again.

I noticed a big difference. The questions tumbled out of them. It was as if they had processed the reality of Jo's death and accepted that she was gone. They were still stricken with sadness but they wanted a new truth. Lejla was no longer asking if we could make Mummy out of wood and bring her back to life, or if we would see her in a different world. Instead they wanted to know why this man had killed Mummy. What had happened to him?

Their questions were not full of hate or bitterness. They were legitimate queries I tried to answer as best as I could.

I knew nothing could be fixed in the sense of bringing Jo back to life. But, as we moved away from the man who had taken her from us, and back to our sweetest and most enduring memories of their mum, I felt sure it had been the right decision. They went to sleep that night more easily than at any time since Jo had died. I looked down at them later and felt a sustaining love – lit with a new certainty of how proud Jo would have been of them.

– 15 July 2016 –

We had decided that the funeral would be intimate. In a couple of months we'd celebrate Jo's life, at the cottage, with all our friends. But only those closest to us would attend her cremation in Batley: Jo's parents Gordon and Jean, Kim and Clare, my parents, my sister, her husband, their three boys, our friends Will and Sarah, and Cuillin, Lejla and me. We met at Gordon and Jean's house. The kids were happy to tell everyone that they had helped me pick the coffin and we had chosen the flowers. The green, white and violet, they reminded everyone, were the colours used by the suffragettes when they had made their call of 'Give Women the Vote'.

The undertakers arrived. We were about to take Jo's body to a crematorium. We were about to say goodbye for the last time.

The undertakers hovered and murmured. I could not escape them. It was time to walk to the hearse.

I held my children's hands. Cuillin and Lejla sat either side of me, having stationed themselves at a window each so they could look out at everyone lining the streets of Batley. It was better that they wanted to look out rather than down at the floor of the strange black car. Jo's family were in the car with us.

The journey began. I could hardly take it in. We were being driven to Jo's funeral.

We had expected that hundreds of people would turn out in honour of Jo – but we were deeply moved that thousands of men, women and children packed the pavements. The diversity of those people was inspiring. Workmen from building sites stood alongside British Asian kids who had been let out of local schools to pay tribute; people poured out of shops and stood beside university students who had travelled from Leeds; everyone thronged together on the streets.

The council had suggested certain spots where people might gather to see the cortège – but road after road was filled. Ordinary people, from extraordinarily varied communities and backgrounds, were united in respect for Jo and all she stood for as their MP. But the tears being shed were more for Jo as a normal person – who had felt empathy for all people, no matter what they did or where their parents had been born, or however fulfilled or disappointing their lives had been.

The hearse drove more slowly than usual so that children could throw flowers on to the bonnet and top. Many people waved to the kids, even as they wept, and Lejla waved at everyone she saw, while Cuillin said something simple but profound: 'I knew that people loved Mummy – but I didn't know this many people loved her.'

It helped the kids to see other people crying and grieving for Jo. Their own heartache felt natural. It remained a terribly painful drive but we found huge comfort in the presence of so many people who had taken time to stand still in appreciation of Jo.

At the crematorium it was different. Apart from the undertaker and his staff there were no people watching.

The kids and their cousins pushed the coffin on a trolley into the crematorium while my dad played the organ. My sister then played an old folk song, 'Sweet Forget Me Not', on the recorder, just as she had done at our wedding. Rather than hiring a minister who had never met Jo, we had decided I would conduct the ceremony.

Focusing all my attention on Cuillin and Lejla, I just said, 'We're here to think about Mummy.' It felt essential to make certain that, rather than attending to our own grief, we should make the funeral as meaningful as possible for the kids. I suggested we sit down and go round the circle. Each one of us shared a specific memory we would always cherish about Jo. The kids wanted to be the first to talk and we soon all became animated.

Most memories of Jo were quite funny – and all were touching. Lejla then stood in the middle of the circle and sang 'Twinkle, Twinkle Little Star'. Cuillin banged out 'If I Had a Hammer' on the melodica, not letting the fact that he doesn't yet know how to play it stop him. My dad played with him and people sang along with varying versions of the tune. One of my nephews played the guitar, another told a story, and then my mum sang (she had been a member of the London Philharmonic Choir for years). The song was 'Ederlezi', a signature piece of music for Jo and me, and it was beautiful. Kim read some poems she had written about her big sister.

We all picked up a white rose and took our turn to place it on Jo's coffin. Cuillin and Lejla said goodbye and then Nick Cope's 'Best Foot Forward', a song they had loved to sing with Jo, echoed around the crematorium. Everyone else left as the song played.

I was alone with Jo. I said a private farewell to her.

It was difficult when I had to turn away and walk out of the crematorium, leaving her behind, knowing her coffin would soon slide into the fire. But Cuillin and Lejla needed me. When I got outside I hugged them and then, once we were all ready, we set off for Healds Hall Hotel in Liversedge. We had arranged a reception for around a hundred people – the extended family and our friends.

We kept it very informal. Gordon and Kim spoke about their daughter and sister, and I spoke on behalf of Cuillin, Lejla and myself. Before the kids disappeared into the garden to play, Kim showed a video from her fortieth birthday just six weeks earlier. Jo and Kim appeared on the screen and started singing. It was classic Jo.

Jo was always a pretty good singer, but Kim (and I know she won't mind me saying this) can't sing for toffee. Suddenly there they were on the screen, the Leadbeater sisters, Jo and Kim, belting out their version of Elaine Page and Barbara Dickson's 'I Know Him So Well'. I looked around the room. People were smiling and laughing. They were remembering Jo as we all knew her, singing next to her sister, just forty-one years old and lost in a joyful moment. She seemed so alive on the screen. I looked up in wonder at her.

10

War Zones

Long before I met her, I had a strong sense of Jo Leadbeater. I almost felt as if I knew her because people spoke about her in such admiring terms. She was the incredible fireball who ran Oxfam International's office in Brussels. I, meanwhile, was a press officer in Oxfam's head office in Oxford. We worked on different issues – my core work centred on the conflicts like those raging in Sudan or Northern Uganda at the time, while Jo was a specialist in trade issues. Plus she was very senior compared to me. It didn't seem likely that we would ever meet.

But then Jo took the job as Head of Policy and transferred to the UK. And in 2005, when we were both working on the Make Poverty History campaign, I heard her voice for the first time, on a conference call.

Make Poverty History was the biggest campaign anyone had ever attempted in the UK development sector. It was focused on increasing aid, cancelling debt and improving trade for the world's poorest countries. The intention was that this would become the most wide-reaching assault on poverty ever undertaken. Oxfam was heading it and was under pressure from the government, the media and partner NGOs, while trying to pull off some of the largest events we'd ever been involved with. Jo was leading the team up in Edinburgh, where the G8 summit was going to be held; the summit was the key moment in the campaign, when world leaders would make their commitments.

All the big cheeses were on the conference call. With so much at stake, tempers were frayed, egos were fragile and the tone of the conversation turned combative. A senior manager suggested that the team in Edinburgh were out of their depth and that, from then on, decisions would be made in Oxford. I remember Jo speaking up very firmly and very calmly. 'No, that won't be happening,' she said with cool certainty. 'I'm going to keep making the calls.' The manager didn't say another word. I was impressed. She was ballsy as hell.

I can't actually recall when we first met in person, but it was soon after she moved to the Oxford office and began to work more in areas of humanitarian crisis. Jo remembered it better than me. At our wedding four years later she joked that, initially, she thought I was 'a bit of a dickhead'. It was fair enough. I saw my role at the time as being to try (aggressively if necessary) to shake off the organisation's genteel image and encourage it to be more outspoken, which didn't always win me lots of friends. But we both had reputations for getting things done, and when we liaised on Oxfam's response to the devastating Boxing Day tsunami, we started to appreciate fully each other's work.

We only really clicked personally when she turned up,

unexpectedly, at a practice evening for the band I had helped form as a pretty hopeless accordion player. Diddley Dee was a terrible name, but we thought it showed we played folk music without taking ourselves too seriously. The joke wore off but we kept playing because we had such a good time.

On a Tuesday evening in October 2005, I walked into my friend Simon Gray's front room in Oxford and discovered Jo was already there. I was surprised, but pleased. Other people occasionally turned up to eat and drink with us while we played, but I wasn't expecting Jo.

I had always found her attractive but there was such a disparity between our roles that I hadn't thought of her as a potential romantic interest. She was also four years older than me. Yet, at thirty-one, Jo had the spark of someone ten years younger, although she could never have been described as immature. She chatted and laughed a lot – but still had presence and a seriousness at her core.

In March 2006, as our friendship developed, I texted her to suggest we go out for dinner. I waited a few minutes, slightly anxiously, before Jo replied. She invited me over to her place and said she would cook. This was evidently a date and I was very excited.

I turned up on her front step in Cowley in east Oxford with two bottles of wine. Jo showed me round her new house: a nice old Victorian terrace on Church Cowley Road. She seemed very happy to be getting settled in Oxford.

Jo started telling me about her time in Brussels and got so carried away with her stories that when she checked, her lasagne was burned to a crisp. I thought it was very funny. We spent the rest of the evening teasing each other while also talking about Oxfam and serious stuff we had done or hoped to do. We both felt an energy between us, part romantic, part political, part intellectual. It was an electrifying evening and, at the end of it, we kissed for the first time.

On the Saturday after our scorched dinner Jo visited me on my narrowboat in Port Meadow. (I've always loved boats, ever since I was a Sea Scout. Luckily for me, with her characteristic embrace of adventure, Jo learned to share my enthusiasm.) Port Meadow is an idyllic stretch of land, full of wild horses and flowers. We went for a long walk up the river and through the thick Wytham Great Woods. The sun lit up the darkest corners and, as we walked, we talked.

We had a great deal in common – whether it was the work we loved, the causes we championed or our zest for travelling to lesser-known parts of the world. Jo and I were both political, but not solely interested in UK party politics. We spoke about Afghanistan and Iraq, Sudan and South Africa. The longer we walked the more honest we became. Jo told me she didn't feel like an Oxfam legend. She worried about whether she was good enough to do the work at which everyone thought she excelled. Her doubts were expressed with such heartfelt sentiment I did not wave them away. They made me admire her even more. Jo also talked about her adventures and her aspirations. She mentioned that one day she might like to represent her home town as a Labour MP. We talked about camping and hiking. It was uncanny. Our interests overlapped to a degree I'd never experienced before, but, more than that, so did our energy. I knew immediately that this was something different. I felt for the first time that I might fall in love with this woman.

I ended up telling her much more about myself than I normally did to anyone. I confessed that, as a kid, I was naughty and often in trouble at school. The thing that helped me was being a Sea Scout. Even as a boy I loved camping and making fires, climbing and paddling boats. The scouts also led me to Bosnia and Croatia and some of my formative experiences.

I told Jo how my life had changed fundamentally when, in the summer of 1997, aged just eighteen, I first went to Croatia and worked with traumatised Bosnian kids. The 'civil war' which had ended two years previously had been portrayed as mind-bogglingly complicated and part of generations of slaughter, but it was, in fact, an aggressive and sometimes genocidal attack by Serbian-backed extremists who wanted to live in an ethnically pure state.

I shared with her my feeling of fury about the culpability of the international community but, as I told Jo, I also recalled being taken aback by how much difference it was possible to make to the lives of these kids. They would barely talk, but would throw a Frisbee back and forth for hours, yearning for a sense of fun in the midst of such all-encompassing bleakness.

I threw myself into playing with them, with an energy

that amused them. But those games gave me a new sense of purpose. Normally, when you watch the news and see conflict in Bosnia or Syria, it's easy to think, This is another world, and I'll never experience such unimaginable horror. I saw how it was relatable and even unremarkable. The banality of evil rang true. But I also started to feel that I wasn't powerless. I couldn't fix things, but I knew I could have a positive impact on people's lives, even if that was just by throwing a Frisbee.

The following year I helped run a camp for forty Bosnian kids from Srebrenica. This was harder even than the previous year. These kids had survived the first act of genocide in Europe since the Second World War, and you could tell. At night the camp was punctuated by the screams of kids suffering awful nightmares. We worked with child psychologists but our main focus was simply to try to give them a good time, a break from the brutality of their lives and their memories. When I was asked to help organise the next year's camp I readily agreed. I had found something I fervently wanted to do.

Every summer, for more than a decade, I worked with my friends to organise camps for a couple of weeks at a time. I spent most time with Bosnian kids from Srebrenica and Croatian children from around the eastern town of Vukovar. I became obsessed. At my peak, I probably spent three months a year in Bosnia and Croatia. I would go out for a couple of months in the summer and then return for a month over New Year. By that time I was studying politics at the London School of Economics, but at one point

I seriously considered dropping out of university. How could I justify spending my time reading Hegel when I knew I could do so much practical work to help the children I had come to love in the former Yugoslavia?

On New Year's Eve in 1999, when I was just twenty-one, the millennium was greeted in muted fashion in a snowy village called Vozuća. This was where the survivors of the genocide at Srebrenica had come to try to rebuild their lives. You could feel the dark stain of history wherever you looked. I realised that some people are capable of great evil but also that most show bravery, generosity and goodness of spirit.

Jo and I spoke about so much on that sunny day in Port Meadow – moving on from the Balkans to Northern Uganda to Oxfam's trade policy to where we'd like to hike. It was a very natural conversation and, reaching the boat, I felt invigorated. I thought, When last did I talk to someone like Jo? When did I feel I had so much in common with another person? The answer was never.

By the end of March 2006 we were a couple. We had only been going out for a few weeks, but we were spending more nights together than apart. On St Patrick's Day, preparing for a meeting the next morning, Jo opted for an early night rather than joining me and my friends from Diddley Dee in the pub.

Simon, Rob and I went to a down-at-heel Irish bar in Oxford. The Half Moon was the kind of pub we loved. There were instruments on the ceiling and so Simon – by far the most talented musician among us – started playing the fiddle even though it had only three strings and no bridge. 'Why don't you boys go and get your instruments and I'll give you booze all night if you play?' the landlord suggested. I cycled across the meadow to fetch my accordion while Simon and Rob picked up their fiddle and guitar.

We played at the Half Moon until three in the morning. People danced and sang along, while we played on a table and drank Guinness and champagne. After it was over the old Irish landlord came outside to thank us. In a thick and slightly slurred accent he said, 'You know what, it's boys like you who keep the craic alive.'

I weaved back to Jo's house on my bicycle. She was half asleep. 'Hello,' I slurred in a thick Irish accent, 'it's Brendan O'Cox here. Boys like me keep the craic alive.'

Jo smiled sleepily and gave me a kiss. But every time she drifted off, I'd tap her cheerfully on the shoulder: 'Hello. It's Brendan O'Cox here. Boys like me keep the craic alive.'

She found it very amusing when Brendan O'Cox keeled over and fell fast asleep. The craic was over – at least for the night.

It soon seemed right for me to leave Oxfam. Neither Jo nor I were keen on being colleagues as well as partners for too long. I had also been offered the chance to become the director of an organisation called Crisis Action. It sounds very grand – especially as Crisis Action now consists of forty people in eight countries – but back then it was just me. Its founding principle was that to have an impact on armed conflict, it was pointless working as a single organisation – you needed to build powerful coalitions. Crisis Action was established as a response to the failure to prevent genocide in Rwanda and Bosnia, and the same failure to stop the rush to war in Iraq.

I loved the way in which Jo encouraged me: 'You should definitely do it, Coxy. It's a brilliant idea.'

Jo was away on an Oxfam trip to Afghanistan and Pakistan and we decided we'd wait for her to come back before I handed in my notice. Everything was going swimmingly.

But soon afterwards I took a phone call from Afghanistan. Jo was having second thoughts about us. She had come out of a relationship not long before we got together and wanted to make sure I was serious, rather than just having a fling. Jo and I had both had hectic love lives in the past and she didn't want to be a notch on a bedpost.

One of the things I liked most about Jo was that she told you exactly how she was feeling, but this made me incredibly nervous too. I couldn't bear the thought that we might lose one another. I tried hard to explain that what we had together was different – I hadn't felt like this before.

Jo didn't say much. I could still sense the threat of falling away from each other. We agreed that we'd talk about it when we were together, and I told her again how certain I felt about her.

She hesitated, and then said she would try to clear her head. We could talk more when she got home. I didn't sleep well until she got back.

We met up at her house in Cowley on her return from Pakistan. I was still worried, but as soon as we started to talk I could see that Jo's doubts had gone. We hugged and kissed. We were staying together, and we were going to live an incredible life as long as we lived.

Jo had always been fearless, but she told me that the solidity of our partnership gave her a firmer base from which to push herself even harder. Whether she was in Afghanistan or Chad, Gaza or Darfur, she was driven by her desire to make the world a better, safer and fairer place. She was deeply practical – always asking the question What should we do? not just What should we think? – and she refused to accept that roadblocks to progress couldn't be navigated.

Gaza was another landmark experience. As was typical with Jo, she could empathise with those on both sides of the conflict. She felt that too often people joined 'clubs' of opinions rather than really looking at the details of the situation. Many of her colleagues pigeonholed themselves as 'friends of Israel' or 'friends of Palestine'. She thought it was possible to be both. She understood the importance of Israel having security for its citizens, but she was also aghast at the treatment of Palestinians when she saw it first-hand in the West Bank and Gaza.

Jo often spoke about her time in the Gaza Strip. She

had entered through a steel cage that felt like a giant cattle container, as Israeli soldiers with machine guns stood above her on raised platforms. Once in Gaza, it was hard to escape the stench of sewage being pumped on to the beach. She met people who were highly capable but without any prospects. They had no chance of leaving the Strip.

Her main aim was to understand the situation so that she could revise Oxfam's strategy in Gaza. Jo met with the Israeli military and politicians and listened to their justifications for the treatment of Palestinians. She understood the history and didn't minimise the threat to Israelis, but she felt the injustice endured by the Palestinians acutely.

Gaza made Jo confront the shortcomings of international aid in the midst of a conflict where politics was both the cause and the solution. She did all she could to use Oxfam's influence to alleviate some of the day-to-day suffering in Gaza.

Darfur, in Western Sudan, presented an even more discomfiting chain of confrontations. When Jo visited, Oxfam's aim was to pressure the government authorities and the rebels into stopping their brutal attacks on Sudanese civilians, and allowing humanitarian access to the victims.

The chief perpetrators of these war crimes were the government-funded Arab militias known as the Janjaweed which, in translation, means 'man with a gun on a horse' or, more colloquially, 'devils on horseback'. The Janjaweed systematically destroyed Darfurian villages, polluting water sources and raping and murdering innocent civilians. It is estimated that 480,000 people were killed and 2.8 million people displaced as a result of the conflict.

Jo learned that the war had been fuelled by battles for access to Darfur's scarce water supplies and land resources. Desertification had spread across the region, drying up wells and destroying grazing areas. The nomadic Arab tribes that made up the armies of the Janjaweed began to attack the black Sudanese farms and round up the dying herds of cattle. In response the non-Arabic Sudan Liberation Army, drawn from the Fur, Masalit and Zaghawa tribes of black people, fought back and also tried to bring down the government.

The conflict in Darfur was labelled genocide by some human rights groups and by the US government. What is undeniable is that the commanders of the Janjaweed ordered their soldiers to unleash carnage against the black villages of Darfur. The violence was horrific and it became increasingly dangerous for aid workers to enter Darfur.

Jo and I both travelled to Sudan and Jo was particularly scarred by her visit to Kalma Camp in Darfur. A relocation camp – a sprawling and desolate tented village with few basic amenities – Kalma was ten and a half miles from Nyala, the capital of South Darfur, in south-west Sudan. The heat was punishing, but evidence of atrocity and death was far more harrowing. Ninety thousand people from different tribes were crowded together. There was little food and water; but overwhelming misery.

Jo sat with women who had somehow managed to

escape their decimated villages. Many had been gang-raped by the Janjaweed. This savagery had also occurred on the fringes of Kalma – women had been raped again when they'd gone in search of firewood. The horror was so deep that the women could not talk much about their repeated ordeals. Their faces were waxy with sorrow and they withdrew into themselves, as if that might help bury the trauma. Jo offered her hands and the women held them as they all sat together in silence. She would often say in later years that she could never forget the look on their faces as they stared mutely back at her.

I remember a particular visit Jo made to Darfur, and to Kalma Camp, in the first year of our relationship. She took some eminent British politicians to the heart of the battle; Jo wanted them to bear witness to the carnage of genocide and rape. She didn't care which party they were from, she simply felt outraged that the international community, including Britain, had done so little in Darfur. Throughout her life, Jo would build alliances with whoever she could. David Cameron – who had recently been elected as Conservative leader – had agreed to visit, and Jo made sure he understood what was happening; that the killings and gang-rapes continued. Aid workers were also being targeted by the Sudanese government and forced to leave the country. It was a febrile atmosphere and Jo knew she and other aid workers were being spied on in an effort to gather evidence against them as grounds to expel them from the country.

Jo was used to intimidation in her work. When she had

travelled from Rwanda into the Democratic Republic of the Congo, her passport, and that of her colleague, was seized at a border crossing. The DRC soldiers frightened her. In the end their passports were returned and they moved on.

Such incidents galvanised rather than deterred Jo. She was sunny and optimistic in her character but, especially after Gaza and Darfur, her politicisation was hardened by a new edge of impatience. The world needed to change; the international community could no longer sit back while men, women and children were killed en masse. Every time she travelled she put herself in the shoes of those suffering: the woman raped gathering firewood; the dad with no job struggling to feed his family; the teenager without prospects. And in every case she returned from her trips determined to tell the stories of those she'd met and to push governments to step up to their responsibilities.

11

A Celebration

The early morning mist thickened into a cold and sinister fog and our view from the cottage across the river valley was ruined. The grey clouds rolled in like battleships. Bleak drizzle and fog should belong to November and the harshest winter. But this is Britain, and our plans for a gentle autumnal farewell to Jo were in trouble.

Jo loved people and so for her memorial we needed a weekend overflowing with friends and family, laughter and memories. But looking after 200 people for two days, without running water, mains electricity or road access, requires military planning. My mum, Stacia and our friend Iona, who had worked as a chef, were in charge of the food and they had asked everyone to bring a plate to share. Mum had also baked twenty cakes, while my brother-in-law Andrew, Will and I had cut up logs and carved out enough seats for everyone at the long line of tables. My neighbour David led on preparing a spit-roasted pig from the local farm.

A working team of us had done much of the prepping the previous Sunday, cutting down the ferns and creating space for a large campsite. The kids and I had then arrived a few days before the party weekend to start setting up. We were joined by the family and willing friends, and we felt ready – before the fog, which turned to soaking rain.

Sitting on a log, watching the rain beat down steadily as the morning slid away in the mud, I felt dismal. How were we going to celebrate a woman as sunny as Jo in such miserable conditions? I promised myself that, somehow, we would still throw Jo a party to remember.

Our guests were meant to arrive around four o'clock that Saturday afternoon and, miraculously, the rain stopped and the cloud began to lift half an hour earlier. It was still a treacherous climb down the hill to our cottage, however. But no one fell and there was lots of talking and laughing as, steadily, the small crowd grew into a large gathering.

There were masses of children, which would have thrilled Jo, and when they were not careering on the death swing or climbing rocks they were caught up in a craft workshop set up by our friend Charlie. She lives on the mooring and is a skilled set and prop designer. She helped the kids make kites and lanterns which we would light later.

Most of the adults and the remaining children planted bulbs in the woods, along the paths and in the garden. The bulbs are flowering as I write this and keep popping up in unexpected places.

Just before dinner we held a 'Jo Quiz'. I think most

people had been secretly dreading it, being unsure what mad idea I'd come up with next, but they were fully involved once it began. I read out the questions (most of which came from Cuillin and Lejla) while the kids took turns to list the options (correct answers written in bold).

1. What was Mummy's favourite possession?
a) Her Karen Millen dress
b) Her Jimmy Choo shoes
c) **Her black kettle**

2. And her favourite drink?
a) Gin and tonic
b) **Elderflower champagne**
c) Sloe gin

3. What degree did Mummy start at Cambridge?
a) PPE
b) SPS
c) **Archaeology and Anthropology**

4. What rude word did Mummy used to say (no multiple choices here for obvious reasons)? **(Bugger)**

5. Was Mummy chased by chimpanzees, **elephants** or pirates in Borneo?

6. When getting engaged did Mummy forget her:
a) **Bike**
b) **Map**
c) **Dinner**

7. What was Mummy's favourite pastime?

a) Cleaning

b) Doing admin

c) Sleeping

8. What was Mummy's winning majority in the election?

a) 4,000

b) 6,000

c) 8,000

9. When Mummy entered a swimming competition did she win?

a) A medal

b) Half of the medals

c) All the medals

10. Did Mummy prefer to eat?

a) Pheasant

b) Squirrel

c) Eel

11. When Mummy and Daddy were stopped by the police in the car was it for:

a) Not paying their tax

b) Not having insurance

c) Not having an MOT?

12. What was Mummy a bit afraid of?

a) Heights

b) Caves

c) Adventures

13. Who did Mummy love most in the world?
a) Jeremy Corbyn
b) Nigel Farage
c) **Cuillin and Lejla**

14. What type of tree did she want to be?
a) Buddleia
b) **Oak**
c) Apple

15. The tie-break question: Who can make the best Mummy monster face?

It was a relief to see everyone enjoying themselves. We marked each other's quiz papers and a team of Yorkshire friends and family won the prize: a *Love like Jo* poster.

As the light faded and the first stars were seen in an inky sky, our friend Eloise Todd, who had partied for many years with Jo in Brussels, slipped into her familiar role as DJ. She played songs we had all loved and everyone began to dance as our cobbled-together sound system boomed around the valley. Our makeshift dance floor was heaving, with children too, and I thought of how Jo would have – should have – been at its centre.

The blackness of the river valley was illuminated by the light installations and glitter balls our arty and disco-y friends had set up in the garden. A bonfire added to the glimmer as the kids roasted marshmallows.

Eloise and I had cooked up a scheme where she spliced together some of the interview Jo had done with Martin

Kelner on Radio Leeds a few months earlier. It was about an hour long with a *Desert Island Discs* format, and Jo and Martin had interspersed their conversation with some of her favourite records. We started the dancing to a set of songs introduced by Jo.

Hearing Jo again upset me. I loved the sound of her voice, her Yorkshire accent ringing out, but it also bit into me.

'Well, this is actually probably the only time at school when I rebelled,' Jo told us. 'Don't tell my headteachers. Hopefully they're not listening but I nicked off school in the sixth form and went to a Michael Jackson concert. It was the first and only time I probably did anything naughty. This song reminds me of those days – it's also just a beautiful, moving song from someone I love to dance to.'

I danced with Cuillin and Lejla when Eloise played Michael Jackson's 'Man in the Mirror'. I smiled when it was time for another specific Jo choice – 'Hard Out Here' by Lily Allen.

'I think this is a brilliant song from an amazing woman who is a bit of a feminist icon and I'm a massive feminist,' Jo said. 'I think we should all shout out for the girls out there . . .'

We jumped around and danced as we celebrated Jo. Her last song on the Radio Leeds show was 'Jolene'. She told Martin Kelner that 'This is when I lived in New York and did a big road trip around the Deep South in America. So this is my driving song and it's a good song.'

In the early hours of a chilly September morning in 2016 the fog had begun to roll across the river again. But

I could see the two of us, Jo and me, in Tennessee, Mississippi and Alabama in the winter of 2008, driving a convertible as we sang along to Dolly Parton's 'Jolene'.

Our garden dance floor was awash with tears and memories. 'Jolene, Jolene, Jolene, Jolene,' everyone sang as if, somehow, through the spreading cold and fog, we might bring back Jo.

As a finale, one of our neighbours had planned a firework display from the opposite bank of the river. A team of willing – if somewhat drunk – volunteers crossed over to set up the fireworks, and as they worked they sang sea shanties that echoed round the steep-sided valley. The sound was haunting. At last, with a whoosh, twelve huge rockets were sent skywards followed by a cacophony of ground-shaking booms. Lejla and Cuillin looked up with delight in their eyes.

– 11 September 2016 –

We woke the next morning to a perfect blue sky. It turned into a day so hot that some of my friends got sunburned. Soon after breakfast, I gathered about fifty people together and we went for a mass walk. I led them to our favourite view of the valley, where we had erected a bench in Jo's memory. We all shouted 'Love like Jo' from the top of the rock. Cuillin and Lejla enjoyed it so much they made us shout it again and again. Our voices bounced off the hills and reached all the way to the cottage and the river below.

Love like Jo . . .
Love like Jo . . .
Love like Jo . . .

At 11 a.m. it was time for the ceremony. Thomas, our friend from the mooring, had made an exquisite casket for Jo's ashes out of teak taken from an old ship. Cuillin and Lejla had helped him, and they had designed and drilled and screwed and sawn together in his studio. The box was large enough to hold the ashes and, as suggested by the kids, a bottle of Jo's elderflower champagne.

Finn, a six-foot-tall fifteen-year-old who lives on the boat next to ours on the mooring, and my best friend Will had agreed that they would take the casket across the river into the field opposite. They would leave it under a lovely old hawthorn tree for me, Cuillin and Lejla to collect. The flaw in the plan was that it had rained so heavily all week that the river was close to flooding. As soon as Will and Finn were on the water their canoe, carrying the casket, was swept downstream.

Having managed to get to the other side and place the ashes, Will and Finn paddled desperately to get back, sweating and shouting, moving forward by a centimetre or two with each stroke. It took them fifteen minutes to travel 200 metres upstream. I was worried: how would the kids and I get across the river? I had no choice. The ashes were now on the other side. I had to get them. Jo would have been highly amused if I had arranged her memorial but left her ashes on the wrong side of the river.

Poor old Will climbed back into the canoe. We gave a paddle each to the kids, and told them to do all they could, while Will and I caned it.

We paddled furiously and made it across, and then the kids and I headed for the hawthorn tree. Cuillin and Lejla helped me carry the casket back to the canoe as we heard Kim thank everyone for coming to our celebration of her sister. She finished her brief speech and, as we sat down again in the canoe, we heard Eloise cutting back to Jo's interview on Radio Leeds and the first song she had chosen – 'Ederlezi' by Goran Bregović.

I felt heartbroken – but also inspired – hearing Jo's voice echoing around us, especially on the river. 'So this is a folksong from the Balkans. My husband spent a lot of time working in the Balkans, after the war, with kids from Srebrenica. I then spent a lot of time going out there with him when we got married. So it's quite a meaningful song. It was sung by my wonderful mother-in-law at my wedding . . .'

My mum stepped forward, at the top of Jo's garden, and sang from her heart the song that had echoed through our lives: first in the Balkans, then at our wedding, in our home on the boat, at Jo's funeral and now, once more, at her memorial.

Everyone lined the riverbank. Led by Finn and other friends from the mooring they sang an old sea shanty called 'Haul Away Joe' – of course, for us, it was 'Haul Away Jo' – with a sweet blend of voices and harmonies.

Way, haul away, we'll haul away together
Way, haul away, we'll haul away, Jo!
Way, haul away, we'll haul for better weather
Way, haul away, we'll haul away, Jo!

Returning across the river was much easier as the shanty reverberated round the valley. Cuillin and Lejla held the casket as Will and I paddled. When we landed we headed for the garden – Jo's garden – near Beater Barn, where we would bury her ashes.

I spoke to everyone. I have no recollection of my actual words but I tried to talk about how much Jo would have loved this weekend. I also spoke about the garden and how she had relished working in it. Three years before, when we moved in, it had been an overgrown extension of the forest. Together, we had reclaimed it. Lejla would help her mum every weekend (pulling out 'the bad boys' as they called the weeds) and now we were surrounded by plants and flowers Jo had grown. On the very last weekend Jo had spent at the cottage she and Cuillin had gone picking wild flowers in the fields across the river.

All the kids had come to sit with Cuillin and Lejla, who were sitting around me. I choked up because I had not written out my speech; I had nothing to read and needed to think about every word I said. But I got through it and, as I ended, my tears fell on the ground.

My family held me and it helped that Diddley Dee played, led by Simon and Rob. I lifted up the casket and, with Cuillin and Lejla, guided it gently into the open earth. I hadn't really thought what to do next, but suddenly all the kids started placing handfuls of soil around the casket with amazing tenderness and love. Cuillin and Lejla led the way, burying their mum's ashes in the garden she adored.

We finished with a rendition of 'Jerusalem', which we had also sung at our wedding. It remained full of resonance, reflecting Jo's patriotism, her love of nature and her belief in a better world.

Once the ground was restored people came up to place a stone that they had brought with them in personal remembrance of Jo. Over two hundred stones, laid one by one, marked the patch of earth where Jo's ashes were buried. Cuillin and Lejla helped arrange them. Some were Yorkshire stones, while others were from the Cotswolds or much further away. Friends of ours had flown to England from across the world and Jo's ashes were covered by stones from countries as different as America and Lebanon.

I knew the lines of tables would soon be filled with plates of food. But, first, we needed to toast Jo with the elderflower champagne she had made. A sophisticated palate would not pick out Cox's Champagne, or Beater's Bubbly, as belonging to a particularly vintage year, but Jo had made it, and she loved it, so it was the only thing that would do. I hadn't worked out what I wanted to say – and Lejla beat me to the perfect toast.

In one of the most sublime moments of the weekend, little Lejla lifted her glass high above her head and shouted out three simple words: 'Love like Jo!'

'Love like Jo!' we echoed.

12

Adventures with Jo

Jo loved the random nature of our first great adventure in early summer 2006. We had only been together for a matter of weeks and we were off to Cuba, without any plan or accommodation. All we knew was that we were flying in to the far east of the country and would hitch our way west, rough camping wherever we ended up at night, before flying out of Havana. It turned out to be a whirlwind of a holiday that took in rum, salsa and spontaneity.

Cuba was gorgeous and fascinating. I remember how, towards the end of a long day of walking and getting lost, we found an interesting old tree in the jungle around which there was a large clearing. We agreed we had found a perfect place to camp for the night. It was only later that evening, while Jo cooked over the fire and I went for a little stroll, that I noticed something spooky. As I approached the tree from a different direction, I saw that there were small skulls, shrunken objects and bizarre offerings around its base. Our lovely tree was a voodoo shrine. I didn't want to freak Jo out and so decided not to say anything about it until the morning.

In the end I was the one who quietly freaked out. Lying in the dark, hearing all kinds of crackles in the surrounding bush, I stayed wide awake while Jo slept deeply. I was so spooked that, fearing we might be attacked by followers of a cult, I kept a knife close to my sleeping bag.

Jo was very cheerful the next morning while I was shattered.

'What's up?' she asked.

'Go and have a look around the other side of the tree.'

'Why didn't you tell me we were in a voodoo shrine?' Jo soon exclaimed. 'It's wonderful.'

And she was right. Our entire three-week trip was extraordinary.

Jo and I had our first argument in Cuba – over how best to start a fire. She had been a Brownie and a Girl Guide, while I had been a diligent Sea Scout and had lived on a boat for years with fires as my only source of heating. We debated different tepee structures and the merits of removing the bark when damp. We both felt we should be in charge of fire-lighting and things got a bit tense as I criticised her kindling-to-tinder ratio. By the time her first effort went out we were barely on speaking terms. After a quiet dinner we laughed under the mosquito nets about our squabble. It felt right that our first argument was about fire-lighting.

There was another lovely moment towards the end of our holiday. We were hoping to hitch a lift when we walked past a woman's garden. She came running over with two mangoes. We were surprised, but when I reached into my pocket to pay for them, she smiled and indicated that they were a gift.

They were the juiciest, sweetest mangoes Jo and I had ever eaten. We gorged ourselves, the juice running down our hands and arms.

'Don't you just love Cuba?' Jo said with a sticky grin.

I did. I also decided that I loved Jo so much that, a few nights later, sitting in a dark and noisy restaurant, having had a delicious meal and smoked my first ever cigar (one of those classic big Havana specials that cost only a couple of dollars in Cuba), I came close to asking her to marry me. We had already decided, in our informal way, that we were destined for many more adventures in a long life together. I was certain about Jo. We'd both had plenty of short-term relationships but this was different and I felt the urge to seal its permanence by proposing to Jo on the spot.

We had spent the night dancing to salsa and we were both glowing and smitten. Then I felt another surging conviction: Jo and I were made for each other. There was no need for me to rush anything. I would find a much more romantic way to ask her to be my wife.

Jo knocked back her drink, wiped away the sweat and smiled at me.

'Hey, Brendan,' she said. 'Let's have one more dance . . .'

Jo and I gave each other confidence. Together we felt unstoppable. Her old insecurities never vanished, and she would regularly question herself, but she learned to control her self-doubt with a combination of my reassurance and her own experience. I was bolstered by our deep partnership and the energy we generated together. Beyond our shared enthusiasm for adventures and new experiences, Jo and I were bound together by a sense of social mission. By this time I was running Crisis Action, commuting between Oxford and London, while Jo continued to shine at Oxfam. Our projects often overlapped – as in August 2006 when my main initiative on the war in Lebanon echoed some of Jo's work.

That month we conquered our first mountains together, up in Glencoe. We were ambitious and tackled the Aonach Eagach Ridge, one of the narrowest ridges in Britain. It offers spectacular views but it also requires a clear head for its dizzying heights. I had attempted it twice before and wimped out both times (once nearly killing Will in the process). On the way up I put my knee out and we talked about turning back. 'Don't worry,' Jo said, 'I'll carry the bag and you can lean on me.' So we completed the ridge with Jo carrying the bag and me limping along behind her. As we overtook a party with full ropes and harnesses, I looked like a chump and Jo like a wonder woman.

On the way down conditions were abysmal, but Jo and I were lost in a brainstorming blizzard of ideas. We forgot all about the weather as we talked about Lebanon. Tony Blair, who at the time was still Prime Minister, had refused to call for a ceasefire. The conflict, waged between the Israel Defence Forces and Hezbollah, had cost the lives of 1,200 Lebanese citizens and over 150 Israelis. Other European leaders campaigned for a ceasefire but Blair believed Israel should be allowed more time to crush Hezbollah. I had not been leading Crisis Action for long, but I knew this was an issue where we had to try to pool resources as a way of putting pressure on the British government.

Fed by a mixture of relief that we had managed the climb without incident, exhilaration and surplus adrenalin, our brains were buzzing. We decided the best approach was to try to 'out' MPs over their positions on the ceasefire and publish the results online. I would set up the portal, Jo would bring in Oxfam and together we'd get the rest of the NGOs on board. A week later, working with a coalition of dozens of organisations, we'd contacted every MP and assembled a comprehensive lobbying exercise. MP by MP we peeled support away from the government line and pretty soon junior members of the government were contacting us to let us know they favoured a ceasefire. The media started to write about a government revolt and the pressure grew.

We spent that autumn commuting between Oxford and London. Jo still kept Beaterville, as she called her house in Oxford, while I had moved my boat down to a winter mooring in Victoria Park, east London. I remember one particularly cold night in November. It was my birthday and we had had a lovely evening on the boat with my parents, who had come for dinner. Jo and I bedded down on the sofa bed, next to the fire. I was awoken by a curious sound.

'What's that scratching noise?' I asked.

Jo woke up and listened hard. 'I'm not sure . . .'

'What do you think it might be?'

'Squirrels,' Jo said.

I was unconvinced but, when the noise stopped, I drifted off again. Half an hour later it resumed. 'Are you sure that's squirrels?'

'Yeah,' Jo said emphatically. 'That's definitely squirrels.'

The scratching continued. 'Jo, that's not squirrels.'

I slid off the bed, opened up the door and put my head out just in time to see two men running off with our solar panels. They had spent the last hour using a little hacksaw to cut though the chain that held them in place.

A few weeks later, with the solar panels replaced and secured to a much bigger steel chain, we were asleep again. The scratching noise started.

'Jo, Jo,' I hissed.

'Squirrels,' Jo said sleepily.

'Bloody hell, Jo,' I whispered furiously. 'Remember the solar panels?'

I pulled on my pants and added a balaclava. I looked absurd but Jo was worried.

'Brendan,' she whispered, 'don't go out.'

'I've got to.' I reached for the ice axe we used up in the mountains. Surely the sight of a man in just his pants and a balaclava would scare them off.

I opened the door softly. I was just about to launch into a headlong charge when I saw an astonishing sight. A furry tail gleamed in the moonlight.

'I can't believe this,' I said.

'What is it?' Jo whispered.

'A squirrel.'

It was very quiet and then I heard Jo's voice. 'Thought so . . .'

Some of our most important adventures took place in the Balkans. In 2006 we went to Croatia for New Year. It was very important to me to show Jo the orphanage where I had spent years volunteering, and to introduce her to the kids I had known for almost a decade. I remember playing with her and the kids in the woods at night. Jo and I were pretending to be mosquitoes and were making buzzing sounds as we chased the kids through the dark. Jo kept flying after a boy called Dalibor; he was fast, but Jo was a runner and she steadily closed the gap, their feet echoing in the woods. As he swerved on to a new path, Jo followed him – and ran slap-bang into a tree. I winced when I saw the cut across the bridge of her nose. Bright red drops of blood fell on the white snow. I would have been more worried had Jo not started joking with the boy.

We spent New Year in the village, as I had done for many years. The bulk of our time was spent working in the village orphanage and the houses where six or seven children were looked after by 'SOS mothers'. There were 112 kids in the village and I knew at least fifty of them really well. My task every December was to organise games in the snow, and Jo threw herself into the fun. She learned the word for 'sausage', which is *kobasica*, and repeated it constantly. The kids thought she was hilarious and kept shouting 'Yo! Yo!' so she would say it again. They could never say 'Jo' because the letter 'J' is pronounced as a 'Y' in Bosnian/Croatian.

On New Year's Eve, we were outside with the kids again and a frozen snowball caught Jo in the face. She got off the deck with a swollen eye to match her boxer's nose, grinned, shrugged and said 'Kobasica!'

Three weeks later Jo was back out again in the heat and dust of Chad, which borders Darfur. Our plan was to meet up in Ethiopia, where I was on a work trip. It was typical of Jo that, despite the danger, she liked to go for a dawn run even if the pop of gunfire could be heard in the distance. After her run she would slip off her shoes to walk back into camp and we assume that this is how she contracted Strongyloides, because this parasitic worm burrows its way into the body by entering the soles of a person's bare foot. It was only later that doctors from the London School of Tropical Medicine, who did many tests on Jo, discovered she was also suffering from Giardia. She had picked up a potent cocktail of tropical diseases.

The Strongyloides parasites embed themselves in the small intestine and then spread through the lymphatic system. Some enter the superficial veins close to the surface of the body and are carried, in blood, into the lungs where they enter the alveoli. Once there they are coughed up and swallowed into the gut. That's where they really get down to business and breed.

I remember Googling and reading out the symptoms and prognosis to Jo. I got to the bit where it said 98 per cent mortality rate and we both fell silent. I read it again and was relieved to find that that only applied in cases of immune-system failure when the worms then infected the vital organs. Nevertheless, it was a serious disease. Jo's already petite frame shrank to six and a half stone, and she was hospitalised. The next few months were an ordeal. Her mood dipped as she struggled to shake off such a debilitating illness. Even by the summer of 2007 she was so fatigued that depression had curbed her natural optimism. Her diary entries show how low she felt in the aftermath of Strongyloides.

24 June 07

This whole illness thing has really hit me hard. I have this horrible sense that I'm letting B down by not being strong enough. He's being great and I'm sure it's in my head but it's really bugging and upsetting me. I love him completely and want to be his superwoman – but just can't do it at the mo. B asked me whether I am happy. Well, generally, yes I am but, God, I've been having some real downs this week. I'm quite stressed and dropping balls left, right and centre.

A few days later, in a typical Jo-ism, she started her latest diary entry on a sweet note:

Munching liquorice allsorts at Reading station . . . mmmm.

But the demons soon flitted across the surface again:

Everything feels up in the air at the mo, like I've got some decisions to take.

Career: Where's it going? What do I want to do that I'm not doing now? What's this empty, unsatisfied feeling about? How do I solve it?

Home: Can't do this whole split life/2 lives thing – esp not with my energy levels as they are. I want one home with B.

My life, though, is brilliant. I've found the love of my life. I'm doing things I knew nothing about. I'm my own person with my own principles and passions.

This year has passed in a daze of not feeling quite right and pushing myself to get on with it. I need to acknowledge that I've been really ill. It's not something I should feel guilty about. What's that about!!

Brendan: I wrote to him the other week – some pretty honest things. Hope he digested it. It took me a long time to write with such honesty. He scares me sometimes. Scares me with how much I need him. I want him. How much I want us to be together on a journey through our lives. Life is very complicated, isn't it? It's beautiful and amazing but it's complex. Or maybe we just make it so.

And then on 8 August 2007:

Haven't written for a while. Am totally recovered.
Yee-hah! Really feel well again. After six months
in a daze it feels great.

We had just returned from another trip to Croatia where we had run our latest summer camp for the kids. It was an uplifting week as Jo's energy returned in the Croatian sunshine. She (and I) made some decisions out there. She had been offered a new role with Oxfam, based in New York. We were going to go to the States. She'd also decided that at some point she definitely wanted to stand as a candidate for the Labour Party in Batley and Spen. The idea would still ebb and flow in the years to come, but this was the clearest she had ever been about what she might do next.

Have decided to stand – final decision whilst I was
in Croatia. It's the right thing to do. Will have to
work out the detail with Coxy. So good to do NYC
and as many adventures before I stand. Have been
buzzing all day with a sense of completeness.
Mmmmmm. Lots going on. I'm 100% better. Work is
great. Totally loving it.

The dark, tangled threadworm of Strongyloides was dead. In its place the familiar bright, clear light of Jo was back. All was right in our world again.

* * *

By early September I had my own plan in place. I had decided to propose to Jo. I had never met anyone like her and I knew I wanted to spend the rest of my life with her. But I wanted the proposal to be right, to be in keeping with who we were and who we would become together. I decided to propose to Jo high up in the mountains. We were off on another Munro-climbing mission and I had settled on An Teallach as the perfect spot for us to get engaged. An Teallach is one of the most scenic of all Munros, and a challenging traverse. Soaring over Loch Toll an Lochain, and overlooking an area known as the Great Wilderness, in its shadows lies Shenavell, reportedly the best bothy in Scotland. I could not imagine a more fitting location for my proposal. I went out and bought a £20 ring from Argos, as a substitute for the real thing that we would choose together.

I was pretty sure Jo would say yes, not because I have a high opinion of myself, but because by this stage we were inseparable. Ever since Cuba eighteen months earlier, we had spoken about our desire to spend the rest of our lives together.

Jo had no idea of my plotting. I told her I would take care of the food, wine, water, stove, camping and climbing equipment. She just needed to bring the map and dinner for the first night on the mountain of what promised to be a superb cycling and walking holiday.

I gave her a big kiss when we met at Euston Station. She looked a bit frazzled so I asked if she had managed to bring us dinner. 'Sorry, Coxy,' Jo said. 'I was in such a rush.'

A strange uncertainty rippled through me. 'Jo,' I said casually, 'you did bring the map?'

The map was the most important item of the journey. I had reminded her repeatedly that she should pack it near the top of her rucksack.

'Bugger! I knew I'd forgotten something.'

I stared at her in disbelief. Jo was carrying nothing but her rucksack on her back. I spoke slowly, trying to remain calm. 'Jo, where's your bike?'

'Oh, no . . .'

I could see her mind whirring as she tried to work out what had happened to it. She finally remembered that she had left it chained to the railings outside Oxford Station.

'So,' I pronounced gloomily, 'we're going on a cycling holiday without your bike . . .'

We got on to the sleeper train and I lay on my bunk, feeling dejected. The proposal was ruined.

'I'm really sorry,' Jo said after a while.

I grunted. I still didn't feel like opening the bottle of wine I had bought for our dinner but I nodded when Jo suggested we go to the buffet car.

She slipped her hand through my arm and I almost smiled. 'I could do with a drink,' I said.

Over a few drinks we made a new plan. I gave up the idea of cycling for a day, climbing An Teallach and then slipping a ring on to Jo's finger in the lovely bothy I had read about. Instead we would aim for a set of Munros in the Fannaichs to the west of Inverness, the only place I happened to have a map for. It was wild and remote and we could enjoy a long walk instead of cycling.

'Looks good, Coxy,' Jo agreed.

We woke the following morning to discover a flawless day outside our carriage window.

'It's probably bucketing down in An Teallach,' Jo said cheerfully.

The sun kept shining in the Fannaichs on our first day of walking, along an old track that led to a dam at the foot of the valley and then up on to our first peak. We lay down and enjoyed the sun on our skin. We climbed three peaks that day and whistled at some breathtaking sights, including a golden eagle flying low over our heads.

We walked all day until, on the flank of Sgurr Mor, the sun began to dip and the cloud lowered. We started looking for somewhere to camp. We were at 900 metres above sea level, in the middle of a boulder field. As we searched we stumbled across a tiny rock shelter. It was about five foot long and three foot wide and high. It was like something out of *The Hobbit*, only much smaller.

We looked at each other and smiled. I thought, What a spot to get engaged. We crawled into the shelter and while I cooked some pasta, Jo started to fill all the gaps in the rocks with our possessions to keep out the wind. We barricaded the small entrance with our sleeping bags and I lit two candles. Next I opened the wine, a real treat given we normally jettisoned everything non essential to save weight – even to the extent of breaking off the handles of toothbrushes.

It was a delicious pasta dish (most things taste delicious on mountains) and, as I refilled our glasses, I looked at Jo in the candlelight.

She was smiling and wearing her ridiculous mountain hat which I loved, even if it did make her look like a gnome. It had turned into a magical evening and I knew I wanted to ask Jo the most serious question I had ever asked anyone.

'Will you marry me?'

Jo's eyes were full of love, and she simply said, 'Yes.'

She started crying when I brought out the Argos ring. Jo just kissed me when I tried to explain that we would buy a proper ring on our next adventure in Vietnam. That made me cry too and we started laughing between the tears.

Neither of us knew what we were doing and I slipped the ring on to the third finger of her right hand. We took some amusing selfies with Jo waving and showing off her hand, the ring gleaming in the candlelight. Pasta sauce still stained the corners of our smiling mouths.

It was one of the most memorable nights of our lives. We curled up in our arctic sleeping bags and talked about our lives together. The shelter wasn't quite big enough so my legs spent the night outside. The next morning, we packed our bags and before we left I carved two letters and a unifying mark in the rock at the entrance to the shelter:

J + B

13

The White House

– 22 September 2016 –

My handwriting is so terrible that trouble, I guess, is inevitable. I just had not expected it to cause problems in America. My mind was scrambled by exhaustion and grief but there were no valid excuses for thinking I could simply write a letter to the US immigration department which Jessie, our nanny, could use to explain why Cuillin and Lejla were travelling without a parent. My handwritten scrawl does not look as though it belongs to the upstanding father of two small children on their way to see the President of the United States.

I remember Googling the requirements for kids entering the US with a chaperone, rather than a parent, and finding nothing beyond a suggestion that I just needed to write a letter of authorisation. I picked up a pen and wrote 'I hereby authorise . . .'

If anyone had been able to read it properly they would have understood I'd travelled to New York two days earlier in order to attend a summit on refugees. I explained that

I would meet Jessie, Cuillin and Lejla at Dulles International Airport on 22 September. Until then Jessie would be in charge of my son and daughter on the flight from London to Washington. I signed the letter and assumed all would be fine.

It was hard for Jessie to bring the kids on a transatlantic flight without me – especially as she hated flying. When they reached the immigration desk at Dulles Jessie handed over my letter to a suspicious official. He sounded incredulous when he asked, 'What's this?' Jessie explained but he shook his head, took their passports and sent them to a holding room with a dozen other people.

I was unaware of any difficulties while I waited on the other side of the arrivals hall, looking up expectantly whenever a new group of people shuffled through from behind the glass doors with their suitcase-laden trolleys.

I stood on my own, missing Jo, longing for the arrival of Cuillin and Lejla.

After another half an hour I was beginning to worry, when my phone beeped with a text from Jessie. She had let me know an hour earlier that they had landed safely, but in this message she told me they were being kept waiting while the issue of the letter was investigated. It seemed as if she and the kids could be held for a long time.

'Yeah, it's likely to be around six hours at this time of day,' a female official confirmed when I went looking for information about what might be happening.

'Six hours!' I exclaimed. It was near midnight, UK time, and the children would be worn out. The plan was that we would get them to bed in Washington soon after 7 p.m. local time, and they could sleep all night without jet-lag spinning their little body clocks out of control. But everything depended on a speedy transfer to our rooms at the British Embassy. Any delay and I would have to introduce two fractious kids to Barack Obama. A poignant invitation had the potential to become a nightmare.

It had all gone smoothly at first. After the call with the President I had spoken to the British ambassador in Washington, Kim Darroch, whom I knew from my work at Downing Street. Kim said he would arrange the logistics of our visit to the Oval Office, and after a few days he came back with a suggested date from the White House: the afternoon of Friday, 23 September. We were also invited to stay at the British Embassy. Those simple arrangements meant I never considered any potential problems at the airport.

I felt like a dunce as I looked helplessly at the immigration official who had just told me that my exhausted children, and Jessie, could be detained for six hours. Jo and I had always avoided trying to gain any preferential treatment, but I thought we would all end up in tears if I didn't sort out my mess.

I explained what had happened and that we were going to see the President. 'Would it help if I got the White House to call somebody here?' I asked.

The official looked surprised. 'Oh,' she said, suddenly seeming to realise that we really were on our way to meet the President. 'Let me see what I can do . . .'

Ten minutes later the three of them appeared, escorted by a police officer. Cuillin and Lejla were smiling, rather than crying, as they ran into my arms.

I was wide awake with the kids at three o'clock the following morning. It was 8 a.m. UK time. I tried to get them back to bed, explaining that they'd had only five hours of sleep. The kids refused to shut their eyes. They sang songs and ran around.

At 5 a.m. I was really worried. How would they be in another ten hours? I could imagine the kids knackered and irritable as Obama tried to talk to them.

The loneliness of being a single parent feels acute when you're tired and your kids are at their most unreasonable. I felt lonely that morning. Cuillin and Lejla would not go back to sleep.

Finally, long before seven o'clock, and in need of reinforcements, we knocked on poor Jessie's door.

I apologised but the kids barged straight in, shouting, 'Hello, Jessie! Wake up, Jessie!'

We were lucky with Jessie, especially when she showed such kindness after Jo's death. With Lejla due to start nursery in September Jessie had planned to start a new job. But then Jo was killed and our lives were torn apart. Jessie kindly offered to change her plans, and put everything on hold, because she knew how much Cuillin and Lejla needed her and the continuity she would provide. The psychologists had advised us to change as little as possible, and losing their nanny on top of what had already happened would have been a huge blow to their security. I gratefully accepted her generosity when she agreed to keep working for us for another year. She was an outstanding nanny: calm, kind and full of genuine love for our children.

We all felt better once we were in the embassy breakfast room where a special table had been laid for us. Jessie took a photo of me, Cuillin and Lejla. We each held up our glasses of chilled orange juice to say 'Cheers!' The kids beamed at the sight of all the croissants, muffins and pancakes, let alone the fruit, cereal, eggs and sausages.

– 23 September 2016 –

Washington, DC, looked stunning beneath a perfect blue sky at 8 a.m. We took the kids to the Lincoln Memorial. As we approached the marble statue of Abraham Lincoln, the breath caught in my throat. Early morning sunshine fell across the statue in a narrow band of light, illuminating Lincoln in that magical beam.

It was so bright that, looking tiny in front of the mammoth statue, the kids covered their eyes. Cuillin wore a red T-shirt, 35 emblazoned across the front, and shorts. Lejla was in a sundress. I snapped away, taking pictures of the kids with Lincoln.

I gave them their first impromptu history lesson of the day and told them how Lincoln had been special in the way he had helped free black slaves way back in 1863.

The only thing that really mattered to Cuillin and Lejla was that their mum would have liked a lot of what he had done. I explained that Jo liked Martin Luther King even more and that, in 1963, he had made his famous 'I Have a Dream' speech on these very steps. I didn't waffle on about the significance of King but, instead, entertained the kids with my version of his rolling oratory in the deserted memorial. I flung open my arms and recited the one passage I knew, trying to make the kids laugh as I reached for the echoing quaver of King's delivery:

I have a dream that one day even the state of Mississippi, a desert state, sweltering with the heat of injustice and oppression, will be transformed into an oasis of freedom and justice. I have a dream that my four little children will one day live in a nation where they will not be judged by the colour of their skin but by the content of their character. I have a dream today!

The kids laughed at my funny voice and terribly bad acting. We spent another hour playing games in the grounds and slowly made progress down the Mall. We stopped at the bottom of the Washington Monument and I showed them the place where Jo and I had stood in January 2009 to watch Obama's inauguration in the freezing cold. They were too hot and bothered to be interested, but I remembered it with fondness.

The morning had flashed past and the temperature outside had risen to thirty degrees. We had lunch and then

Cuillin and Lejla began yawning. We took them back to the embassy where it was easy to persuade them it was time for bed. They didn't stir until two hours later when I switched on the light.

Unlike at three in the morning, they now looked utterly blitzed. They wanted more sleep.

'You can't, kids,' I said. 'We're going to see the President . . .'

Slowly, they woke up. They had chosen what they wanted to wear and were happy with their Oval Office outfits – a checked shirt, long shorts and trainers for Cuillin and a pale blue dress for Lejla, the bottom half covered in images of palm trees, brightly coloured houses and exotic animals and birds.

'You look gorgeous, Ledgie,' I told her as I slipped on her tiny white socks and black shoes.

I wore a suit and pale blue shirt but, as always, avoided a tie. Obama was a chilled-out President.

I had met Obama briefly twice before. I knew he would have no recollection because the first time was just in a line of people whose hands he shook. On the second occasion, while working on the G20 summit in London in 2009, we had spent an hour in the same room, but I'd been one of many advisers and we had not spoken personally.

I suggested to the kids that we go through the drawings they had done for the President. The initial plan had been that they would each present Obama with a couple of their very best pieces of art as a thank you to him for being so kind. I had told the kids how much Mummy would have wanted them to do something really lovely for him. They took my words to heart and, over a few days, each produced about fifty personal drawings for the President.

'Wow,' I'd said, looking down at that small museum of art. 'But, kids, we can't give a hundred drawings to the President.'

'Why not?' Lejla asked.

'Because he's very, very busy. He won't have time to look at a hundred drawings.'

'Fifty?' Cuillin suggested.

'I think we should give him just two from each of you.'

'What about all the others?' Lejla asked.

'We can keep them,' I said.

'Good,' Lejla said.

At home we had whittled down the selection to a shortlist of ten each, which we had packed carefully at the bottom of my suitcase. It was now time to choose the winners from each pile. They could then give the President a gift of their two best pictures.

It was still a tricky task but we narrowed it down. Lejla was pleased with her two but Cuillin had three drawings. He pointed to his favourite. I also liked it the most and said how happy the President would be to receive it.

Cuillin shook his head. 'No, it's a bit too good. I want to keep it.'

'Are you sure?'

'Yes,' Cuillin said.

'Okay. But let's take it with us and at least show it to

the President. Then we'll hear what he thinks and let's see how you feel then.'

Cuillin nodded. I was sure that as soon as we were in the Oval Office he would want to offer his best drawing to Barack Obama.

We gave each other a little high-five. The business of negotiation and artful diplomacy before a big White House meeting clearly wasn't as hard as everyone told me.

Cuillin, Lejla, Jessie and I arrived at the White House. Everyone was kind, especially to the kids, and we were taken on a tour. I liked going into the West Wing and we looked around before we went down to the Situation Room. I told Cuillin and Lejla that this was where the President came when there was trouble and he spoke to leaders around the world and to the people in charge of the army.

The kids were impressed.

We went to the Press Briefing Room and then the Roosevelt Room before we were taken to a holding space where we would wait for the President. I was happy to have a break. I didn't want Cuillin and Lejla to get tired and so I said we should all sit down, eat the cookies they had left for us and read a book together.

I opened *James and the Giant Peach.* Quiet descended as I began to read out loud. The kids listened attentively, chewing thoughtfully. How unreal it felt to be reading Roald Dahl while waiting to meet Barack Obama in the Oval Office. I felt another familiar stabbing pang for Jo; but I thought how proud she would have been.

We lost ourselves in the world of the giant peach and twenty minutes flew past.

The door suddenly opened. 'Please come through, the President is ready to see you.'

We all stood up and I reached for the children's hands. We were just about to walk in with Jessie when the aide spoke softly.

'I'm sorry,' she said to Jessie. 'Family only . . .'

I felt disappointed for Jessie. She had been thrilled by the prospect of meeting Obama and it was the best possible thank-you gift that the kids and I could have given her, but only my name, and those of Cuillin and Lejla were on the official list of visitors. Jessie did the gracious thing and sat down again while the kids and I were swept into the Oval Office.

Barack Obama was warmer and even more approachable than I had hoped. He set us at ease – so much so that Cuillin asked if it was true that British people had burned down the White House. Obama grinned. 'Yes, you did burn it down,' he said cheerfully, 'but it's much nicer now. Do you like it?'

'Yeah,' both kids replied in unison.

I cursed myself. Served me right for telling the kids that British troops had set fire to the White House in 1814. Reminding the current President of that attack was not quite the opening I'd had in mind. But Obama charmed the kids and showed them round his famous office, asking them their ages and talking about how much he had admired their mum.

The sense of occasion had rubbed off on Cuillin and Lejla because they were extraordinary that afternoon, as if they sensed the significance of the day. But, rather than being sombre and quiet, they were full of life and questions. They behaved impeccably and allowed me the space and time to have a long conversation with the President.

He was as humane as he was supremely skilled in conveying his admiration for Jo. His sadness for our loss was palpable but never sentimental. We then spoke about political extremism and how to fight back against it. Obama explained that he would set up a foundation when he left the White House in January 2017 and that he was committed to working at the community level to bring people closer together. I knew a senior member of the team establishing the Obama Foundation and we agreed that I'd follow up with her on some of the specifics. We spoke about my own plans. I discussed my belief that we needed to work harder on establishing an inclusive kind of patriotism that would draw in people who had been marginalised in the past.

We joked about how Jo and I had played a 'key role' in his rise to the presidency. He had been briefed on the fact that we had joined his campaign team in North Carolina as volunteers, in the fall of 2008. I amused him with stories of Jo running around crazily, rounding up little old ladies to vote for him on polling day as the clock clicked down in a tight electoral state.

As our time together came to a close, I told Obama that

Jo would have loved seeing Cuillin and Lejla with him in his office – and how kind it had been of him to invite us.

'It was the least we could do,' he said. He then looked across at the kids still playing. 'You and Jo have done a great job with them . . .'

He called the kids over and said that he had a few gifts for them. He gave them each a bag stuffed with stickers, badges and sweets. There was also a White House Frisbee and a presidential seal. As we were leaving, Cuillin said, 'Dad, what about the pictures?'

I suddenly remembered that I had left the drawings in the holding room with Jessie, so I ran back to fetch them and grabbed the opportunity to sneak Jessie in with us.

Obama gave her a great welcome and Jessie smiled as she shook his hand and he spoke to her. The kids and I, meanwhile, got ready with the artwork. Cuillin hesitated over his best drawing.

'Cucu,' I whispered, using my nickname for him, 'shall we give him the best one?'

He looked down at his drawing.

'What do you think?' I prompted softly. 'Should we give it to the President?'

Cuillin looked up at me and whispered: 'No, Daddy. It's too nice.'

It was such a decisive 'No' that I nearly laughed. 'That's okay,' I said.

Once he had received their drawings and praised them with that winning sense of Obama-esque gravitas and sincerity, the President leaned down to hug my children.

Jo (*left*), aged four, and Kim, aged two, with classic haircuts.

Jo and Kim on their way to Brownies, spring 1984.

School trip from Heckmondwike Grammar: Jo (*far left*), in her teens, outside Number 10 Downing Street.

Jo with her parents, Gordon and Jean Leadbeater, at Pembroke College, Cambridge, on her graduation day, summer 1995.

After university, Jo (*in grey T-shirt by window*) went to Borneo with Operation Raleigh where she worked on conservation projects and helped build a stilt house.

Jo meeting children in Khayelitsha township, South Africa, which she visited in 2001 with Glenys Kinnock. This trip had a huge impact on her.

Jo and Kim during Jo's hen weekend in Yorkshire.

The rock shelter where Jo and I got engaged and spent the night. It was so tiny that I slept with my legs outside.

Moving on to our new barge *Ederlezi*. Shortly after this I managed to steer the boat into a lock at full speed.

Our second wedding day, at the black barn. I had needed to use all my powers of persuasion before the owner agreed to let us use it.

Jo with her fourteen best women all dressed in the colours of the Suffragettes, green, white and violet.

Jo and I on the summit of Sgurr Alasdair on the Cuillin Ridge. We continued along the crest before tackling the hardest peak in the UK, the Inaccessible Pinnacle. We only found out later that Jo was pregnant.

Jo and Cuillin on a ferry in Newfoundland in August 2011. We had spent the previous night sleeping in our car because we'd arrived too late for the motel.

Wild camping after a hard day's canoeing down the River Wye, August 2015.

Picnic time on Bowling Green overlooking Symond's Yat West.

Jo with her mum and dad on election day, 7 May 2015.

Briefing Jo on what the numbers seemed to indicate as she arrived at the count in Huddersfield on election night.

Jo taking part in a Macmillan Cancer Support tug of war between a team of female MPs and a Macmillan ladies' team, June 2016. The Macmillan ladies won.

Jessie, our nanny, the kids and I in our speedboat on the Thames, 15 June 2016. Cuillin and Lejla are on lookout duty.

Gordon and Jean, Kim and Clare visiting the sea of flowers in Birstall, 18 June 2016.

An amazing outpouring of compassion at a memorial to Jo in Trafalgar Square on what would have been her forty-second birthday, 22 June 2016.

Our boat covered in flags and flowers, with the *Yorkshire Rose* alongside. She had been freshly painted and filled with rose bushes by our neighbours on the mooring.

One of my favourite pictures of Jo and the kids in the woods near our cottage.

Making elderflower champagne with the kids.

Cuillin, Lejla and I with President Obama in the Oval Office, September 2016.

We now have a lovely photograph of Lejla reaching up with her left arm to embrace President Obama while her right foot arches behind her. Barack Obama holds her drawing of the blue sea, full of colourful fish, in his left hand. His right arm encircles her. Cuillin, Jessie and I are beaming in the background.

It was Cuillin's turn next and he fell happily into an Obama hug. My gaze drifted from that happy scene to the prized picture we would be keeping. I couldn't stop smiling, making a mental note to present this very drawing in a frame to Cuillin on his eighteenth birthday. We would never forget the picture that was too good even for a great President.

14

America

Life felt pleasantly open-ended for Jo and me on the first full day, 1 September 2008, of our American adventure. We both loved the United States, and New York in particular. We bought a diary to commemorate our trip, and it seemed fitting that Barack Obama's face should be emblazoned across the front cover, with the word HOPE beneath his image. Obama and hope seemed entwined in a year full of such promise that it hurts to think of everything we have since lost.

Jo's new position as Head of Humanitarian Campaigning at Oxfam International was a new challenge for her, building on all the years she had worked for the organisation in Brussels and Oxford. It also meant we would work more closely together and, like my job, it could be done from anywhere. At the time Crisis Action was opening small offices in key cities around the world, and New York was top of the priority list. It made sense for Jo to be based close to the UN as well, so we decided to move together to New York for six months. We had not quite worked out what would happen once that time was up, but we decided simply to soak up every experience until we got married in September of the following year.

Jo captured the dreamy quality of our lives in New York when she wrote to her grandad Arthur on 9 September. At ninety-four he was increasingly frail, but Jo hoped that he would live long enough for her to see him a few more times on our return.

Hello from New York Grandad!

I'm sitting in my apartment, which is about five minutes from the Empire State Building. Brendan and I have been living here for a week and a day and we're really getting into the swing of things.

The first thing I did when we landed was buy a nice photo frame and put my favourite photo of you and me (taken all those years ago!) up on the wall. There you are holding me at the bottom of our garden opposite the barley fields. I must say that you look much better than I do – with my chubby cheeks and very bad haircut!

The second thing that Brendan and I did was head off on a long walk across New York – we walked for miles all over town: taking in Broadway, 5th Avenue, the Brooklyn Bridge and Times Square. It's all breath-taking and you feel like you're in a film.

Next week we're going to see the New York Yankees play baseball. I don't yet understand the rules of the game but I'm hoping we can find a nice fan who can explain it all to us. We are also trying to see some American football soon – maybe the New York Giants. I will let you know how they compare to Huddersfield Town.

On the work front – I'm really enjoying things. Both Brendan and I are doing quite a lot of work with the United Nations which is really interesting and we're meeting lots of new people.

I love you very, very much Gramps and will imagine you sitting in your chair reading this little note.

Lots and lots of love,
Jo xxxxxxxxxx

In between work and relishing everything the city had to offer, we got swept up in the visceral battle of a US presidential election. The debates felt like sporting theatre and we liked to watch them live in a bar full of Democratic voters who hollered for Barack Obama over John McCain and Joe Biden over Sarah Palin.

In her last ever email to Grandad Arthur, Jo wrote about the election:

Everyone here is obsessed with the upcoming US Presidential election. You hear people talking about which candidate they are going to vote for as you walk down the street, in the office and all over town. My preference is for Barack Obama and the Democrats. However, lots of people here are talking about Sarah Palin – the Republican Vice-Presidential candidate. You may have heard about her – she's a gun-toting, moose-hunting, mother of five from Alaska and she has got everyone in a tizz.

We had already offered our services to the Obama campaign and had decided to go to North Carolina in election week. Before then everything fell into place. I found an office for Crisis Action beside the United Nations headquarters. Jo's office was next door to the Chrysler Building on Lexington Avenue. Our American dream seemed sweeter with every day.

But, on 21 September 2008, real life returned. Arthur Leadbeater died in his old-age home near Liversedge. Jo flew home for the funeral at Dewsbury Crematorium. She was glad her grandad had enjoyed her New York emails but, as she wrote from Yorkshire, his death hurt her terribly:

I still feel achingly sad. I have to keep popping out for a little cry. But the funeral itself was lovely. Dad did a great job. The vicar gave an incredibly moving summary of Arthur's life and lots of people came to show how much they loved him. I will miss him dearly but I am so grateful to have had him as my gramps.

As fall descended in mid-October, Jo and I travelled upstate to the Catskill Mountains for the weekend. As we so often did when halfway up, or down, a mountain, Jo and I had a memorable conversation. It was our first really serious chat about children. I was just weeks away from my thirtieth birthday and, at thirty-four, Jo was more conscious than me that time was pressing. We both still felt young and work was going so well we wondered if we should wait a few more years. We didn't want all our adventures to end. But the more we talked, the more we felt that having children together would be the greatest adventure of all.

By the time we reached the top of Hunter Mountain we had resolved that, soon after our wedding, we would try to start a family. It felt good. When we finally stepped inside the cable-car that would take us down, I held Jo close. We looked at our surroundings anew. A canvas of red, orange and golden leaves spread out beneath us. The world was very beautiful.

Early on Sunday morning, 2 November 2008, we caught a flight to Raleigh in North Carolina. Jo was invigorated by Obama and I shared her belief in the forty-seven-year-old man who, we felt, was rejuvenating hope for the world, and who we hoped would become the first African-American President.

North Carolina hadn't voted for a Democratic candidate for thirty-two years, since Jimmy Carter became President in 1976.

We reached Raleigh just before noon. Jo wrote:

*We were straight off to the volunteer Obama HQ
downtown. Amazing buzz – loads of people milling
around, wanting to help, and be involved in an
historic win. Brendan and I ended up canvassing
with a guy called Larry who was nice enough –
though, rather bizarrely, on a diet which meant that
he wasn't eating but insisted on talking about food
all the time. We did one round of canvassing in a
middle-class neighbourhood – big spread-out houses,
pretty positive responses. Then went to Hill Street to
pick up some more addresses and set off again –
after a little jerk-chicken lunch stop, without Larry.*

The following morning it was my birthday. I didn't know
it at the time of our Hunter Mountain trip, but Jo had
gathered some of the remarkable leaves, pressed and framed
them, and she gave them to me as a birthday present and
a memory of our biggest decision together. The frame now
sits by the fireplace in our cottage in the woods.

*A lovely day. We were knocking on doors and doing
voter ID. Lovely forested area, great leaves, blue sky,
big lawns and big houses. Even here, though, a lot of
Obama supporters. We walked for hours, from door
to door. Only one bad reaction – an old guy called
me a socialist but clearly had no idea what it meant.
He also went on about abortion. God, I hope we win.*

On election day we got drenched. It rained all day but we didn't care. Running from one house to the next, feeling the gathering excitement, it felt as if we were doing necessary work. Most people had already voted but each time we reached someone who hadn't, or would find it difficult to reach the polling booth because they were frail or unwell, we switched into Beater-and-Coxy mode. Jo was brilliant. She charmed everyone we met into voting – and I helped them into the car so that they could be driven to the polling station.

Jo had a lovely way of chatting to people, asking how they were doing and what they thought of the various candidates, before she launched into how extraordinary Obama appeared to her. She was much smaller than everyone else but her presence was huge. As Jo reached the clinching conclusion of her pitch she would turn to me, as bedraggled as a patient old Labrador left out in the rainy yard, and say, 'This is my fiancé Brendan. We've flown all the way from the UK to support Barack Obama. We believe so passionately in all he can do for the United States and the whole world. Won't you consider going a mile down the road to vote for him?'

Even the doubters would end up grinning and nodding. One previously reluctant voter said, 'Well, I guess we could ma'am, seeing as you've come all this way.'

'You have such a pretty accent,' the next newly convinced Obama voter told Jo.

'I'm from Yorkshire,' Jo explained.

'Not London, England?'

'Well, we live in London but I'm from the north of England – a lovely place called Yorkshire.'

Before Jo could do any more for the Yorkshire Tourist Board, I urged her on. We had more voters to hunt down. The rain fell still harder, but we were relentless as we moved from one street to the next.

Eventually there were just twenty minutes left until the polls closed. We ran down the streets of an African-American neighbourhood with dozens of Obama supporters. The North Carolina vote still hung in the balance. Jo ran like the wind and she pulled in more voters than anyone else. There were less than ten minutes to go when she bundled a family of six into two cars. We got them to the station a few blocks away and they all voted – with one minute left on the clock.

The mad dash was worth it. Totally soaked, we headed downtown to the hotel for the Democrat Party rally. It was a big ballroom with TVs set up everywhere and everyone nervously sipping on beers and munching free popcorn – eyes glued to the coverage on CNN.

There was an awesome atmosphere and we huddled around the TV waiting for the magic number to be announced. He won Pennsylvania, then Virginia! Then Ohio, then the West Coast came in as the polls closed. And that's when they predicted an Obama victory!

And then, suddenly, it was confirmed – OBAMA IS PRESIDENT-ELECT.

We gathered in the ballroom to watch him speak.
For me, it was one of the best political performances
I've ever seen. He pitched it perfectly. He was meas-
ured, humble, inspiring – and it felt like a moment
in history that has already changed the world. I
cried – as did many others. Everyone hugged and
celebrated. We got chatting to one African-American
woman who had experienced segregation in her life-
time. What a journey.

The woman must have been in her seventies, and her ten-year-old granddaughter sat on her knee. She began to cry as she said to the little girl, 'When I was born they wouldn't let us sit on buses . . . and now we're the President . . .'

Jo looked up at me, her eyes glistening. It felt as if we had just witnessed the climax to a peaceful, once-in-a-lifetime revolution.

The vote for North Carolina took longer than most states to count. It was only late the following morning that the result was confirmed: 2,142,651 people in the state had voted for Obama; 2,128,474 had supported McCain. The winning margin was the narrowest of all Obama's victories in 2008 – with a difference of just 0.33 per cent.

Jo looked at the results, high-fived me and whooped: 'Yee-hah!'

Gordon Brown had been Prime Minister for nearly eighteen months when, in late November 2008, I was invited to fly back to London to meet him. He needed a new adviser on Africa and international development and my name had been added to a shortlist. I was still startled, but excited, when the formal request arrived from Number 10 suggesting a time and date for me to be interviewed by the Prime Minister.

An even bigger surprise emerged when I told Jo. 'I'm not sure I'd want that kind of job if I were you, Brendan,' she said, sounding very unlike the Jo I knew and loved.

'Really?' I said.

'I don't think it's as good as you think it is . . .' Jo said quietly.

I was bemused. Just a few weeks earlier, amid our hectic campaigning for Obama, we had said how ready we felt to take an even more active involvement in formal politics. We were a partnership, politically and romantically. I reminded Jo that a possible position at Number 10 gave us a chance to have a direct impact in shaping the British government's attitude to development, where we had done so much work over the years.

She shrugged. Weren't we having a fantastic time in New York?

I had loved our first few months in America. But, if I turned down this opportunity, who knew if I would ever be offered another?

Jo's frostiness melted. 'I'm sorry, Coxy,' she said. 'I guess I'm just a bit jealous . . .'

It was typical of Jo that she should be so candid, even when she rightly felt she was probably better equipped than me for the role. Jo and I had different strengths. She was smart and creative, a force of nature who made things happen and who took people with her. I was better at writing speeches and political strategy. Her knowledge was superior to mine when it came to issues around development, while I knew more about conflict zones and humanitarian crises. But we both could easily sharpen those areas where we were less confident. It was a job that seemed made for either of us.

As soon as Jo uttered her confession, she switched tack entirely. 'Of course you must go for it, Coxy. You'll be bloody brilliant.'

From then on, a team again, Jo did everything she could to prepare me for the interview. She was seriously good, and as incisive as she was generous. With Jo's help, that first week of December 2008 turned out to be momentous – even if her diary entries were initially low key.

Tuesday: B on a flight to London – off to see the PM. Miss him lots.

Weds/Thursday: Bought a Xmas tree and decorated the flat!

Friday night: Coxy's back! We went to drinks at the UK Ambassador's Residence – nice evening but I drank way, way too much champagne.

But the big news of the week?

COXY GOT A JOB AS THE
PM'S AFRICA ADVISER!!
Yee-hah!

Our time in the US would be capped at six months and then, in early March 2009, I would begin working for the Prime Minister. Jo had also decided it was time for her to leave Oxfam. We had a wedding to plan, a family to start and it felt right for her to move on to something different. So our imminent return to London made us want to see as much of the States as we could.

We took two weeks off over Christmas and New Year to criss-cross the South, and travelled from Winston-Salem in North Carolina to Nashville and Memphis in Tennessee. We paid homage to Elvis and visited Graceland. We moved on.

The Mississippi Delta, with its poor and depressed African-American towns, reminded us of parts of Uganda. The next day, five hours from Clarksdale, Mississippi, we reached Selma, Alabama, from where, in 1965, Martin Luther King had led the march to Montgomery in support of the Voting Rights Campaign. Black people, then, did not have the right to vote in Alabama.

Forty-three years later an African-American man was just weeks away from becoming the President of the United States, and we felt revived.

We made one more trip before we left New York for London. Early on the morning of 20 January 2009, Jo and I took the train from Penn Street Station to Washington, DC.

It was a freezing day but millions of people had descended on the capital.

As Barack Obama was sworn in as President, I thought of Jo and me running down the streets of Raleigh, North Carolina, on that rainy November election night. Applause rang out from millions of people. Jo and I clapped hard and stamped our frozen feet. Despite the extreme cold, we felt completely fired up. Three days later we flew home for the start of a new life.

15

The World Darkens

I sat for a few moments in the dimmed light, watching Cuillin and Lejla, thinking how calm they looked as they drifted away into sleep. The boat rocked gently from side to side as if we were safe in a giant steel cradle. It felt very peaceful. The world outside, by contrast, seemed chaotic and treacherous.

I had put the kids to bed later than usual as it was the night of the US presidential election. A few of my friends had joined us for dinner and they were planning to stay up into the early hours with me to watch the results roll in from America. The desolate feeling I had carried the last few weeks, amid the creeping realisation that Donald Trump might actually be elected President, ebbed a little. My friends cheered me up and the polls continued to predict victory for Hillary Clinton. I promised the kids I'd wake them early the following morning to tell them who had won. Their visit to the White House, and sharing their drawings with Barack Obama, had given them an unusual interest in the outcome.

Cuillin was still two months away from his sixth birthday, and Lejla had just turned four the previous Saturday. But they knew how much their mum would have wanted Clinton to trounce Trump. Away from the chatter of the adults, I had read another few pages of *The Twits*, told them a story about their mum from our time in America and then sung them to sleep.

We know lots of people in the United States and, while the vast majority share our political perspective, a handful are Republicans. They are good people who are economically conservative. But they all said that they would vote for Hillary in an attempt to stop Trump: they had no wish to see a zealot in the White House. Trump was endorsed by the Ku Klux Klan and had no compunction in expressing bigotry towards Mexicans, Muslims and most other minority groups within the US.

Jo and I spoke incessantly about the election. We did not think that Clinton was as inspiring as Obama, but most of our Democratic Party friends believed she would be a competent and intelligent President. We also knew that female candidates are often judged more harshly than their male counterparts, and so the unfavourable media and public approval weightings needed to be viewed from that perspective.

After Jo was killed I did not think about the US election for three months – until we went to visit Obama. The idea of Trump sitting in the Oval Office suddenly seemed disturbing rather than, as it had done a year earlier, vaguely comic. All through October and early

November I listened to a ridiculous number of programmes about the race to the White House. On my bicycle I would pedal through the London traffic with a podcast from the US in my earphones as I absorbed the warped reality that, no matter what he said, Trump seemed unsinkable.

There was a similarity to Brexit in the sense that millions of people felt so disillusioned by conventional politics they were looking to send a message to the elites that govern them. Yet the rise of Trump worried me in a way that Brexit did not. While some pro-Brexit voices like Farage used thinly disguised prejudice and intolerance to whip up hatred, there were many others such as Boris Johnson, Daniel Hannan, Gisela Stuart and even Douglas Carswell who made a case for leaving the EU from a very different starting point. I might have disagreed with their argument but I wasn't repulsed by it.

Trump was different. His naked bigotry was an assault on fundamental rights and principles of equality that I had previously believed were sacrosanct in America.

Once the kids were asleep my friends and I cracked open another bottle of red wine as we waited for the first results. Soon after midnight, a friend who worked for a senior figure in the Clinton campaign texted me: 'We've got the private exit polls in and it's looking good.' The text included all the predicted numbers for each swing state. Clinton was 1 per cent down on Trump in the key state of Ohio but she was ahead in all the others which suggested a substantial victory.

I still remembered the 2004 election when John Kerry

stood against George Bush. I had been in Florida as one of Kerry's volunteers, and on election night a campaign colleague shared the internal exit polls showing us significantly ahead. I had high-fived people in the corridor. The next day I felt like an idiot.

The unease soon magnified. Early results were disappointing. Trump was up. Florida was too close to call. The election was slipping away from Clinton even if she was ahead in the popular vote.

A short, dreamless night of sleep was ended by Lejla calling out, 'Daddy, is it morning?'

I checked my phone for the time and saw the news. Donald Trump was President-elect.

'Daddy, Daddy,' Cuillin asked when I went in to see the kids, 'what happened in America?'

They both looked worried when I explained the news. Trump had been spoken about on the boat for so many months – even in that very different life when their mum was alive – that he had come to be associated in their minds with everything that was wrong and dangerous. I tried to reassure them. I told them it wasn't our country and, in any case, people and the constitution would try to stop him. I'm not sure I convinced them and I definitely didn't convince myself.

Cuillin asked me if all would be okay for two of his closest friends at school who are both Muslims. 'Don't worry,' I said, remembering how I had told him about Trump's boast that he would stop Muslims entering the US. 'He won't actually do that now he's the President.'

As I hugged the kids and then made breakfast, I felt deeply unnerved.

Later that day, with them both at school, I recognised again how people can become unsettled. I had done it myself. But I thought about Jo and what she would have said to me, and to everyone else, had she still been alive. It seemed right to post a few tweets in her memory on a bruising day.

Jo & I talked about #Trump winning & what we would do. Right now she'd say 'don't mourn, organise' & reassert what we hold in common.

History will judge us on how we respond. This must galvanise the political centre – not shatter it. There is too much at stake.

I also wanted to post some brighter and more amusing news.

Thanks to the person who bet on #Trump winning & donated the winnings to Jo's fund with the message: 'At least some good will come out of it.'

*

For us, the ordinary pattern of life had resumed – at least in the sense that Cuillin and Lejla had been back at school for two months. They showed remarkable resilience even when telling me how much they missed their mum. Cuillin captured our bitter-sweet heartache. He said how much he liked thinking of all the happy times he'd had with Mummy – but how they often made him want to cry because he knew he could never have them again.

They loved hearing about Jo. Every night, when they were in bed, I read them a story. We devoured Roald Dahl, one book at a time, and I'd follow ten minutes of reading aloud with a 'Mummy Story'. Sometimes my story would be a retelling of a Finley the Fieldmouse adventure which Jo had dreamed up for them. But I could never match her in the imaginative storytelling stakes and the kids liked it when I stuck to real life. They enjoyed hearing about Jo when they were babies – or before they had been born. We'd had so many escapades before we became parents that it was easy to tell them something new about their mum: the day she was nearly bitten in the face by a snake; the time she was stretchered off a mountain; her tropical disease. Occasionally I'd tell them a story about Jo from a time long before she met me.

September had been a milestone in our family. It marked Lejla's first day in the nursery class of the same school where Cuillin started as a Year One pupil. It's a great school in east London and reflects the population of the local community. Around 70 per cent of the pupils are from a Bengali background and there is a mix of white, black and other Asian kids, which means that Cuillin and Lejla meet boys and girls from all kinds of cultures. Most importantly, the teaching is brilliant.

I felt that Jo and I had made the right choice because Lejla was happy there from her first day, even if we all struggled with the fact that her mum wasn't there to see her head off to school. Cuillin also soon readjusted to being back.

At least there had been some consistency in our lives. Since Jo had become an MP, I had taken on more of the childcare. I took three months off to look after the kids and to support Jo as she went back to work. After more than a couple of years of maternity leave, it was my turn. The kids were used to me being around to look after them, therefore, but I found the new pressures hard. Jo and I had often spoken about how difficult it must be as a single parent. And now I knew we had been right. It was relentless.

I felt lucky to live on our mooring where we have such a community, and other mums and dads happy to help me on a daily basis. I am also fortunate that we have Jessie, my parents, my incredible sister and her family, as well as Kim and Clare – who stay on the boat when I have to travel – and Jo's parents, Gordon and Jean, in Yorkshire. But I had not found the right balance. I was trying to overcompensate because, even when my parents were on the boat one night a week to help me, I tended to avoid a break. I love being with the kids and so it is an easy choice for me to stay with them. Part of me also feels that, in the absence of Jo, I should always be there for Cuillin and Lejla, to make sure they are having a good time and feel totally loved by me.

I am weary now. I feel shattered. I often lie in bed, wide awake at 3 a.m., thinking of Jo. Luckily, I am fairly resilient and don't need too much sleep. I still have a great deal of energy for Cuillin and Lejla. But the daily slog is grinding.

Jo and I would often spar over whose turn it was to pump out the toilet or fill the water tank. She argued that she normally did all the tidying so would I mind doing it again? I was sceptical that tidying was such a chore. A few months after her death I thought differently. I could now spend all my time, when not chatting to or playing with the kids, simply tidying up the mess.

More fundamentally I struggled with my own grief, and the children's.

I spoke at length to Julia Samuel, the child psychologist, and to friends who have lost a parent or someone they have loved. Friends like Dan Jarvis, Flora Alexander, Mabel Van Oranje and Roger Harding, as well as my dad, whose own father died when he was a child, gave me great advice and opened their own pain to me with supreme generosity.

I would pepper them with questions. What do you remember? When was the hardest time? Do you wish your surviving parent had spoken more or less about what happened? I wanted to learn all I could.

There were two extremes I was keen to avoid. The first was to lose myself in grief and fixate on the loss. The second was to put my emotions in a box, *Book of Mormon*-style, and crush it as a way of trying to escape the pain.

I had to resist the first option for the sake of the kids. The second was more of a risk. I was busy and focused on making sure the kids were okay and that something positive came out of Jo's death. But I also struggle to be open with my emotions at the best of times. I know this can be damaging. My dad spoke a lot about how the death of his father had hardly been spoken of, and he had failed to grieve as a result.

So we spoke about Jo every day. With the help of my sister, we made memory boxes. As well as asking them about how they felt, I told the kids how I was feeling. We cried together. Lejla in particular seemed to benefit and, sometimes, she would ask if we could all cry together.

I missed Jo in a way I could hardly describe to anyone. It seemed as if a hole had been blasted deep inside me. We were such a partnership – as parents and a couple – and also in the way in which we shared everything: from our day at work to how we were going to tackle Jo's next big speech on Syria, or the latest great adventure of a family holiday in some distant location.

We were incessant list-writers. We would scribble down our plans for the next few months at regular intervals. These ranged from trying to think of ways to undermine Putin's strategy in Aleppo to deciding what we would eat for dinner on Tuesday night. How could the Labour Party extricate itself from the mess of Jeremy Corbyn's leadership while we changed our schedules so we could both make it to a parents' evening at the kids' school? Grand schemes and necessary domesticity rubbed along together.

I gave up writing lists for a while. It was impossible to feel any ambition or excitement without Jo. We had always spurred each other on. The energy of encouraging each other, pushing ourselves to accept challenges we wouldn't have taken on alone, had always thrilled me. I was teaching myself to accept her absence, though every night I missed her beside me. Each night I would remember how, before we fell asleep, even when we'd had a row, she would cross her leg over mine. I had to try to block the absence from my head so I could finally lose myself in sleep.

– 14 November 2016 –

In the world beyond our little boat, the final assault on Aleppo had begun after weeks of fraught quiet in the second largest city of Syria. Aleppo, having existed for over 3,000 years, was one of the world's oldest cities. It had always been crammed full of people while, as a thriving crossroads of trade and transport, it functioned for countless generations as Syria's commercial and cultural hub. Already brutalised, with entire districts in the east abandoned and reduced to crumbling grey cathedrals of rubble and ash, Aleppo now faced total oblivion. Vladimir Putin had issued a deadline of Friday, 4 November for all rebels to leave the eastern half of a broken city. He and the Russian military had indicated that all corridors out of Aleppo would be left open until then – an offer dismissed by the rebels who said the escape routes were already impassable. They vowed instead to intensify their attacks on the unscarred western half of the city which, under government control, had been spared the aerial bombardment.

Russian aircraft carriers had been stationed along the coast for weeks and, in late October, John Kerry, the US Secretary of State, had warned that Aleppo would be 'bombed into smithereens' unless Putin agreed to a fresh ceasefire. But President-elect Trump and President Putin had apparently spoken on the phone. Hell was about to be unleashed on Aleppo.

Three hospitals were hit on the outskirts of the city as the Russian defence minister, Sergei Shoigu, said missile strikes were aimed primarily against Islamic State militants in Idlib province. He made no mention of Aleppo or its 200,000 trapped civilians who would soon be subjected to a bombing campaign of unprecedented savagery.

There were only thirty doctors left in Aleppo. Grainy footage shows them carrying out amputations on children without anaesthetic or proper sterilisation. A dire shortage of blood, intravenous fluid, antibiotics and pain-relief medication meant the exhausted doctors struggled to help the traumatised casualties. By mid-November 2016 the organisation Physicians for Human Rights had documented 382 attacks on medical facilities in Aleppo – of which 344 had been carried out by Syrian government forces and Russia.

Aleppo was not only in the grip of a medical siege, food supplies were also being blocked and malnutrition had begun to spread. Still worse awaited.

Russian jets bombed a children's hospital and a blood bank in east Aleppo. Twenty civilians were killed and a further forty-seven were injured. Some of the bombs unleashed chlorine gas. 'A horrible day for the children's hospital,' the centre's director, Dr Hatem, said on Facebook. 'Me and my staff and all the patients are sitting in one room in the basement, trying to protect our patients. We can't leave because of all the aircraft still in the sky. Pray for us please.'

While President Assad claimed in a bullish statement that 'Trump is a natural ally' and that his forces, in conjunction with Russia, were about to crush all opposition, a simpler text message seeped out of Aleppo. Abdulkafi al-Hamdo, a teacher in the city, induced a shudder with just five words: 'Horror is back to Aleppo.'

Jo had felt a deep personal involvement in the Syrian crisis. Her finest speech in Parliament had focused on the atrocities suffered by ordinary people. She took on her own party and the government over a collective failure in Syria. At the table where I'm writing this she had often said to me, as she prepared for Parliament or another interview, that Syria would come to define this period in our history. We look back and, with incomprehension, ask: 'How did people let the Holocaust happen? How did we let Rwanda happen? How did we let a million people get slaughtered with machetes when we could have stopped it overnight?'

As I sat listening to the news coming out of Aleppo I could hear Jo express her feeling that, in years to come, our children and their children would ask us: 'How on earth did you let that happen?'

Parliament, the world and the people of Syria needed Jo's voice. She would have strained every sinew to try to protect those innocent people. But she was no longer with us. Jo was gone.

16

Two Weddings

Back in London after our stint in the States, Jo and I found ourselves in the bizarre situation of spending parts of our working week together at Number 10 Downing Street: I was working for the Prime Minister, Gordon Brown, and Jo for his wife Sarah. After Jo's decision to leave Oxfam, she was delighted when she was asked to become the director of the Maternal Mortality campaign that Sarah Brown had founded with the White Ribbon Alliance – a charity that strives to enable every pregnant woman in the world to give birth safely. It was a cause that Jo believed in vehemently and she threw herself into the work. Part of her role was to charm people into joining the campaign even when there were seemingly insurmountable cultural and political differences. She was uncannily good at forging coalitions with people ranging from first ladies of various African countries to NGOs to supermodels such as Naomi Campbell. She encouraged them to help her raise awareness of maternal mortality as well as obtain significant funding to tackle the crisis. She often met Sarah at Number 10 and we would cycle home together after long days.

One night in the summer of 2009, when I was waiting for her to emerge, I decided to play a trick on her and enlisted a willing accomplice in the shape of one of the policemen on duty outside the Prime Minister's residence. He had made a quip about the fact that I always seemed to be hanging around for Jo and, remembering that she had forgotten her bike lights *again* that morning, I asked him if he could arrest her for cycling without lights. 'Just as a joke?'

'I don't see why not,' he agreed cheerfully.

He assumed his best intimidating look as he saw her, and raised his hand. Jo thought he was gesturing to someone else and kept riding towards the iron railings and the gate that led on to Whitehall.

'Madam,' he said loudly, 'you need to stop right now.'

Jo glanced over at me. At the gate I spread my hands wide to indicate I had no idea what was happening.

'I'm checking the lights on your bicycle, madam,' the policeman said.

'Oh, I'm sorry,' Jo said in her most contrite voice. 'I don't have a light on my bike today.'

'No lights at all?' the policeman asked.

'I forgot them this morning. Sorry . . .' Jo's voice trailed away.

'I'm afraid, madam,' he announced gravely, 'you will need to accompany me to the station.'

'You're not arresting me, are you?' Jo asked, her face creased with panic.

The policeman turned to look at me and I burst out laughing.

Jo paused and then, shaking her head, said, staring at me, 'You bastard.'

She then apologised to the officer for her language and the lack of a light on her bike. 'He put you up to this, didn't he?' Jo said, pointing at me as I ambled over, still grinning.

Naturally, Jo was not arrested. As the sun hadn't entirely gone down, the officer let Jo off with a wink. But my hoax worked to some extent. For at least a few months afterwards Jo was much better when it came to remembering her cycling essentials in her daily rush

We were living in a rented flat on Clapham Manor Street which we knew couldn't match Manhattan for glamour. I thought it was fine but Jo wanted to live on a boat again, and I didn't need much persuading. The following week we went to look at a potential boat. She was almost a hundred years old and a bit of a mess. The previous owner had apparently fallen asleep with candles lit and set fire to her. He had since disappeared, which meant we could buy her at a cut-price figure and, in any case, even buying a nice boat was many times cheaper than the average London flat. We both fell in love with the idea of restoring her and decided we could just about raise the money.

We were very happy refurbishing *Ederlezi*, as we decided to rename her, and living along the Grand Union Canal and Regent's Canal. We'd move every two weeks to a new mooring somewhere between Kensal Green and King's Cross and spent winter in Paddington Basin where, stuck behind the mass of St Mary's Hospital, our solar panels never saw the sun and we survived on candles for light and the woodburner for heat. We cycled to and from Downing Street with few problems, unless Jo forgot her lights and ended up the victim of a comic arrest.

I always teased Jo about being forgetful, but when it came to the things that really mattered, she was remarkably organised. We did not know any other women who had already switched all the paperwork to their married name three months before their wedding. Jo Leadbeater officially became known as Jo Cox when we were still twelve weeks from marriage. My future wife wanted to ensure a seamless transition in her working life.

In some ways it was a surprise to me that she changed her name: Jo was an avowed feminist and I had no expectation that she would. We discussed how we might merge our names to make a new surname: Coxbeater, Beatcox, Leadox. For obvious reasons we decided against that path.

We were talking about it on a long train journey back from Scotland, running through options, when suddenly Jo blurted out, 'I just love Cox.' It was one of those moments when the whole carriage goes quiet. People didn't know where to look.

One day, when Jo and I were walking in the mountains early in 2008, about four months after we had got engaged, we discussed our wedding. Where should we get married? We spoke about the kind of experience we would love and soon the idea of Knoydart came up.

Knoydart was the setting for one of our most intense hiking experiences. A mountain range and peninsula located in the north-west of Scotland, it is one of the most remote parts of Britain. It is exquisitely rugged and often tagged as 'Britain's Last Wilderness' because it is only accessible by boat, or a sixteen-mile trek through untamed country.

Jo and I were very excited and we immediately called our parents to tell them our choice of wedding venue. We knew the impracticalities of the location meant we could only expect our immediate family and two closest friends to join us, so we decided that we would also have a far bigger celebration for about 250 people in the south a few months later.

My parents, Gordon and Sheila, were accustomed to our madcap ideas, therefore they were enthusiastic. Jo's mum and dad, Jean and Gordon, needed more convincing. Their hopes for a lovely wedding in Yorkshire, with a hotel reception, had been dashed.

We appreciated their doubts. Everyone needed to travel by train to Fort William, from where we would go by minibus to reach Kinloch Hourn, which takes about two hours with much of the road a single track. We would then get on a fishing boat along Loch Hourn and take it to the bay in Barrisdale. From there we would hike to the bothy a short way inland. My future in-laws must have thought their lovely daughter was marrying a madman.

The Leadbeaters, however, loved Jo and after an initially fraught reaction they caved in gracefully. Everyone we invited agreed to the trek: Gordon and Jean, Kim and her then boyfriend Mickey, my mum and dad, Stacia, Andrew, their three boys, Jo's best friend Sarah Hamilton and my best man Will Paxton. Including Jo and me, fifteen of us made the wedding, where we were joined by Sylvia, the humanist celebrant from Inverness, and Billy the fisherman who steered the boat across Loch Hourn.

Before we married, we succumbed to modern tradition and parted for a weekend. My friends took me to North Wales where we stayed in a bunkhouse and went gorge-climbing. Scaling a waterfall and then climbing a mountain was my idea of a perfect stag do. But on the Saturday night, somewhat inevitably, we ended up in a nightclub in Bangor. It was probably the worst club any of us had ever been to, although my reaction was admittedly coloured by the fact they had dressed me up as a transvestite Elvis. We still had fun – if not quite matching the eclectic style of Jo's hen weekend.

The women started gently in Haworth, which is the heart of Brontë country. Jo was in her element. She loved the Brontë sisters' books, and she loved her friends, all fourteen of whom were going to be her best women at our second celebration – Jo was emphatic that she didn't want any bridesmaids. Our two weddings would be decked out in the colours of the suffragettes, so it seemed fitting that, just as I had a best man at my side, Jo would have her best women. The accent was on the plural because Jo had many close friends, and bringing them together in Yorkshire meant a huge amount to her. They came from her childhood in Yorkshire, her university days at Cambridge, her years of working in Brussels and London – and included, of course, her sister.

They had a lovely meal in Haworth, with Jo introducing everyone from the diverse corners of her world, and she took time to say how much each woman had done for her over the years. The following day they went for a walk through Brontë country before they got ready for a Saturday night out in Leeds. A boozy meal was followed by a karaoke session where everyone wore cowboy hats, and then they went clubbing.

The next morning, to complete Jo's interests, they did a 5K run for a cancer charity. Shaking off her hangover and despite a huge turnout, Jo finished well up the field. Her passions for family, for Yorkshire, for feminism, for books, for singing and dancing and drinking, for running and having fun, for helping charities and hanging out with her best friends, were all fulfilled. Jo's last weekend as a single woman captured her essence.

A week later, we made it to Knoydart. We planned on spending two nights there, and we rented the only cottages there were. They each had electricity and a woodburner, but we still had to lug bedding, food and drink as there was nothing else around for miles.

When we arrived it was mild and sunny, and we convinced everyone to have a walk around the base of the mountain once we had unpacked. The response to my cheerful cajoling would have been different if a cold rain had been slanting down.

We still hadn't worked out exactly where we would hold the ceremony. I would have loved to have married Jo at the very top of Knoydart, but I knew that asking my future in-laws to go mountain-climbing in their wedding gear would be one step too far.

As we wandered down to the shore, I noticed a rocky little island about twenty metres across. You could walk to it at low tide, but when the water came back in, we would need Billy the fisherman to take us across. We decided that would be the spot. The only person who lived in the bay full time was a deer stalker, who very kindly lent us his 4x4 to save Jo having to walk miles in her dress. He used it to haul dead deer off the mountains, but I knew Jo wouldn't mind clambering into it. She would be driven down to the loch to board the fishing boat. We would be married on the island in the middle of the loch.

That night, once we had all eaten together, and played a few games, Will and I took some beer and our sleeping bags and went climbing the surrounding slopes. Sleeping on top of a mountain the night before my wedding seemed like the best idea in the world – even as darkness fell and we got a bit lost. We ended up camping at the summit of a hill rather than on the mountain itself. As if to underline how misguided we had been, it started to rain. It was a bumpy night and I was woken around 5 a.m. by midges and drizzle.

But when the mist and rain rolled away across the sea,

all the discomfort felt worthwhile. A glorious day unfolded in front of us – as if a work of art were being painted while we watched. The sky shifted in tone and texture like a giant canvas brought to life by splashes of changing colours. We began to feel warmer, too, as pale shafts of hazy sunshine lit up the loch and turned the cottages below a yellowy pink.

Knoydart looked tranquil and magnificent as we saw one of the cottage doors open. A small, slight figure emerged in the light and slowly, but with gathering conviction, began to run.

'Look,' I said to Will, and pointed at Jo. 'At least she's not running away.'

Will and I bundled up our sleeping bags, collected the empty cans and strolled down to the cottages. I had started to feel a burning sensation in my legs and when I came to get dressed I had a certain foreboding as I pulled off the trousers I had worn overnight. There were at least fifty deer ticks embedded in my legs. I spent the first part of the morning extracting the blood-fattened pests, swearing as I did so.

'Hope I don't get Lyme disease on my honeymoon,' I muttered to Will, between curses.

Every last stubborn tick was yanked out of my blistered skin – and I was relieved I would be wearing a formal suit for the wedding ceremony.

Will and I were deposited on the island first. We were kept waiting as Jo and Sarah had a lot of fun while Jo got ready. They drank champagne, Jo finished writing her wedding vows and Sarah tried to tie the bride's hair up using just one bobble. Sarah is a documentary film-maker rather than a stylist – but it was just what Jo wanted.

'I am so crap at this,' Sarah said, 'but, Jo, you look amazing.'

Jo kept laughing as, next to a farm shed, and using a tiny mirror, she and Sarah did her make-up.

Sarah was right: Jo looked stunning. Holding the wild flowers we had gathered the day before, she negotiated the 4x4 and the boat in her elegant wedding dress and smiled at me as she, her mum, dad and Sarah sailed across the loch. My mum sang 'Ederlezi' as they approached, bringing a little of the Balkans to the Highlands. As that song of hope drifted across the water, I thought again how blessed I was to have Jo.

The water was shallow now and Billy had to jump down to pull the boat ashore and then help Jo out. My sister Stacia, who is a spectacularly good recorder player, played 'Sweet Forget Me Not'. The imposing mountains surrounded us and the loch glimmered in the sunshine. Jo and I were emotional, and we struggled a little to say our individual wedding vows out loud. Wherever we looked we saw smiling faces we loved, and eyes shedding happy tears.

Our wedding rings cost £10 each: right from the start we had wanted to be clear that we valued each other, not tokens of cold metal. As a surprise, I had arranged to have an inscription engraved into both of them. The message was as simple as the rings were plain: *27 June Knoydart*. They were handed from one person to the next – everyone had the option to say something personal to Jo and me, or simply press the rings between their hands.

We read the vows we had written to each other and then a cup of rum was passed round. The celebrant concluded the ceremony and, to cheers and applause, she confirmed we were now husband and wife.

We were married, Jo and I, Beater and Coxy, and champagne corks popped. Jo looked incredible in the bright sun of a June afternoon. The wind blew in from the sea as we looked out to the mountains together. She was serene, defiant, contented. I felt lucky beyond my wildest dreams.

The tide had ebbed and we were able to walk back to the shore. My mum made a late lunch and then Jo and I went up the mountains for a brief walk. She climbed nimbly, even in her wedding dress. We could have walked all afternoon but we wanted to get back to our family and friends.

Once we had changed we spent the rest of the afternoon playing in the streams with our nephews, building dams and being just like kids ourselves. It was hot enough to dunk ourselves in the stream water. The day ended with a lovely meal and with everyone agreeing that, in our madness, Jo and I had ended up with our perfect wedding.

The next morning there was even time for us to climb one of the smaller mountains with our nephews, seeing how wondrous Loch Hourn looked again in yet more sunshine, before we made the journey back to Fort William – just in time to catch the sleeper train down to London.

As soon as we got home, we were back into planning our larger wedding celebration. A year earlier we'd found the perfect place, near my parents' house, but there had been a problem: the owner didn't want to hire it to us. When we were kids, we called it the black barn. It was thatched, with huge, ancient oak beams on the edge of woodland I had played in as a child. The farmer now used it for storage and to shelter visiting school groups. It had electricity but apart from that was just a stripped-down black barn with a cement floor. Outside there was a giant fire-pit and land where we could camp with most of our 250 guests. Jo and I loved sleeping outside in a tent in any case but, also, we wanted an affordable wedding as many of our guests were flying in from far away.

Jo fell in love with the black barn and we went to ask the farmer and his wife if we could book it for a night. They were kind, and apologetic – but very firm. The farmer told us that he had already rented it out three times in 2009. There was a limit on the number of times a year the property could be hired out without breaking their licensing agreement.

Jo was so disappointed we decided to leave looking for an alternative for a few weeks. We had found the perfect venue and couldn't bring ourselves to settle on somewhere else that we knew wasn't right. I used that time to email the farmer regularly. Jo had no idea what I was doing because I didn't want her to get her hopes up. But I wrote emotionally charged emails about why using the black barn would mean such a lot to us. My secret weapon was a series of photos I sent the owner of me, aged around five, cradling tiny lambs in the very same barn. Eventually, I wore him down and he very kindly agreed to our using the barn and his land in exchange for a donation to charity.

It was such a surprise for Jo, and she was elated.

Her fourteen best women and many of my friends were included in the planning and were asked to do various tasks in our DIY wedding – from arranging the flowers to acting as DJs to helping put up tepees. Each table was named after a Munro we had climbed and the black barn was lifted by the colours of the suffragettes. Diddley Dee played live and sixty tents were erected around the central tepee where Jo and I slept. Some of our guests, being less hardy campers, stayed in local pubs and hotels.

We sang 'Jerusalem' and also 'The Red Flag', and we didn't mind that not everyone joined in with our leftist sing-song. But we were all moved by a reading from my friend Angela Cropper. She had been born into poverty in Trinidad in 1946, one of twelve children whose dad had died when she was four years old. Angela became the first person in her family to complete secondary school and go on to university, and she eventually established herself as one of the world's great environmental leaders – as well as an independent senator in Trinidad and the Deputy General Secretary of the UN's Environmental Programme.

To Jo and me, she was the most dignified, thoughtful and quietly powerful woman we had ever met. Angela had been very special to me ever since I was granted a scholarship that she had set up in memory of the son she had lost. She read Jack London's 'Credo' with serious grace – and captured the spirit of Jo:

I would rather be ashes than dust!
I would rather that my spark
should burn out in a brilliant blaze
than it should be stifled by dry-rot.

I would rather be a superb meteor
Every atom of me in magnificent glow
than a sleepy and permanent planet.

The function of man is to live
not to exist.
I shall not waste my days trying to prolong them.
I shall use my time.

17

The Trial

– 14 November 2016 –

The trial opened at the Old Bailey. I had thought long and hard about whether I should be there. Right from the day of her death, I had decided not to focus on the act of Jo's murder. There was nothing I could do about what had happened, and it caused almost a physical reaction whenever I did think of it. I wanted to remember Jo as she lived, not how she died. I also didn't want to fixate on the perpetrator. He was a sad, pathetic man and he wasn't worthy of anyone's time. Neither was there much to learn from the trial. We already knew that the man had shot and stabbed Jo repeatedly, shouting 'Britain first' as he killed her. I wasn't interested in what he might say in an attempted justification of his hatred.

On the other hand, I didn't want to run away from the trial, I wanted to make sure the jury knew about Jo and I wanted to be there for witnesses, should they need me.

I spoke to Fazila and Sandra – Jo's team who were with her on the day and who were to give evidence. They assured me I didn't need to be there for them. Kim said that she and Clare, along with Jo's mum and dad, would attend the trial to represent the family.

In addition, one of Jo's closest friends from her Cambridge days, Jane Brady, a fiercely intelligent barrister, would send daily courtroom briefings to keep me updated on the legal proceedings. There seemed no doubt that the defendant would be found guilty of murder, but I wanted to be kept informed of any unexpected developments.

In the end it was a simple decision. While I would attend the closing of the trial in order to have a chance to talk about Jo, I would skip the rest so I could focus on the kids and on remembering Jo in the way she would have wanted.

It felt particularly important not to give up everything that had defined Jo and me as a couple. Our dream of climbing all the Munros had been stopped short but I began to feel that the best thing I could do was leave London and head for Scotland and the mountains. I had climbed thirty or so Munros before I met Jo, but I had agreed to start all over again from zero so that we might have the shared pleasure of conquering every single one of those 282 mountains together.

Every morning on the boat, on a pinboard opposite our bed, I looked at the map of the Munros on the wall. There were 98 blue pins, each representing a mountain we had climbed. They were still vastly outnumbered by the 184 black pins that belonged to the Munros we had not yet scaled. The closer the trial loomed, the more appropriate it felt to go up into the mountains, in memory of Jo, and add another couple of Munros to reach that milestone of a century.

I headed for Glasgow. From there, with my friends Will and Simon, we would travel to the Highlands and take on the hills.

I would have to face the courtroom soon enough.

– 17 **November 2016** –

Ben Oss was the second peak of our first day's climbing and would have been Jo's hundredth summit. I had promised Will and Simon we would start with a walk rather than a climb, but it had snowed heavily which made everything exhausting and much more treacherous. We were sweating while icicles formed in our hair and ice frosted our eyelashes.

As we approached the summit, I reached into my bag and pulled out Jo's hat. She always wore it on the Munros and at the cottage. It was from Peru I think, a woolly affair that had long ear flaps that you could tie under the chin. I have dozens of pictures of Jo with her smile framed by the outsized blue hat.

I promised myself that I would carry it with me whenever I went up into the mountains.

At the summit I used my ice axe to carve '100' in the snow. Slightly to the left I plunged the wooden shaft of Simon's axe deep into the snow. Immediately above the

three magical digits, I carefully positioned Jo's hat on my
ice axe, its ear tassels dangling down while the hat itself
sat proudly against the pristine backdrop of the snow. I
took a photograph which, later, I posted on Twitter:

> This would have been Jo's 100th Munro, Ben Oss.
> She would have loved the adventure, the snow and
> the peace.

Then I started to cry. My body was shaking as I held on
to Jo's hat. Simon and Will were visibly upset too but gave
me some space to just be. I thought about Jo and all the
potential she had. The unfinished Munros were one of
many of life's projects that she would leave incomplete.
I thought about the adventures that had been denied us,
the fun we would have had. I felt for her. I used her hat
to wipe away my tears before they froze.

We turned north to climb down into the snow-covered
corrie below, where we planned to camp. But by now the
sky was white and the cloud was coming down fast. Soon
we were in full whiteout conditions. There were no cliffs
on the plateau we were crossing, which was reassuring,
though it also meant there were no easy way markers. We
were using a compass with a GPS as a back-up, but as the
temperature plummeted, the GPS first flickered and then
died, its battery sapped by the extreme cold.

We decided to set up camp for the night where we were.
It was only just after three-thirty in the afternoon but
there was no choice other than to hunker down and see

out the worst of it. By 4 p.m. we had used our plastic plates to dig out a hole in the snow on which to pitch the tent, had had something to eat and were ready for bed.

Will was shaking with cold. Not for the first time, he didn't have the right kit and, without gaiters, snow had filled his boots. He was so frozen that I had to help put warm socks on him.

Eventually the tent started to heat up. The wind whipped around us and as I dozed fitfully I imagined what Jo would have made of it. I knew she would have loved the adventure and the craziness of it. The three of us wondered whether anyone else had decided to camp on top of a mountain in the snow and thought probably not. Simon started telling us some of (what he considered) his all-time best stories, Will and I quickly drifted off to sleep.

Early the following morning Will's boots, left outside his sleeping bag, had turned into blocks of ice. We chipped away at the two frozen hunks with our axes until, at last, the boots were free and I could get Will's double-socked feet back into them.

I felt responsible for the group. Will and Simon were fit, strong and up for a bit of danger but they hadn't done much mountaineering before and had only agreed to make the trek into the Munros to show their sustained support for me. Simon had even driven all the way from Exeter to Glasgow to meet us. I worried Will might get frostbite in his toes if we stayed out another night. When I suggested we spend the next night in the valley, there was an audible outpouring of relief. I resolved to return my friends safely to their families. I didn't want to put myself at risk either.

Before we began the descent, I packed away Jo's hat. I knew I would soon be up in the Munros again. I could no longer have Jo with me but I would climb many mountains with our children, and together we would remember her, as we imagined what she would have made of our latest adventure.

– 19 November 2016 –

I had followed the trial at a distance. It started slowly and I was surprised only by the fact that the defendant decided not to go into the witness box.

A month earlier he had refused to answer when he was asked what he pleaded regarding each charge. As a result of his silence, 'not guilty' pleas were entered on his behalf in answer to all four charges. His guilt on each count was obvious but, in declining to enter any plea, he had forced a full-blown trial. I thought at the time that the point of this was to use the courtroom to make a statement about his belief in 'white power', 'British purity' or a similar rant to try to justify murdering Jo. We knew from the police investigation that he had read about the trial of Anders Breivik – the white supremacist who killed seventy-seven people in Norway's worst peacetime atrocity and who had published a manifesto during his trial. We expected something similar. The defendant in Jo's case, however, was cowardice personified. Offered the chance to give evidence himself, he chose instead to remain silent.

We learned some predictable facts during the prosecution's case. The defendant had connections with white racist groups from around the world, particularly with extremists in the United States and supporters of a return to apartheid in South Africa. His home in West Yorkshire was studded with Nazi memorabilia.

In the days before he murdered Jo, he had spent time in Birstall Library searching the internet for information about the Waffen SS – the armed wing of the Nazi Party, the Ku Klux Klan, as well as serial killers and matricide (his racism has been linked back to his mum's relationship with a black man when he was growing up). He also studied Jo's Twitter page and researched the IRA's murder of the Conservative MP Ian Gow in 1990. He viewed website pages about guns and the use of .22 ammunition. One of these provided answers to the question: 'Is a .22 round deadly enough to kill with one shot to a human's head?'

The most compelling evidence was supplied by Sandra Major, identified in court as Jo's constituency caseworker, and Fazila Aswat, described as 'the MP's assistant and office manager'. Fazila and Sandra were also Jo's friends. Sandra gave evidence after Fazila and explained that the three of them had driven together to the library in Birstall where the defendant had made use of the computer facilities. Jo was due to meet some of her constituents there.

Sandra told the court that, as they climbed out of the Vauxhall Astra, she saw a man walking towards them. 'He had a gun in his hand. He raised his arm and shot Jo in the head. Then he got a knife out of his bag. It was black. Jo was lying on the floor, and she tried to sit up. He just started stabbing her while she was lying on the floor. I was screaming. Jo was shouting, "Get away! Get away you two! Let him hurt me – don't let him hurt you."'

It was a final act of astounding bravery and selflessness from Jo. Even in the face of the worst danger she had ever experienced, she was more concerned about others. It didn't surprise me, but it made me feel overwhelmingly proud of her.

Fazila's account had been equally distressing: 'I said, "Jo, you need to run." She said, "I can't run, I'm hurt." Then he came back. He shot Jo from close range. It was at the end he stood up and said, "Britain first. Britain will always be first."'

A courageous former miner, Bernard Carter-Kenny, who was seventy-seven, had been stabbed by the defendant as he tried to help Jo. Bernard's statement was read in court: 'When I saw Jo roll into the road, I saw blood. I jumped out of the car. My first feeling was he was kicking her. He had a knife in his hand. People were shouting: "Get help, get help."'

The pensioner ran across the road and tried to stop the attack. But Jo's killer turned on him, stabbing Bernard in the stomach. 'The blood started pouring between my fingers,' Bernard said. 'I saw the blood and thought: Oh my God. I just flopped on to the steps of the sandwich shop. I was lying on the floor.'

The attacker then walked away. Two West Yorkshire policemen, Constables Craig Nicholls and Jonathan Wright, were the first to find him. He raised his arms and said: 'It's me.' As they moved to handcuff him he said, 'I am a political activist.'

The court heard that, in his bag he carried a sawn-off .22 rifle. There were two rounds of ammunition in its magazine and a third in the chamber. The rifle's safety catch was off. Two bloodstained knives were also found in the bag.

Jo had been shot three times. She was also stabbed fifteen times.

The love of my life had died early on the afternoon of 16 June 2016.

Jo Cox was described in court as the forty-one-year-old Labour MP for Batley and Spen, a wife and a mother of two young children, aged five and three.

– 22 November 2016 –

On the day of the judge's summing-up I arrived at the Old Bailey on my bike, met my family in a nearby café and was ushered into the courtroom via a side door to avoid the media. Gordon, Jean, Kim and my own parents were all there, as were Fazila and Sandra. So was the defendant. I looked towards him and he refused to return my gaze, shifting in his chair, looking everywhere but at me.

The judge ran through the points of law that the jury should consider as they deliberated on their verdict, emphasising time and again how high the burden of proof remained. Listening to the details of the case was harrowing – I don't know how Jo's family found the strength to sit through it all. I sipped my water and tried to remain calm.

By the afternoon, the judge had decided to adjourn for the day in order to finish his summing-up the following morning. I went home for another night of fitful sleep.

– 23 November 2016 –

The next morning we were all back in our positions. The remainder of the summing-up took less than two hours. The judge asked the jury to consider their decisions carefully and return – if they could – with a unanimous verdict.

For the first time I started to worry. The jury system feels weirdly archaic and slightly absurd when you are caught up in it and think about it deeply. The defendant was undeniably guilty, but what if one of the jurors happened to hold extreme views, another was crazy and a third a simple contrarian? Having fate handed to a random group of strangers like this is an enormous act of faith.

As the jury deliberated, we sat together as a family upstairs, waiting to be recalled. I assumed the process would be almost immediate. The case was open and shut. As the time ticked on I grew more nervous. Was it possible they might have some doubts? What could they be?

After an hour and a quarter we heard the tannoy announcement that we were being called back into court. I was grateful not to be involved in a trial where deliberations took many hours or days. I wouldn't have been able to handle the strain.

We filed back into court. Once again the defendant wouldn't make eye contact with any of us.

The foreman of the jury stood up and was asked if the jurors had reached a verdict. They had. One after another, as each of the counts was read out, he responded simply, 'Guilty.'

In courtroom dramas this is the point where people punch the air and hug each other. None of us moved.

None of us felt any elation.

For us, the verdict changed nothing. A verdict of not guilty would have been horrific but given the nature of the case we knew a conviction was practically guaranteed. It was good to have the trial finished – but that was all. The emptiness with which we went into the trial remained.

Before sentencing I had been asked if I would be prepared to write a Family Impact Statement. These statements were introduced to let the court know the impact a crime had had and help victims of crimes explain how everything from vandalism to murder might have had far-reaching consequences. In this particular case I wasn't sure what it would achieve. The murder of my wife felt every bit as bad as you would imagine, and I knew that people would understand that. Neither did I want to give the defendant the opportunity to revel in the pain he had inflicted.

But I did want to tell the court about Jo. I decided not only to write it, but to speak it in the court, from the witness box.

Our QC – who conducted himself brilliantly throughout – warned me how emotional it would be in that moment, and said that if I were not able to make it through the statement, he was ready to step in. I knew I wanted to do this.

Before I could begin, the defence said that their client wished to speak. I had been expecting this from the start. The judge was cutting, stating that the defendant had had his opportunity to speak from the dock and had refused it. He certainly wasn't going to be given another opportunity now.

I was relieved I didn't have to listen to his attempt at self-justification, and it was gratifying to see how shocked he looked. He had clearly been up all night writing words that he hoped would make him appear more profound than the sad, lonely figure he actually was. He had committed his crime for this very platform, this moment of notoriety – and it would be denied him for ever.

I walked to the witness box and faced the jury. But as I started to speak I turned to the defendant and looked straight at him. He jerked his head away from me even before I began to talk, unable to maintain eye contact. He looked pathetic.

I spoke at him.

We are not here to plead for retribution. We have no interest in the perpetrator. We feel nothing but pity for him; that his life was so devoid of love that his only way of finding meaning was to attack a defenceless woman who represented the best of our country in an act of supreme cowardice. Cowardice that has continued throughout this trial.

I turned to the jury and spoke to them.

We are here because we want to tell you about Jo. Who she was and what she meant to us. You have heard so much about her death, we'd like to tell you just a little about her life.

Jo was interested in everyone. Driven not by her ego but by her desire to help. Connected deeply to her community and proud of her country, but interested in the world. Connected to her roots but not defined by them. Earnestly committed to making the world a better place but with an easy smile and a devilish sense of fun.

I read my statement but I kept looking up at the twelve men and women who were listening so intently. I hoped it helped them warm even more to Jo, to understand her, and to know how much we had all loved her.

Jo grew up on the streets of Batley and Heckmondwike. She'd spend the long summer evenings in the fields across from her house with her sister and friends. She'd often tell our kids about her adventures; one of her favourites was rolling down hills in old barrels. How she made it to adulthood was a miracle.

She was inseparable from her sister and had a close-knit group of friends. Her mum and dad gave her all the love and support growing up that she needed. She had an especially close relationship with her grandad Arthur who was the local postman. She loved going for long walks with him on the weekend, loved how he greeted everyone as friends and his deep connection with the community.

When growing up Jo was painfully shy, so much so that she couldn't even call rail enquiries to find out train times and used to ask her sister to do it for her. So going to Cambridge – and becoming the first member of her family to graduate from university – was quite a shock. It was at this stage that she started to become more political – to realise that who you were and what accent you had often defined your life chances. And that, she felt, just wasn't right. She decided to dedicate the rest of her life to trying to change that, in whatever way she could.

Early in her career she went to work for Glenys Kinnock in Brussels. Here she established herself as a feisty, fun and supremely effective advocate. She moved on to run Oxfam's office in Brussels pushing the EU to do more for the world's poorest. She built a wide group of friends and spent most evenings chatting, drinking and dancing with them.

Jo and I first met when we both worked for Oxfam shortly after she moved to their headquarters in Oxford. We fell in love walking the banks of the River Thames, climbing mountains and living on our boat on the canals and rivers of

Oxford. We were bound together by a love of adventure, laughter and a zest for life.

Our commitment to doing our bit to improve our country and the world deepened our bond and gave us a shared mission. On our holidays we'd go to Bosnia and Croatia to work with kids who had lost their parents – she threw herself into it – so much so that she'd regularly sustain injuries from running into trees or getting balls of ice, masquerading as snowballs, in the face during increasingly chaotic games with dozens of kids.

Jo and I got married in 2009 in one of the most remote places in the UK, a wild peninsula called Knoydart – much to the bemusement of our family who had to hike in in their wedding gear.

One year later, as she abseiled down the Inaccessible Pinnacle, the most difficult mountain in the UK, she realised she was pregnant with our first child.

Our second child was born two years later and spent her first week in intensive care. We didn't know if she would make it. Jo hardly left her side in a week and thanks to the amazing care of the doctors and nurses, combined with our love, slowly she got better.

Jo loved being a mum. She threw herself at it with the energy and enthusiasm that defined her. From time to time the lack of sleep and exhaustion started to get to her – but with a little help she'd soon rebound.

Many people think of Jo first and foremost as an MP and a campaigner. But being a mum always came first. In Parliament she'd vote in her cycling gear in order to be able to be home in time for bedtime, she'd skip votes that were less important even if that sometimes made the whips angry. Our kids came first.

She created a world of adventure for them with long stories she'd make up about Finley the Fieldmouse, with wild boar hunts into the woods and with an ability to throw herself into any role-play that that day's game dictated – from being a mole to a marauding monster. Our children still inhabit the world she created for them.

In 2015 Jo was told that the MP in her home town was standing down. Jo had been asked to stand for Parliament several times before but she never really wanted to be just an MP – she only ever wanted to be *the* MP for her home town. She ran in the selection and by going house to house and just being who she was she won it and became the Labour candidate, later winning the election of 2015.

When Jo became an MP she committed to using her time well. She decided early on that she would work as if she only had a limited time – and would always do what she thought was right even if it made her unpopular. So she walked her own path, criticised her own party when she felt it was wrong and was willing to work with the other side when they shared a common cause. The causes she took on ranged from Syria to autism, protecting civilians in wars to tackling the loneliness of older people in her constituency.

Above all she loved being an MP because of the connection back to her home town. It made her feel grounded again to be back in Batley and the surrounding towns. She especially loved talking at schools. I often teased her about the lack of votes in schools to which she'd reply: 'It's not about votes, it's about getting kids to know that they can do anything they set their minds to.'

None of this means she was perfect – she was far from it. From driving in the middle lane to being late for every meeting. From forgetting her bike for a cycling holiday to absent-mindedly almost burning down our boat on at least two occasions. She could be one of the most frustrating people in the world.

But the things that made her frustrating we now remember with as much affection as the things that made her exceptional.

Jo was a warm, open and supremely empathetic woman. She was powerful – not because of the position she held – but because of the intensity of her passion and her commitment to her values come what may.

The killing of Jo was, in my view, a political act, an act of terrorism – but in the history of such acts it was perhaps the most incompetent and self-defeating. An act driven by hatred which instead has created an outpouring of love. An act designed to drive communities apart which has instead pulled them together. An act designed to silence a voice which instead has allowed millions of others to hear it.

The court was very quiet. I looked once more at the man in the dock. His head was down.

I turned back to the jury. I knew these last lines so well. I barely needed to read them. I just said them out loud in the hushed courtroom.

Jo is no longer with us, but her love, her example and her values live on. For the rest of our lives we will not lament how unlucky we were to have her taken from us, but how unbelievably lucky we were to have her in our lives for so long.

As a much loved friend, daughter, sister, auntie, wife and mum, Jo lit up our lives. And she still does.

I sat down, grateful for the opportunity to speak for Jo. I had tried to bring some of her personality, of her vibrant essence, to the courtroom and the most formal and harrowing of processes.

The judge, who had been studiously fair throughout, then delivered his sentence firmly, speaking quietly, and all the more powerfully for it. The defendant would serve a whole-life sentence; he would never be released, owing to the 'exceptional seriousness' of the offence – a murder committed to advance a cause associated with Nazism. The judge chided the cowardice of refusing to enter guilty pleas and so force the prosecution to prove their case in detail.

I was moved by the most salient truth at the heart of his sentencing remarks. Mr Justice Wilkie drew a stark contrast between the patriotism of Jo and the fascism of the man who killed her. 'It is evident from your internet searches that your inspiration is not love of country or your fellow citizens,' he told him. 'It is an admiration for Nazis and similar anti-democratic white supremacist creeds. Our parents' generation made huge sacrifices to defeat those ideas in the Second World War. What you did betrays those sacrifices. You have betrayed the quint-essence of our country – its adherence to parliamentary democracy.'

The defendant, concluded the judge, had 'affected to be a patriot'. Jo Cox, instead, was 'not only a passionate, open-hearted, inclusive and generous person . . . but a true patriot'.

18

Saving Lejla

Jo was usually full of energy but in the early summer of 2011, she crashed. We had become parents at the start of the year, but for a while it felt to both of us as if little had changed. For six months after Cuillin was born our lives had rolled forward at the same relentless pace. We mapped out new work ambitions while we climbed mountains, and kept up our social lives as before. Cuillin came everywhere with us. In a noisy bar or a crowded restaurant we simply popped his carrier under the table. I was surprised that, no matter the commotion, Cuillin slept peacefully. It was the same whenever we went to Scotland to tackle our next series of Munros. He dozed in a pouch strapped to my chest under my Buffalo mountain jacket as we clawed our way to another summit. The three of us, I thought, were unstoppable.

Jo and I were equals in all that we did. We thought a lot about parenting and how to share tasks between us. But it was a new experience and after six months of living at our usual speed it all became too much.

Jo was getting up at least a couple of times every night

to breastfeed Cuillin. I would stir when he cried but go back to sleep quickly. Jo would climb out of bed to pick up our baby, feed him and settle him – before his next four-hour call. Often he would remain nestled against her all night. Those nights of broken sleep, and her extra load, took an inevitable toll.

Our working lives had also changed. Jo was not sure how much longer she wanted to run the Maternal Mortality campaign and I had accepted a permanent position as director of Advocacy and Policy at Save the Children. I had been working full time for a short spell when Jo's crash came.

She had occasionally complained of exhaustion before but, apart from the period when she had been very ill five years previously, she normally regained her energy after a decent night of rest. This was different. It wasn't just the tiredness. She also began to question the way we lived.

'I'm not sure we should be living on a boat,' Jo said bleakly one night. 'It's too difficult.'

I looked at her in amazement. When we had last lived in a flat, in Clapham, Jo was desperate to get back to the river within weeks.

'Maybe we should move to Yorkshire?' she said, as if depression and fatigue would be wiped away by going back to her old life.

Her instinct to go back home when she was out of her comfort zone or exhausted had been there since Cambridge. I suggested that she just needed some proper rest but I also knew I had to help her to balance things better. I reduced my hours at work and took Cuillin off more frequently in the mornings so Jo could go back to bed. Gradually she started to return to normal. A few weeks later she said, 'What was I thinking?' as if the desire to escape the boat, and London, had been uttered by someone else. But I saw a warning sign. I needed to support Jo to conserve her strength now that there were three of us.

'The holiday will do us the world of good,' Jo said cheerfully.

I smiled and nodded hopefully, thinking of the potentially hectic break we had booked months earlier.

'We're off on another Coxy, Beater and Cuillin adventure,' Jo told our gurgling baby. Cuillin cooed and smiled – blissfully unaware of the wild dogs and steep mountains awaiting us in Transylvania. Rather than heading for a sun-lounger in the south of France, or a tranquil villa in Tuscany, we would fly to Romania. A change, I hoped, really would be as good as a rest.

'The only specific warning I want to issue about walking in Romania relates to the sheepdogs,' the author of our guidebook wrote conversationally, before going into more chilling detail.

I have been attacked innumerable times in Romania – forcing me to defend myself desperately. I've been badly bitten several times. The breed is called the Carpathian Mountain Shepherd Dog and is there to protect sheep from wolves and bears and so, if they spot a lone walker, they will run at the person in a pack while emitting ferocious barking. They usually try and bite the walking or running person. Keep your distance from sheep as much as you can, carry a few stones and practise throwing them at stationary targets in quiet moments. Do not hesitate to throw them as soon as the dogs come within range. Do not turn your back on the dogs – ever.

If you are unlucky enough to sustain a dog bite you will need immediate rabies injections. Above all, abandon your soft western impressions that large dogs make pleasant pets. In remote stretches of mountain, a pack of uncontrolled Carpathian sheepdogs will unhesitatingly try and kill you. They are frighteningly effective.

'Bloody hell,' I said to Jo on the flight to Bucharest. 'It all sounds a bit serious.'

We had come across dangerous dogs in that part of the world before, on our honeymoon in the mountains of Bulgaria and Albania, but we had never feared for our lives. We told each other that the author was probably being melodramatic. Poetic licence. Still, it's one thing when it's just the two of you, quite another when you have a six-month-old child in tow. When we got to Bucharest I bought an eight-inch hunting dagger, just in case we got into difficulty. And then we promptly forgot about the warnings because we fell in love with Romania. The countryside was astonishingly beautiful and the people were warm and welcoming.

We were walking in the Carpathian Mountains, which

ring the southern edge of Transylvania, and felt relaxed in the gorgeous setting. Cuillin was asleep in his pouch as we cut across a pretty meadow. I saw a dog at the far end and had a quiet word with Jo. It was best to avoid even a solitary dog. She agreed and we slipped into the forest to take the long way round the meadow.

The forest was lush and peaceful and we enjoyed a diversion that must have taken us at least a mile out of our way. As the woods opened up we took the only path available to us. We had been walking along the track for fifteen seconds when we heard the barking.

I looked round and saw a dog running towards us from 500 metres away.

'Shit, Jo,' I exclaimed when I swivelled to the left and saw another dog, and then another.

'Oh my God,' Jo said as she moved close to Cuillin and me. 'There are more of them.'

A small pack ran towards us from the right.

'Get your stick ready,' I instructed Jo as I reached for the dagger.

We both carried sharp-pointed hiking sticks and Jo and I backed into each other so we could face the dogs rushing at us from different angles. There were eight of them, each one looking massive and demented. Then, in an orchestrated manoeuvre, the dogs fanned out into a snarling circle. We were surrounded.

'Stay calm,' I said softly. 'Use the stick if they come any nearer.'

The dogs inched towards us, the noise intensifying, and

then one lunged at me. It was like watching a nature programme in which a hyena makes a rush towards a wounded buffalo only to stop a few metres away, and then another on the other side of the circle does the same thing, testing the defences. I was not sure how long we could hold them off. I swapped hands, taking control of the dagger with my right even though I had no real idea what I would do with it. I had a sickening sense that, in our complacency, we had made a very stupid decision.

Suddenly, we heard a man shout. The dogs kept barking but they looked in his direction. It was a shepherd. He yelled again, calling his dogs in a guttural voice. Slowly, they retreated. A few still snarled but the shepherd drew them away from us. They ran towards him.

He waved urgently, gesturing that we should walk on while he controlled the pack.

I looked back a few times and saw that the dogs padded around him, their tongues lolling from slavering mouths as he kept a tight hold on them. The relief was dizzying.

'Is Cuillin all right?' Jo asked anxiously as we walked away as quickly as we could without running.

I looked down at the pouch expecting to see a terrified little baby. Cuillin was fast asleep.

It felt as though a disaster had been averted and so, for the next few days, we changed tack. Leaving the Carpathian Mountains we took a train to Braşov, a fascinating city in southern Transylvania. Once we'd got over the dog panic it didn't take us long to resume walking and climbing.

Jo, Cuillin and I travelled across the breadth of

Transylvania, untroubled by any dogs, bears, wolves or even Dracula, as we hitched one lift after another. Cuillin was our magnet. As soon as people saw a young couple and their baby, they offered a lift. They couldn't resist the little bump in my pouch and we met some lovely people on the way to Maramureş in the far north of Romania. It is an isolated area, with few roads, and in winter it is often cut off from the rest of the country. But in the early summer of 2011 it was sublime.

We stayed in a farmstead for the night and a well-dressed Englishman, with an accent that suggested he was probably an Old Etonian, turned up. He spoke fluent Romanian and introduced himself as William Blacker. It emerged that he had spent the last fifteen years in Transylvania and Maramureş. When the Berlin Wall came down, he had jumped in his Ford Fiesta and driven across Europe. Blacker had then worked as a peasant labourer in this rural part of Romania, fallen in love with a gypsy girl and written an acclaimed book called *Along the Enchanted Way*. He was back in Maramureş for a family wedding and, before we knew it, Jo and I had accepted his generous invitation to join them the next day at the celebration.

It was an unforgettable experience. Everyone was in traditional dress – the men wearing straw hats, white robes and moccasin shoes, the women in ornate dresses and white headscarves. William, Jo, Cuillin and I were the only non-Romanians and we felt privileged to be invited. During the wedding procession, the men hit and jangled strange sticks while a gypsy folk band played. We were invited to the bride's house and were welcomed in as a bottle of plum brandy was shared around. It seemed rude not to take a swig and, that night, we went to the reception in one of the barns, where everyone danced. Jo and I loved it while Cuillin slumbered on.

William invited us to stay at his home later in our holiday. We took a taxi to get there and, in broken English, the driver told us that we wouldn't want to stay there. It was a gypsy village. We paid him his fare, jumped out and discovered a rough-and-ready but very attractive village. William's cottage near the centre, close to a fortified Saxon church, was filled with old Romanian furniture. We loved it. Over the next few days we bought bread, a few eggs and lots of vegetables to cook on his wood fires. We also ventured out to the bar. It was not necessarily a place to linger at night but we enjoyed it in the late afternoon. Jo and I understood why William had asked us to keep the whereabouts of his village a secret. It was wild and untrammelled.

I remember, on our last night there, Jo turning to me and saying, 'What a fabulous place, Coxy.'

The lure of politics had waned, briefly, as Jo embraced motherhood. She wanted to dedicate all her attention to our new son. But her plan to go home one day and try to win the right to stand for the Labour Party in Batley and Spen remained at the back of her mind. Two years before, in September 2009, she had taken her first real step towards parliamentary politics when attending the Labour Party conference in Brighton. As always with Jo, the political began with the personal. She made a bold decision in conjunction with Eloise Todd, her great friend from Brussels, whom we met up with.

The 2009 conference had been dominated by the same old voices. Peter Mandelson had warned that Labour was 'in the fight of our lives' to hold back David Cameron and a Tory Party craving power after twelve years in opposition. It was hard for Jo to take Mandelson seriously when she had clashed so often with him in Brussels. Gordon Brown, for whom I worked at the time, made an impassioned speech promising that Labour was 'not yet done'.

We were of a different generation and to us it seemed that Labour was in real trouble and in need of fresh voices. Jo hesitated, but it was the right time for her to make the first move.

Eloise helped seal that conviction. She and Jo were walking around the conference centre when they spotted a stall for the Labour Women's Network. Jo steered Eloise towards it and said, casually, 'You know they offer courses for prospective women candidates . . .'

'I've heard about them,' Eloise said.

'Should we go on one?' Jo asked.

Eloise laughed, a touch nervously. 'I will if you will.'

Jo smiled at her friend. 'C'mon, let's do it.'

They walked over to the stall. 'Hello,' Jo said. 'We just wondered if it's true that you run courses? Training people that might want to become MPs?'

Eloise could hear how hard it was for her friend to say

the words out loud. Jo sounded embarrassed, as if the woman at the stall might think she was ridiculously presumptuous.

'We do,' the woman replied cheerfully. 'Hold on – let me get you some info about it . . .'

She looked through her information packs before picking out a couple. 'Actually,' she said, checking the details, 'there's a course next month in Newcastle. Do you want to sign up for it?'

'Should we do it?' Jo asked Eloise, with an encouraging smile.

'Yeah.' Eloise nodded.

It took ten minutes to complete the forms. As they walked away, Eloise slipped her right hand through the crook of Jo's left arm. 'Let's get a drink,' Eloise suggested. 'We deserve one.'

Six weeks later the weekend course in Newcastle concentrated their minds. Nan Sloane, who was leading the Labour Women's Network at the time, was passionate about the issue of women's representation in Parliament. She explained that, in 1997, the UK had moved up to twentieth place in the international league table of women's representation. That improvement had been driven by a new intake of Labour MPs; and yet they were burdened with the tag of 'Blair's Babes'.

Twelve years later, Britain had slumped to sixty-fifth in that same table and had been overtaken by Australia, Belgium, France, Poland, Rwanda, Tunisia and Trinidad and Tobago. The percentage of female MPs had doubled from 9 to 18 in 1997 but nothing had changed since. Westminster was still dominated by middle-aged white men who had mostly attended similar schools and universities. The sight and sound of them shouting at each other, or chortling 'Hear, Hear!' in support of their chums, was part of the reason that most people, especially women, were alienated from party politics.

We were closing in on the centenary, in 2018, of the enfranchisement of British women, and it was time for change on the front and back benches. It was time for young women like Jo and Eloise to make a stand.

They were set various tasks – from participating in media training to making a hustings speech – and Jo was the standout performer. She scored top marks in all the exercises and easily overcame the cringe factor of watching herself, in front of everyone else, on a television screen.

One of Nan's assistants took Jo and Eloise aside when they were having a celebratory drink at the end. The mood was merry but the woman sounded sincere. 'If you two are serious about this, you are definite Cabinet material.' Jo laughed. She never took herself too seriously.

The following year, a senior Labour Party player called Jo to encourage her to stand for the seat of Erewash in Derbyshire at the coming election. It was a winnable seat and Jo was humbled to have been asked but she never really considered it. I suggested she should. After all, opportunities like that don't come up often. But Jo was clear that she would feel a fraud representing anywhere except her home town. For her, politics was first and foremost about community – and she wanted to be deeply rooted in hers.

In the late summer of 2012 Jo was six months pregnant with Lejla. It was time to get ready for our next adventure – a new child. We had decided to convert the boat's forecastle into a tiny bedroom for Cuillin and the baby. The day before we went on our last holiday prior to the birth, I cruised up to a boatyard in Brentford to leave *Ederlezi*. While we were away we got a call to say that the workmen had discovered a series of small holes in the hull. Another few weeks of work were needed to repair the boat and make it completely safe.

Once more, while waiting for Jo to give birth, we returned to Reading to stay with my very patient parents. I called the welders relentlessly – stressing how my heavily pregnant wife and one-year-old baby depended on them. On a crisp October morning I picked up the refurbished boat and steered her back down the Thames to our mooring. This time there were no dramatic snowfalls or iced-over canals to overcome. We looked to be sailing towards the calm arrival of our new baby.

On the Sunday night of 4 November 2012 we went to dinner on the boat next door and set off a few fireworks for Guy Fawkes. Cuillin was no fan! We also ate the spiciest squid we'd ever enjoyed and, around 3.30 a.m., Jo shook me awake. The contractions had started. We woke Cuillin and took him to our friends around the corner. Remembering his difficult birth we were nervous.

Jo had decided to give birth in a midwife-led unit, rather than a hospital, in the hope she would enjoy a more relaxed experience. It was a courageous decision, given what she went through last time. After dropping Cuillin off we took a cab to the unit. A TENS machine was strapped to Jo and, at the side of the birthing pool, we ate a little food as it was important Jo maintained her strength. She soon needed it. The contractions rolled down in seemingly endless waves and we were disheartened when, after three hours of Jo doing well with the help of gas and air, she had only dilated two centimetres.

The midwives suggested they could speed things up by breaking her waters. We just needed to make a decision. Should the procedure be done there or in a hospital where she could have an epidural? Jo was brave and tried to argue the case for staying. In the end I convinced her to take the safer route, given our experience last time, and we called an ambulance.

By the time we were in the ambulance Jo was on her hands and knees in an attempt to ease the excruciating pressure because, as with Cuillin, the baby's back was grating against her spine. An epidural helped soon after we reached Whitechapel Hospital but the baby's heartbeat and oxygen levels fluctuated.

Many hours later it was decided that, with the baby in clear distress, there was no choice but to do an emergency Caesarean. The drama was made worse by the Wagnerian organ recital booming around the operating theatre. 'Can we turn off the music?' I asked edgily.

The music was switched off and a resuscitation table was wheeled in at speed. A screen was placed in front of Jo so she and I could not see what was happening. The surgery was quick and we soon heard them moving the baby to the resuscitation table. I was anxious and Jo stared at me in confusion until I started smiling at the sound of a raggedy cry.

A nurse brought the wriggling baby to Jo who stretched out her arms: 'Oh, it's a boy!'

The nurse laughed. 'No, Jo, that's the umbilical cord.'

It was another classic Jo moment. 'Oh!' Jo exclaimed. 'It's a girl!'

Jo held our tiny baby while she was sewn up. It had been another traumatic birth but, as Jo eventually began to breastfeed, I contacted her parents. I then texted my parents and my sister Stacia to confirm that Jo had just given birth to a healthy baby girl.

Stacia apparently looked up in dismay from her phone and said to Andrew, 'You are not going to believe what they have called this poor baby: Lancelot Ethelred Cox. I bet that's bloody Brendan.'

Andrew looked at his wife. 'Yeah, that's Brendan all right. He's got you again . . .'

In fact, we named our baby Lejla Angela Cox. Two days after she was born we took her home to the boat but our joy didn't last long. A few days later, we were hit by a catastrophe which nearly cost us Lejla's life.

After the worst was over, or so we hoped, I wrote a letter to Lejla that she might read one day when she is older. As it is a message of love from Jo and me, it's appropriate to save most of the two pages for Lejla but, looking back at it now, I can see the relief from the opening lines.

Dear Lejla (or Ledge-La as I'm worried you might always be called),

Well. What a start to life. It's day twenty of your life and me and your mum are sat next to your bed in intensive care watching your heartbeat, oxygen and breathing on a big monitor. Every now and then one of the indicators slides into the red and all the alarms go off before you sort yourself out again. To say it's stressful is an understatement. But I imagine it's much worse for you – not that you'll remember it.

I can now look back on the worst experience of my life, at least until the tragic death of Jo just three and a half years later, and remember it with jolting clarity.

We chose Lejla, pronounced Layla, after some of the most inspirational women we had met in Bosnia and Croatia. When I was volunteering there after the war I worked with an amazing woman called Lejla who was a teacher in Vozuća. Another Lejla was the wife of the director of an orphanage in Croatia, whom Jo and I visited regularly. She was a forceful local campaigner who Jo admired. A third Lela came from the orphanage we had worked at in Croatia and whom I had known since she was a toddler.

Angela was our tribute to our friend, the former Trinidadian senator and UN official who had read the Jack London poem at our wedding. Angela's life had been extremely hard even before her husband John, as well as her mother and her sister were all murdered during a burglary in Trinidad. Angela refused to buckle to hatred or bitterness. She spoke out against the death penalty when her family's murderers were brought to trial and, for the rest of her life, she campaigned against the inequality she regarded as being the scourge of the world. Angela never pitied herself and, even in her last days, she whispered more concern for my cold than her own ravaging cancer. She was one of those people who always paused before she spoke and when she did, she communicated such deep wisdom it was hard to respond.

She died on 12 November 2012 but I was glad to have been able to tell her, just days before, that Lejla had been born and would carry her name.

I was a pall-bearer at Angela's funeral in west London. Naturally, I was upset, but deep anxiety soon engulfed me. On my way to the funeral Jo had called me and told me she was going to the Royal London Hospital with Lejla. We had been worried about her cold and Jo had taken her to see our GP. He had advised immediate attention at A&E.

I left the funeral as soon as the service was over and by the time I reached them in hospital Lejla was struggling to breathe. She had been transferred to intensive care.

Our nightmare had just begun.

Lejla had contracted bronchiolitis, a relatively minor

ailment in children but of serious concern in an infant. She couldn't find the energy to feed so a tube was inserted in her nose, and she was strapped to a ventilator. Lejla could no longer breathe for herself.

She deteriorated markedly over the next three days. On the fourth night of our ordeal I asked a nurse, who was part of the excellent intensive care team, if Lejla was going to live. She dodged the question and I feared the worst.

When the consultant arrived I asked the same stark question. *Will she live?*

The consultant talked more generally about all they were doing. I understood. She could not give us any guarantees. Lejla's tiny lungs had collapsed and they feared meningitis and other complications.

Jo and I held each other as we sat next to Lejla. We tried to encourage each other – but we didn't know if she would survive. It was so desolate that we spoke about death. We resolved that, if we lost Lejla, we would always honour her memory, and look after Cuillin, and each other.

The people who lived around us on our mooring were wonderfully supportive. Each night I returned from the hospital I found food on the table. Someone had lit our fire. It was one of those times when community means everything. We were also helped by Jo's parents, as Gordon and Jean looked after Cuillin while we were in hospital.

Jo was very strong throughout those interminable days and nights. She would not leave Lejla. Night after night she sat next to the ventilator, only breaking away when Cuillin arrived.

We talked incessantly to Lejla, and sang to her. I can't even begin to imagine how many times I sang 'Soldier Soldier'.

We also stared at the three monitors that gauged the state of her life in a series of beeps and squiggles. The oxygen levels dipped the most and, fearing brain damage or death, we would push the alarm as soon as the line slid towards the red zone. A nurse would rush in, adjust the ventilator and the monitor would hum calmly again.

At some point at the end of the first week, Lejla rallied. Within another couple of days she could breathe for herself.

Jo and I cried in relief when a consultant looked down admiringly at little Lejla: 'You've got a fighter here.'

Just as I had written to Cuillin soon after his birth, I could finally carry on with our letter to Lejla.

I hope the rest of your life is less troubled than the start has been. If the amount of fight you've shown in the last week continues into the future you are going to be a force to be reckoned with . . . I hope when you read this you'll have lots of memories to look back on; lots of family adventures and personal triumphs. I hope that the highs will be frequent and that the lows will bring insight.

I also told her about her mum, Jo, the mother Lejla would lose before she turned four.

Your mum has had to put up with a lot. But to let you into a secret (I don't want her getting big-headed), she's pretty awesome. From climbing mountains to bringing up kids – she puts all of her energy into everything and you're lucky to have such an awesome role model.

The world and our lives are incredible. I hope you enjoy yours as much as me and your mum enjoy ours . . . We love you unconditionally and can't wait to find out what you want to be, see and do. Go forth, burn the candle at every end and never step back from what you want to be.

From the day that Cuillin was born, Jo saw her primary responsibility in life as being a brilliant mum. We both thought about parenting seriously and spoke to experts (above all my sister) about what we should focus on and what we didn't need to stress about. We even agreed a long set of parenting principles which I wrote down in a letter to Cuillin at the time:

The week after you were born your mum and I went for a long walk with you around the university lake in Reading and wrote down the principles by which we'd try to stick. They include:

- *Be consistent and follow through.*

- *Be patient (that one is particularly for me!).*

- *Don't emphasise gender roles.*

- *Make it clear that you have choices and that those choices have consequences.*

- *Be positive, interested in your interests, enthusiastic and supportive.*

- *Don't worry about small things/nag.*

- *Give lots of varying experience.*

- *Help you be thoughtful and reflective.*

- *Give you the confidence to take calculated risks.*

- *Share with you a zest for life, take you on inspiring adventures*

- *Read to you regularly.*

- *Don't be overly protective.*

- *Don't force our interests on you (though you may have noticed by your name we might have trouble sticking to that one).*

- *Keep ourselves happy and healthy.*

- *Set clear boundaries.*

The letter to Cuillin finished:

Of course, your main advantage in life so far is having an amazing mum. The most energetic,

exciting, adventurous, dynamic woman you will
probably ever meet – certainly that I have ever met.

Jo's decision to throw herself wholeheartedly into parenting came at a cost: it impacted on her career and it left her exhausted at times. But it was the thing of which she was most proud. Jo and I talked a lot about the importance of the early years – especially the first three – when most of the hardwiring of the brain gets done. It's of immense comfort to me to know that Jo and I crafted that wiring together, that her love moulded Cuillin and Lejla into what they are, the foundation of what they will become. It's why when we talk about Jo as being in our hearts and in our heads, we know it's true.

19

The End of the Worst Year

A year unlike any other I could remember was about to end. You could not escape the seeping consequences of 2016 in the round-ups and lamentations of Trump, of fleeing Syrian refugees and a pugnacious Kremlin, of terror attacks and the seemingly endless deaths of famous people. Old media and social media listed the number of celebrity deaths over the previous twelve months, from David Bowie, Alan Rickman and Terry Wogan in January to George Michael, Carrie Fisher and Debbie Reynolds in December.

The names reeled and blurred: Fidel Castro, Muhammad Ali, Prince, Leonard Cohen, Jo Cox, Harper Lee, Johan Cruyff, Zaha Hadid, Victoria Wood, Caroline Aherne, Gene Wilder, Shimon Peres, Zsa Zsa Gabor, Umberto Eco, Arnold Palmer, Andrew Sachs, Ronnie Corbett and on and on until there were fevered debates as to the supposed symbolism of so much loss in a single year. In that fallow period between Christmas and New Year such list-making filled the media. Jo's name and face appeared again and again as if she had joined a starry pantheon of the dead.

Exactly one year before, she had been a forty-one-year-old mum of two small children, a wife, a daughter, a sister and a new Member of Parliament who had begun to make a mark in politics. She was just Jo to us on New Year's Eve 2015 as, down at the cottage, we looked ahead with anticipation and eagerness to all that awaited. Jo resolved to become even more confident, thicker-skinned and accomplished as a politician while ensuring our family remained at the centre of her life. She also pledged to make more elderflower champagne.

A year on I felt that, in the mere five and a half months she lived in 2016, Jo had fulfilled each of those personal goals. As if in fizzing reminder of that fact, some of my visits to the cottage after her death almost resulted in heart failure for me. The kids and I would be playing, or they would be asleep while I worked, and the silence would suddenly be broken by an explosion. It sounded as if an intruder had fired a gun right inside the cottage.

The first time, I jumped up as if someone had actually been shot but, after a while, I just grinned at the fact that another of Jo's fermenting bottles of home-made champagne had exploded. The stoppers were firmly in place so the only way the gas from the fermentation could escape was to smash through the glass that surrounded it. That kick of her champagne lives on in our memories – and always makes me smile when I remember Jo and her fizz.

It also reminded me of how once, again at the cottage,

Jo made stinging nettle soup. As she was too busy to bother finding proper gloves she wore an old woollen pair to deal with the nettles – which meant she had tingling fingers for a week. Jo's enthusiastic domesticity at the cottage always included a bang or a tingle. These personal memories helped sustain me.

As I read my wife's name among that long list of the famous dead, sometimes I drew tiny vestiges of solace from the certainty that, even amid the devastating end, her name and her work endured in new ways. Rather than being forgotten, Jo had been discovered by the world in death. People who had never heard of Jo Cox a year before now understood that her name resonated with meaning for them and millions of others.

Another painful truth echoed. As the wider world eulogised Jo, her absence left those of us closest to her trapped in previously unimaginable distress and grief.

Kim told me later how she had experienced similar emotions on New Year's Eve. She and Clare were travelling from Yorkshire to join us at the cottage. They were planning a leisurely trip and would spend the night in a hotel on the way down, then arrive for lunch the following day and stay over to celebrate Cuillin's birthday on 2 January. Kim felt okay until, as they wandered down for a drink in the hotel bar that evening, she spotted a huge newspaper spread on celebrity deaths. Jo's smiling face stared out of the page at Kim, her image larger even than those of David Bowie and Muhammad Ali. Kim felt desolate again. Clare understood. She had known and also loved Jo for years and she still dreamed of her death most nights. They retreated to their room. There was nothing to celebrate on the last night of the year we had lost Jo.

Cuillin, Lejla and I had enjoyed our Christmas with my parents and Andrew, Stacia and their three boys at the cottage. My family had stayed in a delightful barn for a few days and Christmas lunch had been poignant and special.

Jo and I always spent New Year's Eve surrounded by close friends. This year that felt more important than ever. Eloise and Tom, Simon and Kate, Rob and Emma, Colin and Liz and all their children, had rented a large cottage further up the river. We built a big bonfire, much to the kids' excitement. Eloise had once again brought a sound system over from Brussels and we cranked it up on the back of their van so it pumped out songs that Jo and all of us had danced to over the years. At midnight, we set off a rocket.

Watching it soar up into a clear, starlit sky, and with everyone wishing each other Happy New Year, I suddenly became very upset. My feelings of missing Jo seemed unbearable and, despite not wanting to ruin the night, I could no longer curb the tears. Em, Rob's wife who was close to Jo, just held me. I could be myself with my friends yet I didn't want to make another spectacle of my misery. I hugged Em and then broke away. I needed to be alone.

I moved deeper into the woods. The blackness was broken by the moonlight and the distant gleam of the crackling bonfire behind me. I crouched against a tree and looked up at the sky. All I can remember is that, as I cried, fresh hurt poured out of me. I probably didn't cry for more than a minute because I heard a little voice calling me.

'Daddy? Where are you, Daddy?'

'I'm here, Cuillin.'

'Daddy!' he exclaimed as I scooped him up in my arms. I kissed him. He smiled and nestled into me.

'I wanted to look up at the stars with you,' he said.

'That's a lovely idea. I'd love to look up at the stars with you.'

We sat on a log and stared up at the glittering stars in an inky sky. Cuillin pointed to those he liked best and I helped him identify which of the large unblinking stars were actually planets.

When we walked back to the fire, Cuillin was pleased to see that he was the last child still awake. The other kids, including Lejla, had been tucked up in their sleeping bags.

'Can I stay up a bit longer?' Cuillin asked.

'Why not?' I said as I lifted him on to a metal chair so he could dance to a few more songs.

I eventually carried a happy Cuillin into the cottage to join the others in sleep.

A few of us drank and chatted around the fire. It was nearly 3 a.m. by the time Simon and I clambered into his new tree-tent. Held up by anchor points, and stretching from one tree to another, six feet off the ground, the tent makes you feel as if you're hanging in the air. It was a strange sensation made more head-spinning by the amount of alcohol we had consumed. I drifted off into a dreamless sleep, only to be woken just after five in the morning.

Lejla was giggling and sitting on top of my head. For a

few moments, I had no idea what was happening. Where was I? And how had Lejla climbed into the tent? She soon explained. I had put her in a room in the cottage with Kate, Simon's wife. When Lejla woke she told Kate she was missing me so Kate had brought her over and lifted her up into the tent. It was lovely to cuddle little Lejla but any chance of sleep ended as soon as the other kids heard where we were – between the trees and up in the air. It was a fun way to start a new year.

There was a more important celebration the following day. Cuillin turned six on 2 January. It was also another wrenching milestone. In the six and a half months since her death there had now been birthdays for Jo, Lejla, me and Cuillin, as well as a funeral, a wedding anniversary, a celebration of her life, Christmas and New Year. Each occasion had been crammed with emotion. Jo had always lit up our happiest get-togethers. She would never do so again.

We enjoyed Cuillin's birthday all the same, and the best moment was the sheer pleasure that spread across his face when he opened his main present from me. Cuillin looked down at the Swiss Army knife and smiled proudly. He seemed very grown-up as, carefully, he showed Lejla how, beyond its main blade, it also worked as a saw, a wire-cutter, nail clippers, a corkscrew, a fish-scaler and a screwdriver.

'Wow,' Lejla said, sounding deeply impressed.

The sweet surprises and simple pleasures of life, especially on a six-year-old's birthday, remained as vivid as always to Cuillin and Lejla.

* * *

It was much harder for me to feel the same excitement without Jo. I also struggled with more tangled emotions. Sometimes, during the earliest months of grief, I would fall into the old way of thinking I must tell Jo about this tonight. I would start to compose text messages to her that now, unfinished, fill my drafts folder. Or I would open my eyes in the morning and instinctively reach out for her. Her side of the bed would feel cold and empty and then I would remember. I still sometimes caught myself expecting to see her smiling face when the door to the boat opened – and, instead, it was a kind neighbour or my parents paying me a visit.

I am now dealing with chronic, terminal absence. Jo is gone for ever.

We had lived our days and years together so fully that we never spent much time reflecting on everything we had done. Unlike many people of our generation, we kept up the ritual of printing our photos and putting them into albums – but despite having nearly a hundred, I'm not sure we ever looked at any of them. I suppose we were saving such nostalgia for when we were old and grey and had spare time to reminisce. Jo's death has made me savour, with new feeling, everything we did together. In the last couple of months, with help from my dad and Jo's best friend Sarah, I have indexed all our albums. I feel immensely grateful that the children and I have so much to look back on.

When Jo died, I said that she would have no regrets about how she had lived her life. She had spent it with her foot to the floor and without a brake pedal. Of course that meant occasional crashes, but ultimately they made her stronger and it was an amazing ride.

Like most married couples we had our difficulties – our relationship certainly wasn't perfect. There were times when we found each other intensely annoying. Jo's forgetfulness and my relentlessness sometimes rubbed up against each other badly. We both did and said things we regretted, but it's fair to say that Jo was always the better person. Whatever I had done, she was always full of love and forgiveness, even when I was least deserving of it.

When somebody is snatched from you unexpectedly, the things you never had a chance to say can haunt you for ever. I know people who have lost loved ones who always regret never having had the chance to say goodbye, 'I love you' or 'I'm sorry'.

Hard as it has been to lose Jo, and much as I miss her every day, I comfort myself that there wasn't really anything left unsaid. We had grown better at being honest with each other and confronting the things that had tested us. In doing so we reaffirmed the fundamental underpinning of our relationship. We knew that nothing could ever change our commitment to spend our lives together. We had taken thirty and thirty-four years respectively to find each other, we had two wonderful kids and frankly our approach to life drove most other people mad.

The last Valentine's card Jo wrote me in February 2016 (having initially forgotten Valentine's Day and having got

Cuillin to make a card!) was full of her love. I re-read it regularly now:

> *Your energy, passion, principles, boundless love and support for me and my dreams, your dedication to being the best dad to our gorgeous ones, and your drive and ambition to change the world for the better still blow me away. Our life truly is unique, awesome and full of happiness. I love you more each year. And thank you for everything you do to keep me alive and happy, and to help me succeed in my dreams. I appreciate it and couldn't do it without you.*

And mine to her read:

> *Beatnose! Happy Valentine's Day! I love you even more than I did all those years ago on the banks of Loch Hourn. Thank you for all your love and support over the last year. Looking forward to an even more awesome one to come, all my love as always. Bx*

Our lives were intertwined. Our partnership wasn't just personal it was all-encompassing. Ideas, passion, practicalities, adventure, kids – all moulded into one.

20

Selection Days,
Election Night

It was a Friday night in the early spring of 2014, and Jo and I had big things to discuss. She had received a call telling her that Mike Wood, the Labour MP for Batley and Spen, was standing down at the next election. A selection process to choose Labour's new candidate would soon get under way. We were driving to the cottage as usual and, thankfully, Lejla and Cuillin had both fallen asleep on the back seat before we had even got out of London, so we had time and space to talk properly. I could sense Jo's excitement but also her trepidation. This was her chance to fulfil a lifelong dream, but it had come at a difficult time.

Jo had just recovered from the exhaustion of having two kids and was in the early stages of setting up a new organisation looking at how women are affected differently by policy. I had just finished three months of paternity leave, which I took when Jo returned to work. I had gone back part time, as had Jo, and we were having a brilliant time as a young family. Our income had been reduced, but our lives felt enlarged. Jo was concerned about the potential impact on the kids of standing for Parliament. She always put them first in any consideration and Cuillin and Lejla would only be four and two at the time of the 2015 general election. Jo did not want to let either of them down at a critical stage of their development.

As she spoke, my mind raced with contradictory thoughts. I was worried about the effect on our lives, especially the disruption to our family life. But if I'm honest, I was also a bit jealous. I remained quiet as we drove until, after a long monologue that first leaned towards one conclusion and then back towards the other, Jo asked, after a pause, 'What do you think, Coxy?'

I tried to compose my thoughts.

'Jo,' I said, 'this is your chance. And if you go for it I will back you with everything I have.'

We both cried and she squeezed my hand. We knew that this was a huge decision, a turning point in our lives. Win or lose, it was the moment when Jo took on her demons of self-doubt. It was the moment I put myself second and her first, the moment when we coalesced as a partnership and took forward her ambition as our collective project. And I was proud of her.

Over the next two hours we went from the principle to the plan. The next few days were crucial; she had to move quickly if she was to stand a chance. Who did she know in the local party? What did she mean nobody! Okay, who might introduce us? 'Let's do it properly and drive hard,' I said. 'Let's make sure you win the contest.'

It is tempting, with hindsight, to suggest that Jo always had a plan to become the MP for Batley and Spen, but in reality it was more of a general aspiration. Yes, she had undertaken training for prospective candidates, and by the time her opportunity came she was leader of the Labour Women's Network and she knew people in the Labour Party. But she had never played a role in local politics, so in many ways we were starting from scratch. As a relatively safe Labour seat it would be a hard fight to secure the right to represent it – which is just as it should be.

Our plan was simple. Jo was naturally magnetic and inspiring. She had the empathy, ability and force of personality to gain the support of most people she met. Now, before they pledged their support to other candidates, she just had to meet them. But she would need a campaign. The only way you win the selection process is by convincing the biggest number of party members in your area to vote for you, rather than another candidate. Already getting excited, we decided that we would work as a team and give it our absolute best shot.

I set up a detailed database of every single party member in Batley. There were 243 in total and, looking back, it's amusing how obsessed I became in devising a convoluted system, using different colour codes, for assessing people's potential support for Jo.

We returned to London on the Monday and Jo was straight on a train to Batley. It did not take long to establish that some other possible candidates were already in pole position. A couple of men had spent the last few years getting pledges of support from virtually the entire membership. Mike Wood was approaching seventy and had been the Labour MP since 1997. He was an obscure figure in national politics and belonged to the hard left of the party. Wood had strong feelings about his successor, and they weren't pro Jo.

Jo met with as many people as she could in the first few days and most of them seemed to like her. The constant refrain was 'If I hadn't already pledged my support I'd be 100 per cent on board.'

When Jo rang me I tried to be encouraging. 'Keep plugging away', I told her, but I feared it was all but impossible for her to win.

Then news came that the Labour Party head office might insist on an all-women shortlist. Many people are wary of the idea of such positive discrimination, and I can understand their doubts. Why not just let the best candidates fight it out – that's real equality, isn't it? But when you know how institutions like the Labour Party work, you come to see how necessary such shortlists are. If you ask people to close their eyes and think of an MP, nine out of ten people will see a man. It's an implicit bias that will only change as representation does. And despite huge progress women still carry most of the domestic and parenting pressures so have less time to build the relationships essential to win. Although Jo hoped that one day we wouldn't need all-women shortlists, she had always believed in them as a jump-start for equal representation.

When the party made the ruling it suddenly opened up

the field. Jo genuinely felt for the two men who had aspired to be the next Labour candidate. She visited them to say how sorry she felt for them personally, even if she agreed with the principle of the decision.

Mike Wood had seemed to resent Jo even before the announcement of the all-women shortlist – and because Jo led the Labour Women's Network, he might have assumed that it was her doing. It seems that most MPs try to stay neutral in selection contests when they leave office. Given the network and resources they have it's only fair, though I'm sure a lot will express a preference privately, if asked.

The contest was now primarily between Jo and Alison Lowe, a Leeds councillor who lived in Birstall, whose politics were closer to Wood's. Lowe was a good worker and we respected her, but there was a nasty and personal tone from other quarters right from the start. Jo was shocked as she always got on with everyone. Her opponents tried various routes: that she wasn't local (not an easy one to sustain); that she was out of her depth (her CV made short work of this); that she wasn't left wing enough (Jo was happy to take on the arguments). Then Wood took what I felt to be the extraordinary step of sending a letter to all members urging them to vote for Alison Lowe. The leader of the Labour Group on Kirklees Council sent a letter in response telling members it was up to them whom they elected, not Wood.

Her opponents clearly didn't know Jo. She visited ten houses a day, drank her own body weight in tea and talked from morning until night. She was as happy debating the details of foreign policy as having a good natter about what was happening locally. Bit by bit, as she always did, she won people over.

A sympathetic Labour Party member in Batley, Jo Broadhead, urged her to meet Fazila Aswat, a local charity worker then based at the Royal Voluntary Service. Fazila's father was a former Labour councillor who had arrived in Yorkshire from Gujarat in India in the 1960s. He had worked hard and eventually earned enough money to bring his wife to England. Fazila was born and bred in Batley and Jo Broadhead stressed she could be a vital conduit into the Asian communities.

Fazila and Jo struck up an instant rapport and an initial meeting lasted two hours. Their shared experience of charity work and backgrounds in Batley and Heckmondwike forged a bond deepened by a wider political interest. They discussed community work and cuts to government funding and Jo displayed a solid grasp of local affairs – especially in regard to the alarming fact that Batley and Spen was, nationally, the twelfth most deprived area in terms of health. Fazila offered to help Jo make inroads into the network of Asian Labour members. It was a huge boost.

By now Jo had a mini campaign team of devoted supporters, though none of them had known her three weeks previously. It was wonderful to see. While Jo went from door to door, I compiled the database, drafted her leaflets and speeches and each evening we'd go through the next day's plan. I was astonished by her progress but I knew we couldn't be complacent. I constantly ran and re-ran the numbers, always with a conservative set of assumptions. Gradually we got close to the magic 50 per cent figure that would make us unstoppable.

There were low moments as well. One member apparently tried to ridicule Jo, spending two hours peppering her with obscure and aggressive questions on subjects ranging from the budget of the local library to the best sanctions with which to target the Burmese government. He hadn't accounted for the fact that Jo was on the board of Burma Campaign UK. She was more than happy to discuss the intricacies of Burmese politics, about which she was considerably better informed than he was. She got through that experience as she had done other bruising encounters, but she hated the hostility and that night she came back in floods of tears.

'Maybe I'm not cracked up to be an MP,' she sobbed.

For once I did the right thing, just held and reassured her. The next day she was once again fired up and ready to go.

By the day of the hustings, Saturday, 10 May 2014, Jo had met 239 of the 243 local party members, in old-fashioned door-to-door politics. The other four were either abroad or deceased. I was extremely cautious but, even in my more pessimistic forecast, I thought Jo was at least ten votes ahead of Alison Lowe. She just needed to speak well and handle any questions that would be thrown her way.

We had worked on her speech for a long time and she delivered it with power and authenticity. It was less a hard-selling pitch than a narrative of her life and why she felt so passionate about representing Batley and Spen.

The count is a tense occasion. Only the candidates and their partners are allowed in the room as the votes are checked by party officials. Jo and I chatted edgily as we watched the unfolding of each new ballot slip. It was initially hard to tell what was happening. Jo looked at me anxiously. She was more nervous than I had ever seen her. Gradually it became obvious to me that Jo had won. And won big. But Jo had been too nervous to look and when Alison went over to congratulate her, Jo asked, 'Who won?'

'You did!' Alison said.

Jo was in shock. She hugged Alison and thanked her.

I slipped Jo the bullet points of a speech we had prepared for her to deliver in the event of her being selected. She flashed me a huge grin.

By now Jo had recovered her usual poise. With her typical graciousness, she thanked Mike Wood for his years of service. She finished by saying, 'I am hugely proud and humbled to have been chosen to represent the party in the constituency I was born in. I am honoured to represent Labour in Batley and Spen in the next general election. I will not let you down.'

During the 2015 general election campaign, at least in the earliest days, Jo would usually go up to Yorkshire on the first train on a Tuesday morning and travel back to

London late on a Thursday evening. She would campaign hard for three straight days, while spending a couple of nights at her parents' or sister's house. Towards the end of an exhausting process she spent even more time in Batley, determined to knock on the door of as many homes in the constituency as she could.

When we weren't all at the cottage, I would take the kids up at weekends and sometimes join her as she went from one door to the next. I have never met anyone who could match Jo's instinctive knack of knowing how to engage warmly with so many different kinds of people. The key factor in her appeal was that Jo saw everyone as a person with a real life, full of highs and lows, rather than just a prospective voter.

Inevitably, Jo's charm sometimes paled within the immediate family. Her mind worked in mysterious ways. She could be intensely, astonishingly concentrated for long periods of time, but once the pressure eased she would relax and be distracted from day-to-day niceties. If you needed Jo to explain the intricacies of the conflict in Syria she would blow you away with her empathy and attention to detail. But if her mum needed Jo to remember not to put down a hot mug on a newly varnished sideboard, there was a good chance that she would still plonk down her coffee and leave a ring on the surface. If her dad tried to remind her to get up in plenty of time for an early appointment the following day, Jo would still end up being twenty minutes late. She invariably left the house in a state of relative chaos as she rushed around asking her mum where she had left some papers or if she could borrow a scarf.

Gordon and Jean had recently sold the family home in White Lee and moved to a bungalow. They were looking forward to a peaceful retirement, and as much as they enjoyed having Jo home it was also exhausting for them. She sometimes drove her mum mad, and there were a few arguments. I remember one in particular. Amid the heat of the early campaign, Jo stormed into the bedroom we were sharing with the kids at her parents' old house in White Lee, to announce we were leaving. She had woken me up and I had no idea what was going on. I went into the kitchen and, with Gordon's help, brokered a peace deal.

Jo appreciated her parents doing so much for her. But she was frequently preoccupied or knackered, worn out from thinking about the people she was about to meet or those she had listened to that day. She began to spend time with Kim and Clare to give her parents some respite from the Jo whirlwind.

But when Jo was talking to older people or schoolchildren, small business owners or religious leaders, she struck a chord with almost everyone. In the past year I have heard countless stories from people she met. Cath Pinder, the chair of the Constituency Labour Party in Batley, remembered how she had walked into a room filled with about twenty British Asian leaders. They sat on the floor and Jo was in the middle of the circle, utterly engaged as she listened to them. She brought gravitas to the proceedings but, once the serious work was done, she embraced everyone in the room.

'I don't get that many hugs from my wife,' one elderly man said, as he beamed at Jo.

She was even more adept with children. She was a wonderful mother, but Jo had a gift when talking to kids of all ages and backgrounds. We would walk around town and passing schoolchildren, whom she had met the week before, would break out into a broad Yorkshire chant: 'Vote Jo Cox . . . Vote Jo Cox!'

Apart from the fact that it became a comic routine in our family – because Lejla developed a pitch-perfect Yorkshire accent as she imitated the children shouting 'Vote Jo Cox!' – we often heard how those same kids had gone home and told their parents that they had met Jo Cox. She had spent hours with them at school and made them laugh and told interesting stories. They hoped their mums and dads would vote for her. Jo Cox was very cool, apparently.

Once she had won the selection, I always believed she would win the seat itself but neither of us wanted to take it for granted. Jo insisted on walking down as many streets, and knocking on as many doors, as possible. Fazila always looked elegant alongside her, in her head scarf and high heels, but every evening she would look down at a fresh set of blisters on her poor feet. Dan Howard and Dathan Tedesco, who had been active in the local Labour Party for years, were instrumental in helping to run the campaign. The whole team was energised and the pace stepped up every day.

We both thought Labour was almost certain to lose the general election, despite the polls. But Jo had better prospects than the Party. The only thing that really worried me about Jo's chance of victory was that the Conservatives had put forward Imtiaz Ameen, a local Tory with a strong network within the local Asian community. I was worried that he might split the perceived Asian vote that Labour had traditionally received. Jo remained confident that people would vote based on their beliefs and values, rather than whether or not they were Muslim.

Jo made no attempt to tone down her world view to placate anyone. In fact even during the campaign she made it clear that she differed from Ed Miliband, the Labour leader at the time, when it came to issues like Syria. She really liked Ed, but she was disappointed when, after he had been asked to list some of his proudest moments in politics, he included a decision not to back military action in Syria. Jo pointed out that it felt wrong for someone to be proud of anything to do with Syria. Global inaction and incompetence had caused huge human suffering, the biggest refugee crisis in Europe for years and the rise of ISIS. She argued for much more active engagement in Syria as the best way of stopping the carnage of innocent civilians.

On election day, 7 May 2015, while Cuillin and Lejla were looked after by Jo's mum and dad, the rest of us hit the streets. Jo was going to spend the day going from polling station to polling station and Fazila would ferry her around.

When she picked Jo up that morning Fazila was stunned. 'Jo,' she said in alarm, 'why are you wearing blue?'

'Don't you like this dress?'

Fazila sighed. 'The dress looks great, Jo. But it is election day. You are standing for Labour. Shouldn't you be wearing red?'

'Oh no . . . I wasn't thinking straight this morning.'

'Don't worry,' Fazila said. 'We'll nip home to mine and get you something red to wear on top.'

Jo wearing something from Fazila's wardrobe was a constant theme. It helped that they were of a similar size, and no one seemed to notice the mixing and matching.

As they began to travel around the constituency Jo posted a photo of herself on Twitter: 'Just tucking into a bacon sandwich.'

Fazila smiled and rolled her eyes. I was more worried. I called Jo up and pointed out that munching a bacon sandwich might not be the best way to win over the Muslim community.

'Oh shit,' Jo said. But we both laughed and she said that most people in Batley were very sane. They would judge her on her policies rather than her choice of sandwich.

Jo campaigned right up to the wire. I was proud of her already and we didn't even know the result. It would not be announced until three or four in the morning, so we took Jo, who was exhausted but in good spirits, back to her parents' bungalow for a sleep.

I couldn't have slept even if I'd wanted to. I was nervous as hell as I headed for the sports hall in Huddersfield that had been commandeered for the count. I arrived as the exit polls were announced. It looked as though Labour was set for a shocking night. One bad result followed another as, anxiously, I watched the Batley and Spen ballot boxes being emptied and the votes being counted. I started to worry. A bad night nationally, a potential split in the Asian vote in Jo's constituency . . . My mind was whirring. The Tories only needed 2,000 local voters to switch sides and everything could change.

Everyone else in our team was more confident. Shortly after 3 a.m. we decided it was time to call Jo to come to the count. When she arrived, wearing an appropriate red dress, I took her to one side. She was calm; I was fretful. I tried to hide my nerves and said the vote looked positive but it was too early to say for sure. I had actually been told numerous times over the previous hour not to worry: 'It's in the bag.' But the thought of Jo hearing such predictions and then being confronted by a different result was unbearable. I tempered the bold claims. Jo's dream of representing the people of Batley and Spen in Parliament was now tantalisingly close.

Jo was extraordinary that night. She walked around the hall, moving from one group to the next, chatting easily to everyone she met. I paced around at the back. Local Labour experts, like Dan and Dathan, were emphatic. 'She's definitely won,' they agreed, beaming.

I still couldn't bring myself to tell her, and insisted that nobody else did either, until we were certain. When Jo came back to me I just smiled and said, 'It's looking okay.'

All Jo's instincts had been right. Looking at the vote breakdown by area, you could see that attempts to split the Asian vote had completely failed. Jo had retained their support because, as she had always said, her constituents from Asian families behaved in the same way as her white constituents: they made decisions primarily on the basis of their values and beliefs, not their group's identity. It was a powerful reminder of how much we have in common.

Finally, the votes had all been counted and collated. The electoral officer summoned the seven candidates.

The five men and two women gathered around him in a small huddle. This was the moment when he broke the news to them first, so that they could prepare themselves for the official announcement in front of the television cameras.

Jo turned away from the huddle. She looked straight at me and winked.

Bloody hell! Jo had won. They all went up on to the stage as excitement fizzed inside me. The names and tallies of votes echoed around the hall.

Karl Varley, Patriotic Socialist, 53.

Dawn Wheelhouse, Trade Unionist and Socialist Coalition, 123.

Ian Bullock, Green Party 1,232.

John Lawson, Liberal Democrats, 2,396.

Aleks Lukic, UKIP, 9,080.

Imtiaz Ameen, Conservatives, 15,769.

Jo Cox, Labour, 21,826.

Jo smiled and stepped forward. She had held the seat for Labour with an increased majority of 6,057 votes, 50 per cent bigger than at the previous election. It was a 1.7 per cent swing to Labour on a night when, nationally, the party had performed abysmally.

Applause rang around the hall. Jo gave her acceptance speech and then, as people shook my hand and clapped me on the back, I lost sight of her for a while.

Finally, as she broke away from the photographers and all those congratulating her, Jo walked straight towards me. She was smiling. Jo stretched out her arms, and I opened my own to welcome her.

'You did it, Jo,' I said softly. 'You did it.'

She hugged me tight as I picked her up in the air and spun her round. My eyes filled with tears of pride.

21

Jo Cox MP

On 3 June 2015, at exactly 5.31 that Wednesday afternoon, Jo Cox, MP for Batley and Spen, stood up in the House of Commons to make her maiden speech. Jo wore the same red dress she had worn on election night, which looked striking against the green benches. Her hair was tied back in a ponytail and, watching her speech again now, two years later, Jo seems very young. She also appears happy and confident as, with a dimpled smile, she looks out at the august chamber before she starts to address her parliamentary colleagues for the first time.

So much had happened in the three weeks and five days since she assumed office that there had been little time for Jo to agonise over her speech. Suddenly, the eyes of the House and her constituency were on her as she was called by the Speaker, John Bercow, in the midst of a debate on 'Devolution and Growth across Britain.'

Thank you, Mr Speaker. It is a great privilege to be called to make my maiden speech in this most important of debates, and I congratulate many others who have made outstanding maiden speeches today.

I am sure that many right honourable and honourable members will claim that their constituencies consist of two halves or numerous parochial parts. I am another in that respect, and Batley and Spen is very much that kind of constituency. It is a joy to represent such a diverse community.

Batley and Spen is a gathering of typically independent, no-nonsense and proud Yorkshire towns and villages. Our communities have been deeply enhanced by immigration, be it of Irish Catholics across the constituency or of Muslims from Gujarat in India or from Pakistan, principally from Kashmir. While we celebrate our diversity, what surprises me time and time again as I travel around the constituency is that we are far more united and have far more in common than that which divides us.

Jo was not especially happy with her speech in the ensuing days and weeks, believing she had not paid enough attention to the craft of writing it. But following her murder just over a year later, snippets of the speech were played over and over again as the epitome of all she had represented. Her observation that 'we are far more united, and have far more in common, than that which divides us' is a line that will always define her. The 'more in common' phrase, in particular, echoes a belief shared by so many during these days of division and darkness.

That belief also encapsulates a critique, namely, when we spend too much time talking about diversity and difference, we unwittingly emphasise all that divides us. Jo knew that diversity was important but she also felt that we need to redress the balance and to talk more about the things that we have in common. Yes, we need to recognise diversity, but the more inspiring story is everything that helps bind us together as a community and as a country despite these surface differences.

Jo's speech was well received and people congratulated her on the back benches. Her phone, turned to silent, lit up with messages from family, friends and other MPs. Jo knew she had been competent but it had gone too quickly and she felt she could have added more poetry and depth. She promised herself she would be better next time.

Each new MP is given a specific date for their debut in Parliament, and I had cursed when I realised that I would be working abroad when Jo spoke in the House in the first couple of weeks. My parents, Gordon and Sheila, went in my place to support her from the public gallery.

Jo allowed herself to enjoy the moment. She took my mum and dad up to the House of Commons terrace and, as the evening sunshine lit up London in shades of yellow and orange, my dad bought a bottle of champagne to celebrate her successful debut. Jo Cox, MP, was on her way.

During the first couple of weeks Jo was followed by a local BBC camera crew who wanted to give their viewers an insight into the life of a new MP. They interviewed Jo in Parliament and came to the boat. They followed her usual routine of getting the kids ready for school. Late as ever, she hurried Cuillin along, lifting him off the boat and on to the pontoon. As she did so, Cuillin let out a squeak: his shoe had fallen off and now bobbed in the murky Thames. Jo jumped to the ground, leant off the pontoon and just managed to fish it out without falling in herself. It was classic Jo, and TV gold.

In the week following the election Jo had appointed her parliamentary team and set up her constituency office in the heart of Batley. She had also brought the team down to Westminster to map out her five-year plan as an MP, over two intense days. It was an exhilarating time for Jo and all those who would work alongside her.

Fazila Aswat, Sandra Major, Dan Howard and Dathan Tedesco would assist her in Batley, while Michelle Smyth, an old friend, would help set up her Westminster office until Ruth Price was recruited as her primary researcher. Jo invited everyone on to our boat on their first night in London. The excitement was palpable, even if some of those closest to Jo, like Fazila, her main assistant, still found it hard to believe that they had ended up working for an MP who had become a friend.

As the mother of three young children, Fazila had taken redundancy from the Royal Voluntary Service in March 2015 with the intention of enjoying a long break before she began looking for a part-time job nine months later. But as soon as her RVS work ended she was swept up in Jo's election campaign. Fazila could not easily resist Jo who, in her beguiling way, told her that, 'You'd be perfect as my office manager. What do you think?'

Fazila explained that, while she was happy to help with the election, she had set her heart on a spell away from work. 'Of course,' Jo said. 'Let's just get the election out of the way.'

Once she was elected, Jo made her next pitch. Fazila's expertise and past experience made her the perfect person to run an MP's office. 'You'll be fantastic,' Jo enthused, 'and I'll be so flexible you'll be astounded.'

Fazila couldn't stop herself smiling but she made herself say: 'I'm still not sure . . .'

'Have a think,' Jo said. 'But I know we'll be fab together.'

When they spoke a few days later, Jo was unstoppable. Before Fazila even knew what she had done she had agreed to take the job. 'There goes my summer,' Fazila said with a helpless smile.

It was easy to be charmed by Jo, but Fazila found that the charm was underpinned by substance. And surprise. Fazila only discovered that her new boss had worked with Glenys Kinnock in Brussels and Sarah Brown at 10 Downing Street once she had agreed to become her assistant. Unlike many politicians, Jo had underplayed her past achievements.

She impressed her team with a strategic and well-thought-out five-year plan for her term in office. They were aware that the new MP for Batley and Spen could be endearingly forgetful about clothes, food and time-keeping, but Jo led the way when it came to planning the detail of the work. She also set herself a series of priorities that included Syria, humanitarian intervention in global crises, loneliness among older and marginalised people and regional devolution.

Jo had been keen not to get pigeonholed as only caring about foreign policy and international development. Her experience might be greatest in those areas, but they were far from the only things she cared about. She wanted to tackle domestic issues before anything else. However, as the situation in Syria deteriorated in 2015, she knew that she could not turn away from what was happening: hundreds of thousands of people were dying, millions were displaced, as a direct consequence of the brutal war waged against civilians by their own government – the regime of Bashar al-Assad. She felt our government had a responsibility to help those persecuted, and also that it was in our national interest to do so. Jo believed that ignoring the suffering in Syria had contributed to the refugee crisis and the rise of ISIS, both of which now had implications for Europe and the UK. She decided to take up the cause and quickly became the leading parliamentary expert and voice on the situation.

Jo could hardly believe so little had been said in the House of Commons since Assad ignored Resolution 2139, signed by all Security Council members of the United Nations, including Russia, in April 2014. This resolution was meant to protect 3.5 million Syrians who had been cut off from food, water and medical supplies. The block-ades, which allowed Assad to use starvation as a weapon, were meant to have ended a year earlier. In the same way, barrel bombs had also been condemned by the Security

Council: being explosives, they are simply pushed off planes and consequently have no real chance of landing accurately on supposed military targets.

Human rights organisations had used satellite imagery and video and photographic evidence supplied by witnesses to prove that, between April 2014 and February 2015, over 450 locations in rebel-held towns and villages in Daraa, and more than 1,000 in the city of Aleppo, had been hit by barrel bombs. Ordinary people, rather than ISIS radicals, were being bombed by Assad. In fact, despite the media depiction, it was Assad who was killing many more innocent civilians than any other groups, including ISIS.

The United States appeared ready to force through a short-term deal as a way of ending the fighting, but this entailed making concessions to Assad that would diminish any chance of a sustainable peace. Meanwhile Europe, including the United Kingdom, seemed to have ended up in the role of a confused onlooker, watching Russia's growing domination of Syria. As long as other governments did nothing, Vladimir Putin and Assad would strengthen their grip on Syria. The worst humanitarian crisis of the twenty-first century to date would continue.

Jo stressed to her team that these global concerns would not dilute her commitment to local issues in Batley, since these had motivated her decision to stand for Parliament and she wanted to spend most of her time focusing on her constituents and how she could help them. She planned to increase her visits to local people's houses and community centres, as well as businesses, churches, mosques and schools, to make sure her constituents regarded her as accessible and aware of their needs.

Jo's deep immersion in local politics meant that she could spend more time with her parents. Gordon and Jean added a loft conversion to their bungalow in Roberttown so Jo could stay with them while she worked in the constituency. When I was travelling and Cuillin and Lejla joined her in Yorkshire she would leave the kids with her parents in the morning and then do a full day's work as an MP. She would arrive home in the evening, just as Gordon and Jean were reading bedtime stories. Cuillin and Lejla would jump out of bed, crying 'Mummy! Mummy!' excitedly, and Jo would roll around on the floor as all three of them laughed together. After she had tucked up the kids and kissed them goodnight, she always told her mum and dad that she felt these were the most important moments of her day.

Fazila had fuelled Jo's instinctive empathy for the lonely. In the first few weeks, amid the deluge of local casework that arrived for Jo to consider, Fazila was struck by the death of a constituent who had been completely isolated. Apart from her goddaughter, who lived in Halifax, the old lady had no one. The goddaughter tried to visit her at least once a month but she had her own family to look after, and a job. She emailed Jo's office to say that her godmother had been let down by the whole system in Batley and Spen.

'Is this a rare incident?' Jo asked.

Fazila began to tell Jo about her experiences at the RVS where she had encountered similar cases. Beyond the emotional impact of loneliness there were associated health issues. People who were lonely tended not to maintain a stable diet, and either overate or, more often, stopped feeding themselves properly. As a result, their physical health, and often mental state too, deteriorated amid the isolation.

'I would love to talk to some of the people you met,' Jo said to Fazila. And so Jo visited Mabel, a ninety-six-year-old woman who had been alone for a quarter of a century. Her husband had died when she was in her early seventies and she had no other family – she had been an only child, as had her husband, and they had not had children of their own. Mabel told Jo that, until she was ninety-two, she had coped well and done all her shopping. But as her mobility had diminished, it had become increasingly difficult and she had been forced to withdraw from ordinary life and rely on social services. Often her only visitors were her care workers. They did their best but they had little time to chat, as they had many other people to see, and Mabel had become more and more lonely.

Jo thought of her grandad Arthur and how even he had complained of loneliness towards the end of his life – despite regular visits from Gordon and Jean, Kim and Jo. She began to imagine the lives of her elderly constituents who had no families to help them.

Tackling loneliness at home, in Batley and Spen, was just as important to Jo as the global ramifications of the

Syrian crisis. She decided to make it her mission. She told me why as we drove through Batley one evening. She talked about Mabel and started to cry. Jo felt other people's pain as her own but channelled that feeling into action. She set about arranging meetings with Age Concern and the RVS, with commissioners of social care and GPs at local surgeries, as well as many elderly people in person. The lives of the threatened and the vulnerable, from Aleppo to Batley, were all deserving of compassion and care. Jo's ethos as an MP was already in place.

Politics, like real life, is littered with mistakes and regret. Jo's decision to nominate Jeremy Corbyn for the Labour leadership turned out to be a terrible error. When the first very short list of potential Labour candidates to succeed Ed Miliband emerged in late May 2015 it appeared there would be a choice between Andy Burnham and Yvette Cooper, whose politics were very similar. Jo liked both Andy and Yvette but she and her friend Stephen Kinnock worried that neither of them could overturn the Tory majority and that, in any case, there needed to be a wider field. She and Stephen wrote a joint letter to say that they would encourage other MPs to put their names forward in an attempt to diversify the leadership choices. If they did, Jo and Stephen said that they would nominate them to help them get on the ballot.

In the coming days a few other MPs entered the race and, as promised, Jo and Stephen nominated one of the new entrants, Mary Creagh, the MP for Wakefield. However, unable to get the required support, Mary then withdrew, which left them with a conundrum.

Jo felt deeply that having pledged to do something, she should follow through on it, but that would mean nominating Jeremy Corbyn, the one MP who was still in the race but struggling to get the required nominations. Jo knew Jeremy a little bit, and she liked him, but thought he would be a disaster for the party. Jo faced a dilemma. She decided that she would keep her word and nominate him, but also make it clear that she wouldn't vote for him. Her assumption, and mine, was that Corbyn had no chance of winning a leadership election. She backed Liz Kendall once the contest began.

It soon became apparent that the electoral college had been turned inside out by a sudden influx of new voters who had paid the £3 required to be able to vote in the selection. This new support from disaffected people to the left of a muddled Labour Party was decisive.

Jo and I were at the cottage, with the kids, on Saturday, 12 September 2015, when we heard the election results on the radio. I can still see us both holding our heads in our hands, and groaning, when the figures were confirmed. Kendall had won 4.46 per cent, Cooper 17.02 per cent, Burnham 19.04 per cent and Corbyn a staggering 59.48 per cent of votes.

Jeremy Corbyn was the new leader of the Labour Party.

Jo looked at me and said, with utter dismay, 'I can't believe it . . .' She felt personally culpable and thoroughly cursed her own naivety.

Three days earlier, on Wednesday, 9 September, Jo had offered a moment of contrasting clarity. During Prime Minister's Questions she stood up and faced David Cameron. This was in the immediate aftermath of the publication of the picture of Alan Kurdi, the three-year-old Syrian child whose body was washed up on a Greek beach. Jo was angry that the government had been so slow to offer sanctuary to children like Alan. It had just caved in to pressure to announce more places for vulnerable refugees, but it was Jo's view that the government was far behind the humanitarian sentiment of the country.

In a devastatingly short question she asked simply, 'Can the Prime Minister tell the House whether he thinks he has led public opinion on the refugee crisis or followed it?'

Cameron was taken aback. Red-faced, he fumbled for words. Jo didn't dislike him, in fact she thought he was one of the more sympathetic Tories and admired his protection of the aid budget, but she longed for politicians to play to the best instincts of the country and not our worst.

Cameron avoided the truth by trying to wriggle away from it, but he looked, and evidently felt, exposed. I have since read that the question had a significant impact on him. He had always approached the refugee problem politically whereas the prevailing public response to the picture of Alan Kurdi was rooted in a deeply human reaction. Suddenly Cameron was behind the curve. Jo had highlighted this and many MPs took note of her acumen.

The Spectator too – hardly a friend of Labour – wrote at the time: 'Bullseye. Or very nearly. Her plan of attack was exemplary. Take the burning issue of the day. Isolate the PM's main weakness. And expose it in a question so brief he has no time to think.'

Jo was a proud member of the Labour Party, but she wasn't a pack animal like some people in politics. She didn't grow up with political parents or immerse herself in student politics, so although she was Labour to the core she didn't think the party had a monopoly on ideas, or on righteousness. She approached each issue on its own merits and looked around to see who could help her create an impact. Jo's most important cross-party work was sparked by Syria and her desire to set up a new parliamentary group to increase scrutiny on the crisis. She had only been an MP for a few weeks when she approached Andrew Mitchell, the Conservative MP for Sutton Coldfield, to ask him if they could discuss issues of international development. They appeared to have little in common because Andrew was of a different generation, background and political persuasion. Jo didn't care. She had been impressed by the work he had done in international development, both in the Shadow Cabinet and as Secretary of State from May 2010 to September 2012. She recognised him as an intelligent man with whom she could make a difference.

It didn't matter to Jo, or to Andrew, that his party was in favour of military intervention in Syria while hers took the opposite stance. They resolved to work together and set up an all-party parliamentary group, the Friends of Syria, which they would co-chair as they took evidence from military commanders, diplomats and officials from the region.

'Jo might have been new to Westminster, but she led the way,' Andrew wrote after her death.

A lot of people in her situation would have been very reluctant to work with a wicked old Tory like me, but Jo never minded. During Commons debates about Syria, we would sit across the chamber exchanging text messages. She was utterly fearless. Last year [2015], we went to see the Russian ambassador in London, to give him a rollicking about the terrible way his country has behaved in Syria. He's a professional diplomat and a pretty tough case. But Jo got the better of him: it was her mixture of charm and steel. The best word I can think of for her is ballsy. The ambassador just didn't know what to make of her, and she left him looking quite discomforted.

As their friendship grew, Jo and Andrew formed a powerful alliance. On 10 October 2015, a Saturday that was spent at our cottage with Eloise and Tom and their children, Jo and I broke away from making cider with our friends to check the final version of the article that she and Andrew were set to publish in the *Observer* the following morning. We knew it would cause a mighty stir in both the Labour and Conservative parties. I thought it was an example of Jo's best work as, setting aside petty party politics, she and Andrew penned a powerful call to action on Syria. While most of the article focused on the humanitarian and diplomatic response, they didn't shy away from the more difficult military question: 'Some may think that a military component has no place in an ethical response to Syria. We completely disagree. It is not ethical to wish away the barrel bombs from the Syrian government when you have the capacity to stop them . . . Nor is it ethical to watch when villages are overrun by ISIS fighters, who make sex slaves of children and slaughter their fellow Muslims, when we have the capability to hold them back.'

As the piece was published, Shadow Cabinet member Diane Abbott responded on Twitter saying it was 'Sad' that Labour MPs wanted to support Cameron in bombing Syria. Jo was furious, not that Diane disagreed with her but that she appeared more interested in party politics than a serious discussion of how to address the worst conflict in a generation.

Two nights later, on Monday, 12 October, I put the kids to bed and then quietly opened the door to the boat to let in our neighbours. Dave and Anna were happy to babysit while I jumped on my bike and cycled hard to the House of Commons. I was sweating as I chained my bike to the railings and ran up to the Strangers' Gallery. It was just before 10 p.m. and Jo was about to make her first major parliamentary intervention as she opened the debate on 'Civilians in Syria'. She had worked hard on it, going through many iterations and testing different arguments. She was nervous because she wanted it to count, to shift the government – and her own party – from their slumber.

I sat in the gallery looking down at her as she gathered her thoughts. She looked up and I managed to catch her eye. Her face lit up. I had kept the fact that I was coming a surprise and I knew that my silent accompaniment and quiet pride would mean a lot to her. I felt very calm. I knew Jo was incredible; and she was ready.

At precisely 10 p.m., the MP for Batley and Spen was called to begin the debate. Jo stood up. Her voice, full of clarity and conviction, rang out as she delivered the finest speech of her life.

Every decade or so, the world is tested by a crisis so grave that it breaks the mould: one so horrific and inhumane that the response of politicians to it becomes emblematic of their generation – their moral leadership or cowardice, their reso-lution or incompetence. It is how history judges us. We have been tested by the Second World War, the genocide in Rwanda and the slaughter in Bosnia. I believe that Syria is our gener-ation's test. Will we step up to play our part in stopping the abject horror of the Syrian civil war and the spread of the modern-day fascism of ISIS, or will we step to one side, say that it is too complicated, and leave Iran, Russia, Assad and ISIS to turn the country into a graveyard? Whatever we decide will stay with us for ever, and I ask that each of us takes that responsibility personally.

Neither side of the House has a record to be proud of. Let me start with my party. One of the reasons it is such an honour to be standing on this side of the House is the deep pride I have in Labour's internationalist past. It is pride in the thousands of people from our movement who volunteered to fight tyranny alongside their fellow socialists and trade unionists in the Spanish civil war; pride in the leaders of our party – and Robin Cook in particular – who demanded action to stop the slaughter of Bosnian Muslims in Srebrenica and elsewhere, in the face of outrageous intransigence from the then Conservative government; and pride in the action we led in government to save countless lives in Kosovo and Sierra Leone. In recent years, however, that internationalism has been distorted, and now risks being jettisoned.

My heart sank in 2013 when, following President Assad's use of chemical weapons against civilians, we first voted against a military response and then supported taking military options off the table. Our failure to intervene to protect civilians left Assad at liberty to escalate the scale and the ferocity of his attacks on innocent Syrians in a desperate attempt to cling to power.

I understand where our reticence comes from. It comes from perhaps the darkest chapter in Labour's history, when we led this country to war in Iraq. Many members in all parts of the House have been scarred by that experience; but Syria is not Iraq. I opposed the war in Iraq from the beginning because I believed that the risk to civilian lives was too high, and their protection was never the central objective. I knew, as we all knew, that President George Bush was motivated not by the need to protect civilians, but by supposed weapons of mass destruction and a misguided view of the United States' strategic interest.

I marched against that war, and have marched against many others. Indeed, before I joined the House I was an aid worker for a decade with Oxfam. I have seen at first-hand the horror of war and its brutal impact on civilians. I have met ten-year-old former child soldiers with memories that no child should have to live with. I have sat down with Afghan elders with battle-weary eyes. I have held the hands of Darfuri women, gang-raped because no one was there to protect them. From that experience, I have the knowledge that there are times when the only way to protect civilians requires military force. I might wish it were not so, but it is.

The history of Iraq hangs over us all; but its legacy is awful enough without supplementing it with a new one of ignoring the slaughter in Syria. We must not let it cloud our judgement or allow us to lose sight of our moral compass while hundreds of thousands are killed and millions flee for their lives.

I shall now turn to the Conservative Party's record. For four years the government has categorically failed on Syria. The failure to develop and implement an effective strategy on Syria left this conflict free to create a horrendous European refugee crisis and provide a haven for the barbarism of ISIS to take root, allowed chemical weapons to be used unchallenged and emboldened Russia. Since the Prime Minister's mishandling of the 2013 Syria vote, the government has let this crisis fester on the 'too difficult to deal with' pile. There has been no credible strategy, nor courage, nor leadership; instead we have had chaos and incoherence. Indeed, it has been a masterclass in how not to do foreign policy and a stark lesson on what happens when we ignore a crisis of this magnitude. Britain – with our proud tradition in international affairs, our seat on the UN Security Council and one of the best diplomatic, humanitarian and military services in the world – has been a political pygmy in this crisis.

None of us has a proud history in this affair. But we must put party politics to one side and focus on what really matters – the protection of Syrian civilians.

Let us stop casting the humanitarian, diplomatic and military responses as mutually exclusive alternatives. They are not. If we are serious about addressing this crisis, we need to stop pretending that any one of them offers a panacea and instead weave these strands into a coherent strategy. Secondly, let us not be duped into believing that we need to make a choice between dealing with either Assad or ISIS. This may seem appealing, but it is not an option.

We must address both Assad and ISIS for two principal reasons. First, a sole focus on ISIS will not end the conflict and the threats to our interests. The Assad regime ignited, and continues to drive, the violence in Syria. This year alone, it has killed seven times more civilians than ISIS, so a strategy that only focuses on ISIS will not end the fighting or the threat to regional stability. It will not stem the tide of desperate refugees trying to get into Europe.

Secondly, a myopic focus on ISIS will not lead to its defeat. Assad is ISIS's biggest recruiting sergeant, and as long as his tyranny continues, so too will ISIS's terror. A sole focus on ISIS, while ignoring the regime's ongoing bombardment of civilians, risks strengthening the Jihadis' narrative, which is fuelled by the idea that the west is colluding with Shi'a forces in Tehran and Damascus in a crusade to subjugate Sunni Arabs. That is why we need urgently to develop a comprehensive and coherent strategy.

There are three core elements to such a strategy. First, the humanitarian aspect. Four years from the start of the conflict, there are now 240,000 dead – some credible estimates put the figure over 330,000 – and more than 12 million people in need of humanitarian assistance. The scale of the human disaster is breathtaking.

The UK's response to the refugee crisis has, to date, been woefully inadequate. Taking 20,000 refugees over five years is simply not good enough. Whether it is the response to the drownings in the Mediterranean or our offer to take Syrian refugees, the Prime Minister has been pushed into climbdown after climbdown, embarrassed into action by the humanity of the British public. It is time for him to lead, not follow.

But no matter what our humanitarian response is to this crisis, it cannot end the conflict. That is why we also need to invest far more in diplomatic efforts to find a political solution. This needs to be a much higher-level conversation . . . A credible political solution has to involve a transition to a new government that represents all Syrians and that enjoys sufficient trust and legitimacy that all but the delusional fanatics of ISIS will be willing to lower their guns and work together to rebuild their country. Russia's recent intervention makes the route to a political settlement more complicated but it does not change the necessity for one. A political solution is the only way to end the conflict between the regime and the opposition in Syria. Only when that conflict has ended can ISIS and other extremists allied to al-Qaeda be defeated.

The third element of the strategy has to be military. While

I do not believe that there is a purely military solution to this conflict, I do believe there will be a military component to any viable solution.

The threat from ISIS – to the region, to the west and to Syrian and Iraqi civilians – is real and growing. I do not believe it to be ethical to watch from the sidelines as Syrian villages are overrun by ISIS fighters who make sex slaves of children, terrorise minority groups and slaughter fellow Muslims. In addition, their call for individual sympathisers to attack westerners requires a robust response.

The estimated 20,000 foreign fighters in Syria and Iraq, many of whom hold western passports and can travel freely in Europe, present a serious threat to us in the UK. In addition, ISIS's spread to new havens in Libya, the Sinai peninsula, Afghanistan, Yemen, Nigeria and elsewhere convinces me of the need for active UK involvement – but only if that is part of a comprehensive strategy to protect civilians and end the conflict.

For moral reasons – and national self-interest – we can no longer afford to ignore Syria. Inaction will only see a growth in the number of Syrians killed, the number of refugees fleeing and the potential threat to British national security from ISIS. I urge all members to look to their party's best traditions and to think about the personal role that they can play to protect civilians in Syria and further afield.

The voices of Syrians have been absent from this debate for far too long. They have been asking for protection for years and no one has been listening. It is now time for us to listen and to act.

22

Batley and Westminster

Politics has always been a brutal business. It is not an arena for anyone easily hurt by words and insults. Jo knew that speaking out on Syria and, in particular, criticising the government and her own party would lead to a backlash. She wasn't surprised to be condemned as disloyal and treacherous, a warmonger or a defender of extremism, a disgrace and an idiot. There were even calls for her to be deselected by members of her own party in Batley and Spen.

Jo's toughest period as an MP, and the time when she suffered most abuse, coincided with the House of Commons vote in regard to military action being used against ISIS in Syria. On 2 December 2015, after a long debate, in which Hilary Benn spoke so well that he was applauded by both sides of the House, MPs had to vote for or against air-strikes being launched at ISIS targets. Benn's speech was such a restrained but powerful rebuttal of his own leader's stance – Corbyn was emphatic that all Labour MPs should vote against military action – that Jo felt even more conflicted.

The Syria vote was framed as a binary choice between two options, both of which ignored the catastrophic role of the Assad regime. Writing in the *Huffington Post*, Jo pointed out that the 'something must be done' brigade were understandably desperate to respond to the fascism of ISIS and the threat to the UK, but less inclined to reflect on the type of action that might be needed.

There's a danger of them falling into the trap of the man with a hammer who thinks everything is a nail. We need a nuanced approach not a one-tactic-fits-all plan. On the other hand there are the 'nothing can be done' sect who see military action as anathema in all circumstances, who view the role of Britain with suspicion and who trace back most if not all injustices in the world to UK imperialism. This depressing lack of sophistication airbrushes from history the role we played in cases such as Kosovo or Sierra Leone – where civilian protection was key – and fixates on Iraq as the sole frame.

Jo had decided on the hardest choice of all: to abstain from voting. It was a decision that would engender anger and derision from both opposing sides of a simplistic vote. Jo had agonised over it. She understood why some people were infuriated but she still believed it was the right thing to have done, as her article tried to demonstrate.

I've always thought abstaining on key debates was due to one of three things: a cowardly opt out designed to avoid accountability, a case of chronic and unacceptable indecision or the judgement to place political positioning over conviction.

So I have thought long and hard before deciding that I have no other choice. The reason is simple: I'm not against air-strikes in principle. In fact as part of an integrated strategy for Syria they are almost certainly a necessary part. But air-strikes are a tactic, not a strategy, and outside a strategy I fear they will fail.

The Prime Minister has compounded this for me by positioning the strategy as 'ISIS first', like we are picking from a menu of independent variables. First we'll deal with ISIS and then we'll come back to Assad. Wars don't work like this. Indeed, by refusing to tackle Assad's brutality we may actively alienate more of the Sunni population, driving them towards ISIS.

David Cameron and the Conservative government won the right to approve the motion for air-strikes against ISIS by 397 votes to 223. Sixty-six Labour MPs defied Jeremy Corbyn while eleven more, including Jo, abstained.

The reaction among certain members of the Labour Party in Batley and Spen was fierce. Amid stray calls for her deselection, others accused her of letting down the Muslim community or failing to have the courage to back her principles. When Jo met her most strident critics in local politics she soon calmed the mood and even succeeded in persuading some that she had good reason to abstain from the vote. She accepted the positive dialogue as a reminder that, during future moments of deep controversy, she should spend more time explaining her position to those who had selected her to represent them. The actual decision to abstain still seemed the most appropriate response to a limited vote in Parliament.

Ritual abuse of MPs can carry a sinister undertow. As we have seen with the increasing number of death and rape threats issued with nonchalant vehemence on social media, female MPs are a target for unhinged trolls. Jo's fate should be a stark reminder of how, in a world often desensitised to the consequences of language, words can still incite tragedy.

Jo grew accustomed to being vilified on the internet. All female MPs, and many male politicians too, are told to expect such vitriol. Jo tried to rise above it but there were occasions, in just over thirteen months as an MP, when she felt compelled to report a particularly threatening tweet or message on her Facebook page.

In March 2016, three months before her death, a man was cautioned by the police for the text messages he was sending Jo. He had no connection to her murderer but belonged more to that group, which is almost always made up of men, who find a perverse pleasure in verbally abusing women in public life.

The language used is brutally misogynistic. Jo's skin had been getting thicker but, unsurprisingly, the abuse sometimes wore her down. At first I encouraged her to ignore it, or shrug off the comments if she had read them, but then Jo showed me her Facebook and Twitter notifications. Alongside words like 'bitch' or 'slag' there was an incoherent anger and poisoned malice to many of the insults.

'I am so sorry,' I said to Jo when I read some of the messages. 'I had no idea it was this bad.'

We decided it would be best to keep those accounts off her phone and let her team manage her social media messages for a while. She still wrote her own tweets and Facebook postings but it was crucial for her sanity that Jo did not have to endure the bile on a daily basis.

As the husband of an MP I came to appreciate how difficult parliamentary life can be for female politicians. Beyond the abuse, there is often an unthinking sexism at work. One of the Labour councillors in Yorkshire said to her: 'Jo, I've seen you wear the same three outfits every time we've met. I think you should invest in some new clothes.' I don't think that particular person would have made such a comment to me about what I wore to meetings.

Jo didn't get upset or angry because she realised that some people belonged to a different generation and that there were more important issues to challenge, but she would often tell me how grating it felt.

She was genuinely irritated, however, by the absurd voting hours in the House of Commons. It was as if the British parliamentary system was designed to make life difficult for MPs who were parents, and especially those with young children. Jo could not understand why they insisted on carrying out a vote at ten thirty on a Monday night and at seven thirty the rest of the week. It was a relic of the era when being an MP was a part-time job that you did in the evenings after your main job. The Monday late-night sitting you could understand – as it gives MPs time to come back from their constituencies – but holding votes at seven thirty made it incredibly difficult to get home for kids' bedtimes.

Jo did everything she could to avoid missing bedtime. She would vote in her cycling gear and then jump on her bike and pedal as fast as she could to reach the boat in time to read a story. But she knew that not all MPs lived a fifteen-minute cycle ride away from the Houses of Parliament. It seemed crazy to her that voting could not take place during an ordinary working day. She had planned, in conjunction with other MPs, to campaign for a change in voting hours as a way of making Parliament more family-friendly.

Nonetheless, Jo loved working in Westminster, even when, while sitting in the House, listening to a debate or to Prime Minister's Questions, her phone would light up with a message.

Stop picking your nose. I'm watching you. xx

Kim always made Jo laugh with her random texts.

The joy of being home in Yorkshire, representing Batley and Spen, was deepened by the fact that it gave Jo a chance to see more of her mum and dad, Kim and Clare, and her old school friends such as Heidi and Louise. But her schedule was exhausting. Working in Westminster, looking after Cuillin and Lejla on the boat and spending the rest of the week in Yorkshire with her constituents meant that Jo's family and friends often saw her at her most chaotic and exasperating. Endless reserves of patience were required when she turned up late at her parents' place in a taxi with no money to pay for it, or offered to treat Kim and Clare to a Chinese takeaway to say thank you for having her to stay, only to be shocked that the delivery driver wouldn't accept a credit card.

Fazila Aswat had also learned to adapt. Jo was serious and effective in mapping out her political strategy – just as she was excellent in being a hardworking and highly visible MP who brought a humane touch to her dealings with her constituents. Fazila only needed to say a quiet word to Jo that an elderly man had had a knee operation or that a woman had lost her father to cancer, and Jo would offer the right words of support and comfort, while also taking time to send handwritten letters. Sometimes she would ask Fazila to post a box of House of Commons chocolates to a lonely constituent. It was Jo's way of letting people know that she was thinking of them.

She was less adept at looking after herself, however. She would dash straight from the school run to the train up to Batley, and work on the journey without thinking to buy any food. Jo would rush to her office, usually about fifteen minutes late, and as soon as she opened the door she would shout up the stairs: 'Hellooooo! It's me . . .'

'Hiya, Jo,' Fazila would answer. 'We're a little late.'

Fazila would have arranged a full day of appointments from 9.30 a.m. until almost 10 p.m., with a fifteen-minute leeway built into every meeting. Even if they made up time there would be points in the day when Jo extended a meeting because she had become so animated by the discussion. It would then be Fazila's task to phone the next person to apologise for running late and blame the traffic – rather than her brilliant but wayward boss.

'I'm starving,' was a familiar refrain from Jo.

At first, Fazila would ask Jo why she hadn't thought of buying a sandwich at King's Cross or Leeds stations. But after a few weeks, Fazila simply took to bringing Jo a Tupperware of food that was left over from her family meal the night before – or she made Jo a packed lunch while she did the same for her kids.

'This is so delicious,' Jo would exclaim between mouthfuls. 'How do you do it?'

Fazila understood that Jo was too busy thinking about the important stuff, the challenges and struggles of her work in Westminster and Batley, dealing with issues as diverse as Syria or bin-collections, therefore lunch and dinner were easily forgotten.

The Labour Party was divided and listing badly under Jeremy Corbyn. The May 2016 local elections should have been a chance for Labour to reinvigorate itself following the humiliating national vote a year earlier. Yet, rather than doing the usual opposition trick of drubbing the government locally after a year in power, Labour suffered a net loss of eighteen councillors. UKIP, led by Nigel Farage, gained twenty-five new councillors.

Jo felt compelled to speak out against Corbyn's weak leadership. Late on the afternoon following the election results, Friday, 6 May 2016, Jo and Neil Coyle, the MP for Bermondsey and Old Southwark, published a comment piece for the *Guardian* under their joint names. The *Guardian* used this headline: 'We nominated Jeremy Corbyn for the leadership. Now we regret it.'

> We helped put Corbyn on the ballot because we wanted a genuine debate within the Labour Party. We didn't expect to be debating things far from the priorities of most voters: unilateral nuclear disarmament, the Falkland Islands, the monarchy and all the rest. Important issues, perhaps, but not ones that swing elections. Why should we be surprised if people are turning their backs on a party that appears to have stopped talking about the things that are relevant to them?

While there were many who agreed with their opinion piece, Jo and Neil were also attacked as 'selfish careerists' and 'egotistical traitors'. Some of the online comments had to be removed because the language was too abusive or threatening.

Jo knew that one option was to join other MPs in asking for Corbyn to resign immediately, but she made the right decision to temper that approach and offer a more open-ended assessment. She liked Jeremy as a person, and shared many of his values, but was deeply worried about how his leadership was damaging the party. Labour could not function as a mere protest group. Jo had spent years working for NGOs and campaigning groups which, through persuasive advocacy, had tried to shape government decisions from the margins. The Labour Party's remit, however, is not to operate on the fringes of political life. Its task is to win power and influence society and the world beyond Parliament. Labour had to get back to being in a position to win elections.

Neil was pilloried for his honest belief. Yet Jo, presumably because she was a woman, suffered three times the contempt and rage. She expected that, and still believed that it was right to speak out. In addition, she felt a particular responsibility because of the fact that she had nominated Jeremy. She was tough, strong and well prepared for the fallout, having reached out to key people locally to let them know what she was thinking. Jo then drafted a letter to all Labour members in her constituency to explain why she had criticised the party's leader. She knew her letter might cause further animosity but she thought it was right to be open and clear with those she represented.

The draft was due to be checked and refined before Dan Howard, her campaign manager, distributed it. Dan and a colleague were fooling around in the Batley office the next afternoon. As a joke, Dan filled in the blank subject heading to Jo's email. He typed: *Why I Knifed Corbyn.*

To his horror, while reaching out to delete the bogus

title, Dan hit 'Send' by mistake. Before her reasoned explanation could be read, Labour members opened their email accounts to see that their MP had sent them a message with that outrageous heading.

As soon as he realised what he'd done, Dan called Jo, who was with the children and me on the boat at the time.

'Jo,' he said, his voice shaking, 'I've sent the wrong email.'

At first Jo thought that he had sent an earlier draft, which contained a few different words. But the blood drained from her face when Dan explained the title of the email he had sent.

'I'm sorry,' Dan kept repeating. 'I'm so sorry.'

Jo was distressed because, having been brave in voicing her true feelings, her honesty had been tainted by a bad joke gone wrong.

I didn't want Cuillin and Lejla to see their mum upset, so I diverted the kids and set them up with a video. Jo and I sat in the wheelhouse as she shook. She had readied herself for the attacks, taken a brave decision to speak out despite them and then her own team had put her in an impossible situation. I tried to be reassuring but I mostly just felt for her. I wrapped my arms around her. Jo lowered her head on to my chest and cried.

After a while, once she had wiped away most of the tears streaking her face, I tried to help her gain some perspective. We plotted a way out of the mess. The email would obviously hit the news later that day, so it was important that she and Dan contacted everyone who had been sent the mistakenly titled message.

Dan offered to resign on the spot; but he had just made a mistake. Instead of resigning, Jo told him, he could explain to members that the headline had been written by him – without her knowledge. Dan agreed immediately. He wrote a press statement in which he stressed that he was 'mortified' by his 'inappropriate' joke.

Jo still looked devastated as I prepared to take the kids to a party to give her some space. I hugged her again.

'I know it's bad,' I said, 'but look, nobody is going to jail. Nobody has died. And we can fix it.'

Jo kissed me. 'Yeah, Coxy,' she said with the first smile I had seen in an hour. 'You're right. It'll be okay . . .'

Life is full of mishaps – most of us have sent a mistaken email or texted the wrong person. Jo began to feel much better early the following week. She and Fazila had been working on the compulsory annual account for her first year in office. They had to divide the one-page summary into a bullet-point breakdown of her activities in Parliament and her constituency.

Jo Cox, MP for Batley and Spen, had founded and co-chaired the Friends of Syria group and spoken thirty-six times in Parliament on various issues relating to autism, the NHS, local hospitals, education, Syria, the refugee crisis and much more. She was the vice-chair of the all-party parliamentary group End Homelessness as well as those groups devoted to Palestine, Pakistan and Kashmir. Jo was on the Select Committee for Communities and Local Government and she had just set up the Loneliness

Commission to highlight the detrimental effect that loneliness has on thousands of people in the UK.

In Batley and Spen she had attended to 4,372 constituency cases ranging from immigration, housing, benefits, education, health and local hospital services to autism, age concern, sport, culture and changes in the postal service. Jo had held fortnightly surgeries and she and her assistants had corresponded with constituents and the wider public via email (in excess of 10,000 messages), phone calls, through her website and social media, and during visits to local schools, churches, mosques, community groups, charities and businesses.

Jo looked up from the stark details on her laptop screen and smiled at Fazila. 'We've done okay, haven't we?'

'You've done brilliantly, Jo,' Fazila replied.

Jo could still remember the disappointments and errors. She was sure she would get better and better as an MP, with every year she served.

'It's just the start,' Jo said. 'We've got so much more we need to do over the next four years.'

Jo wrote down her own assessment of how she had done in her first year. She asked me to read it at the time and it was characteristically honest. She concluded that she had been:

1. Principled (e.g. sticking to principles not politics and standing out on Syria)
2. Inexperienced (e.g. Jeremy Corbyn nomination)

3. Brave (to criticise Jeremy Corbyn and to stick to my position on Syria)
4. Focused (Syria, loneliness, constituency)
5. Stressed (worrying too much about small things, finding it hard to switch off, too dependent on BC and others)

And for the next year she wrote objectives for the type of politician she wanted to be:

1. Brave
2. Principled
3. Focused
4. Respected
5. Grounded

She wrote this list just after she had spoken out against Jeremy Corbyn's leadership, and she wrestled with the fact that standing up for her principles might result in her being de-selected or losing her seat in 2020. She concluded that this was a price worth paying.

I would be very sad on one level. I love the job in so many ways; love the link back to home, Mum and Dad and Kim; love the platform and all that can be achieved. But I really really don't want to be a politician for being a politician's sake. I don't want to be leader or PM. I need to be true to myself. I should just enjoy it while it lasts, not worry about the next election, be true to myself and the people I respect and admire. Put the kids and Brendan first, focus less on the micro and individual knob heads and more on the big picture.

In re-reading this self-assessment now, I am full of pride for Jo for sticking to her principles regardless of whether it would cost her the job she loved. I also know that history will remember Jo as she would like to be remembered: brave, principled, focused, respected and grounded.

23

The Last Day

– 15 June 2016 –

We were keen to have a more real home base in the constituency, rather than regularly driving Jo's parents loopy in the bungalow or crashing with Kim and Clare. Jo found a cottage to let in Cleckheaton that Sandra had once lived in, and she loved it. Invisible from the road, it was tucked away at the end of a pot-holed track behind rows of identikit houses that had been built in the 1980s. It was the quirkiest old farmer's cottage Jo could have dreamed up as her Yorkshire sanctuary, with dark beams and a narrow, twisty staircase. In one of the rooms upstairs there were bunk beds, with dinosaur duvets, for Cuillin and Lejla's visits. In pride of place was the old open fireplace with a cast-iron oven next to it heated by the burning embers. Jo furnished it for less than £500 from local second-hand shops.

The cottage was just a couple of minutes down the road from her old school friend Heidi Toulson-Bennett. Heidi would bring over her young son to play with Cuillin and

Lejla, and would arrive with food parcels for Jo on those week nights when she was alone. As sweet as the cottage looked, the fridge was usually empty if the kids weren't around.

Occasionally Jo, Kim, Heidi and Louise Woollard would get together as the old Heckmondwike Grammar gang reunited. But, mostly, Jo was so busy she would return to the cottage around 10 p.m. and fall into blissfully unbroken sleep. It gave her a chance to catch up on her rest without any little voices calling out to her when they woke.

In the morning, refreshed in a way that she did not always feel after a night on the boat, Jo would go for a run along the winding Yorkshire roads. When she got back to the cottage, glowing and happy, she would take a shower and rush around getting ready for work.

Everything had worked out beautifully. Jo had us, she had the boat on the river, she had our cottage in the woods, she had her long-cherished job in Westminster and Batley, near her family and oldest friends, and now she had a Yorkshire refuge. Life felt just about perfect.

A week before Jo was killed, on the evening of Thursday, 9 June 2016, Kim saw her sister for the last time. Jo rang the doorbell to Kim's house and, having kissed Clare hello, she walked into the front room. She knew Kim was still at work but she felt utterly at home with Clare.

'God, I'm knackered,' Jo said. 'Do you think I could borrow some clothes?'

Clare knew exactly what Jo would feel like wearing and

so, despite being on crutches after a foot operation, she found Jo a hoodie and a pair of Kim's pyjama bottoms.

'Oh, Clare,' Jo sighed in relief. 'Thank you.'

She took off her dress and stepped into her sister's comfy gear. Kim remembers coming home around eight o'clock and seeing Jo's dress draped over the back of a chair. Jo was curled up in a big armchair, her feet tucked under her, as she watched the final EU referendum debate on television. Angela Eagle, Amber Rudd and Nicola Sturgeon represented the Remain campaign, while Boris Johnson, Gisela Stuart and Andrea Leadsom spoke on behalf of the Leave team. Clare, meanwhile, was in the kitchen preparing something for Jo to eat.

Kim looked at Clare and the tiny figure of Jo, in her hoodie and PJs, absorbed by the political debate on TV.

'What the heck's going on here?' Kim asked.

Jo waved. 'Clare's so lovely. She's making me some tea. I'm starving.'

'And you're wearing my clothes,' Kim said. 'Job's a good 'un, Jo.'

Jo smiled. 'Sorry. I can change if you like . . .?'

'It's fine,' Kim said, rolling her eyes at Clare after yet another classic big-sister moment.

Kim gazed at her. Jo drove her crazy half the time but she was also doing incredible work. Two years earlier, when she told Kim and their parents that she was going to run for the Labour Party selection, they were emphatic. They would support her but they wanted to keep away from the political battleground. Instead, they would be there to pick Jo up, feed her, lend her clothes and give her a bed whenever she needed one. Kim, Gordon and Jean wanted to be low-key and private.

That night the sisters had a lovely evening together and Kim drove Jo back to her little cottage. They hugged and kissed as they said goodnight. Jo offered Kim the hoodie back, but her sister said it was fine – she could return it the next time they saw each other.

Jo spoke to her mum and dad for the last time on the night before she died. On Wednesday, 15 June, after she had left Cuillin, Lejla and me zipping along in our little dinghy between Bob Geldof and Nigel Farage on the Thames, Jo returned to Yorkshire. It was time for a final round of campaigning before the referendum and then her normal constituency surgeries. When she reached the cottage in Cleckheaton, Jo discovered the familiar sight of a bare fridge.

She called home just before 10 p.m. 'Hi Mum. I've just got in but I've got nothing to eat.'

'Now there's a surprise,' her mum joked. 'Okay, I'll send your father over. Do you want some soup or a pie, or something from the freezer?'

'No, no,' Jo said. 'It's late. Have you got a banana?'

'Yes, Jo,' Jean said patiently, 'And some custard . . . How about bananas and custard?'

'Ooooh, yes. Thanks, Mum, as always . . .'

They said goodnight to each other. Ten minutes later Jo's dad arrived.

'There you go, Joanne,' Gordon said as he handed over the bag. 'Two bananas, custard, bread, cheese and a pint of milk.'

Jo stood on her tiptoes to kiss her father. 'I love you, Dad.'

Thursday, 16 June was shaping up to be an ordinary if busy day for Jo and her team, aside from one factor: England were due to play Wales in their second group match of Euro 2016. It was a vital game. Kick-off was at 2 p.m. UK time and some horse-trading had gone on between Dathan and Fazila in Jo's Batley office over who was going to do the afternoon shift. It was supposed to be Dathan, but he desperately wanted to watch the football.

'Is there any chance we could swap shifts?' he asked Fazila.

'Talk about lastminute.com,' Fazila kidded Dathan. 'Go on then. If you pick up Jo and do the morning, I'll take over in the afternoon so you can watch the game.'

It was a bright, sunny morning when Dathan arrived at the cottage to collect a cheerful Jo. They headed for the first appointment of the day, a visit to a local school, and Dathan was entertained by her upbeat mood.

'I've not had a sleep like that for weeks because of the kids having chickenpox,' Jo said. 'I went out like a light. I feel incredible.'

Jo was remarkable that morning. After she had amused the pupils at their school assembly, she had been lovely with the elderly men and women she then met at a care home. Jo spent longer than usual talking to everyone.

There was a much more formal encounter next as Jo met with fifteen businessmen to discuss the impact of European manufacturing on their companies. The meeting was so constructive they ended it thirty-five minutes later than expected. She and Dathan needed to rush if they were to get back to the office in time for Fazila to drive Jo to Birstall by twelve forty-five.

'And you've got a big match to watch,' Jo teased Dathan. 'Come on, let's dash.'

Fazila and Sandra Major heard the office door finally open at 12.35 p.m. that afternoon.

'Hellooooo!' Jo shouted up the stairs. 'It's me . . .'

Sandra, who had become increasingly worried over how they were ever going to make it to Birstall on time, waited at the top of the stairs. 'You're late again, madam,' she said with comic seriousness.

'I know,' Jo said as she ran up the stairs. 'But I had such a fantastic morning.'

Fazila and Sandra smiled indulgently at her. Jo brought such energy and enthusiasm into their office that they could never be genuinely cross with her. Fazila, in particular, was used to it.

'We are a little late,' she confirmed. 'But I guess you're starving?'

'You know me too well.' Jo laughed.

'I made a pasta bake for the kids last night, and I did some extra for you,' Fazila said. She heated it up in the microwave as Jo got her papers ready. After the surgery in Birstall she was planning to spend the rest of the afternoon doing some referendum campaigning alongside university students.

Fazila presented Jo with a bowl of pasta. 'Amazing,' Jo said as she began eating. 'And delicious . . .'

Sandra was already walking downstairs. 'You can eat in the car, Jo. We've really got to get going.'

Jo's mouth was too full for her to answer but she opened her eyes even wider and nodded, continuing to eat as she went down the stairs.

Fazila had just locked the office when she realised she had forgotten a box of leaflets. 'Sorry,' she called to Sandra. 'One minute . . .'

By the time she had fetched the box, locked up again and reached the bottom of the stairs Fazila could hardly believe her eyes.

'You've wolfed it all down already?' she said in surprise.

'It was that good,' Jo replied as she placed the empty bowl and the fork on the bottom step. There was no time to waste.

Jo and Fazila kept chatting and, ironically, the topic of their discussion was security. That morning Fazila had considered how best they might increase the safety of their office, because for the previous few weeks she had been phoned repeatedly by a man who was very aggressive in his dislike of their political views. Jo had urged Fazila to contact the police and earlier that week the man had been sent a formal warning that he could no longer call their office.

'That's good,' Jo said as they reached Fazila's car.

Fazila opened the doors to her Vauxhall Astra. Sandra climbed in next to her and Jo sat in the back. While Fazila drove from Batley to Birstall, Sandra ran through the key points of each case Jo would talk over with her constituents. It was an excellent discussion, and Jo suggested that two of the cases could be pertinent to topics she was planning to raise in Parliament.

Birstall is usually a nightmare when it comes to parking, and Fazila exclaimed in relief when she saw an empty bay just outside Birstall Library. She looked at her watch: 12.50 p.m. They had been due to set up at 12.45 but Jo's first appointment with a constituent was at 1 p.m.

'Only five minutes late,' Fazila said. 'Incredible.'

The last minutes of Jo's life were a blur. Sandra and Jo got out of the car first. Fazila opened the back door to collect her handbag and the papers and leaflets. She had just pushed the door shut with her foot and locked the car when she saw a confusing sight.

Jo lay on the pavement. Sandra was near her, screaming.

Fazila stood for a moment in the road, on the driver's side of her car. She initially thought Jo must have fallen. Fazila took a step towards her.

She then saw a man standing over Jo. Fazila shouted at him. Hazy images of Cuillin and Lejla were in her head. 'She's got two little kids,' Fazila shouted. 'Get away from her.'

The man didn't even seem to notice Fazila. He stared down at Jo.

Sandra had just seen him shoot Jo at close range. It was then that Sandra began to scream, in horror, but also in the hope that people would help them.

The man had taken a knife out of his bag. He seemed oblivious to the screaming.

Sandra lashed out at him with her handbag, trying to stop him stabbing Jo. Fazila ran towards Jo, her raw instinct driving her on in an attempt to save her friend.

The murderer turned to Sandra and Fazila. He was ready to stab them too. Sandra could hear Jo's cry, weak but insistent.

'Get away!' Jo said to her friends. 'Get away you two! Let him hurt me – don't let him hurt you.'

The man turned back to Jo. He attacked her even more viciously. He then stood up and waved his knife at Sandra and an Asian man who had run to the scene. They were forced to back away.

Fazila crouched over Jo. 'I really need you to get up and run, Jo,' she said.

'I can't run, Fazila,' Jo said. 'I'm hurt.'

The killer had retreated but now he came back. There were gunshots. Jo slumped down. Blood seeped across the concrete.

Fazila turned cold. The man's voice chilled her even more. She heard him talking clearly.

'Britain first,' he said. 'Britain will always be first.'

Fazila can still hear his voice now, as the nightmare revisits her often. He sounded calm. There was no shock at what he had done to Jo, and no remorse.

The man then stabbed Bernard Carter-Kenny in the stomach. Bernard was a seventy-seven-year-old former miner, who had rushed to try to save Jo.

Fazila cradled Jo in her arms. Her hands and her clothes were covered in Jo's blood. There was blood everywhere. Jo could no longer speak. Fazila kept talking to her but she heard the panic in her own voice. She didn't know what to do and then, suddenly, Fazila remembered that she and Jo had met the chief inspector of West Yorkshire Police three weeks before. He had given both Fazila and Jo his number and said: 'If you have any security issues, ring me straight away.'

She can't remember how she managed it but, still holding Jo, Fazila phoned the chief inspector.

'I need your help,' she cried. 'I'm with Jo Cox and she's been shot and stabbed.'

'What?' the chief inspector said. 'Slow down. Tell me again.'

'Jo has been shot and stabbed and I need somebody to help me. Jo is in my arms.'

'Where are you?' the chief inspector asked.

'Outside Birstall Library.'

The chief inspector was normally based in Huddersfield, but that day he was in Batley. He must have acted with extraordinary speed because, within three or four minutes, the Special Branch arrived. They carried guns and moved quickly.

A young policewoman ran towards Fazila and Jo.

Fazila was crying. She had sensed Jo's last breath. Fazila

felt her sigh and then slip away into silence and stillness. She told me later that she was sure Jo had not suffered any pain after the initial attack. Now she was certain that her friend had just died in her arms. But she wanted to believe she was wrong.

Standing up, in a daze, Fazila knew they needed a miracle. She saw Sandra running towards her. Sandra told Fazila the paramedics had arrived.

'She's not breathing, Sandra,' Fazila said. 'Jo's not breathing.'

Sandra held her. 'There's nothing we can do,' she said softly. 'We must just pray.'

The paramedics began to work on Jo. They pumped her heart and tried to breathe life back into her.

Fazila's phone rang. She looked at my name on the screen.

'Brendan,' Fazila said helplessly as she answered.

'I've just heard Jo's been attacked,' I said. 'What happened?'

'Jo's been shot, and stabbed,' Fazila said. 'I'm so sorry, Brendan.'

'But she's going to be okay?'

'The paramedics are with her right now. I'll let you know as soon as we have news.'

Fazila remembers me calling again a few minutes later. 'What happened?' she recalls me asking. 'Who did this to Jo?'

'It was a man I've never seen before. A white man.'

'Is Jo going to live?'

'I don't know,' Fazila said. 'The paramedics are doing everything they can.'

There was silence on the phone. And then Fazila could hear the sound of me starting to run.

'I'm leaving London now,' I said. 'Call me Fazila. Please call me . . .'

The police told Fazila that the paramedics were taking Jo to Leeds General Infirmary. At least she could phone me again to tell me to head straight there as soon as I arrived.

Fazila was convinced that Jo was already dead, but the thought of me travelling alone on a train from London stopped her saying anything more. And, still, she clung to a thread of hope that the paramedics and doctors might save Jo.

She asked the police if she could go with Jo in the ambulance. 'I don't want her to be alone,' she said.

'It's all right, love,' a policeman said kindly. 'Her mum and dad are here now. You've had a big shock. But you are a key witness. We need you to come to the police station.'

Fazila turned to see Gordon and Jean running towards the ambulance, their faces etched with fear.

There had been less than an hour to kick-off when the phone rang in the Leadbeaters' bungalow. Jean had just brought in a pot of coffee and some biscuits as she and Gordon sat down to watch the build-up to England's game against Wales.

Dan Howard was in shock. But he managed to tell Jean that Jo had been shot in Birstall.

Gordon and Jean are calm people and they maintained their composure even as they rushed from the bungalow. They did not allow themselves to think of a fatal shooting. Jo might have been hit in the arm or leg.

They knew it was serious, however, as they drove down the Leeds Road. Police helicopters swarmed across the sky. Gordon and Jean knew they were flying towards Birstall, and Jo.

The traffic became increasingly clogged. They had only travelled halfway down the Leeds Road when it ground to a standstill.

Gordon pulled into a Texaco garage. He spoke to the man at the garage, explaining why he needed to leave his car, and then he and Jean ran the last half-mile, as fast as they could, into Birstall, heading towards the library in the town centre. They just wanted to see Jo, and hear that she was all right.

A policeman barred their way.

'We're Jo Cox's parents,' Gordon said.

The policeman took one look at their faces and cleared a path. They started to run again, filled with dread. There were police wherever they looked.

Suddenly, they saw Sandra Major. She was with a police-woman, and looked traumatised.

'Sandra,' Jean said. 'What happened?'

Sandra reached out for their hands. She could hardly speak.

'The paramedics are with Jo,' the policewoman told Gordon and Jean.

They began to run again. Two armed policemen stopped them. 'You can't go there,' one said.

'We're Jo Cox's mum and dad,' Gordon said. He was walking now, Jean at his side, making for the three yellow ambulances. The doors to one of them were open.

An armed-response inspector intercepted them and told them Jo was on her way to the LGI. An ambulance siren began to flash and scream.

'I'll take you to the hospital in my car,' the inspector said.

Other police cars led the way, and more followed, sirens blaring.

The policeman kept saying, 'I'm sorry, I'm so sorry. We'll get you there as soon as we can.'

'Don't worry,' Gordon said. 'I know you're all doing your best.'

Kim and Clare were at home, also getting ready for England vs Wales. Clare, a Liverpool supporter, had her foot up on a cushion, her crutches resting against the arm of the settee. Clare was flicking through social media when she shouted to Kim, 'Oh my God! Something's happened in Birstall – a shooting or stabbing.'

'Don't worry,' Kim said, knowing that Clare's aunt Theresa was a teacher in Birstall. 'It'll be all right.'

Clare nodded. 'I'm going to text Auntie Theresa – and make sure she's okay.'

'Good idea,' Kim said. She was about to jog down the

hill to pick up her car from the MOT centre. 'I'll be back before the game starts.'

Kim ran down the road, enjoying the mild summer afternoon. She was nearing the garage when her phone rang.

'Hi, Brendan,' she said, slowing to a stop.

'Kim,' I said. 'Jo's been attacked. Have you heard anything?'

Her voice was calm. I didn't know it then, not being able to see her, but Kim began to shake. She shook so hard she nearly dropped the phone.

Kim knew. It was Jo. She thought of Clare's words. A shooting. A stabbing.

I told Kim that Jo had been shot. Could she try to find out what happened?

Kim knew instantly, and with utter certainty, that Jo was dead. It was a horrible premonition, as well as a flashback to how tiny Jo had looked in Kim's hoodie and pyjama bottoms a week earlier. How could she survive a shooting, or a stabbing? Kim didn't say any of this to me. She promised instead to call me as soon as she knew more. I told her they were taking Jo to the LGI.

By the time she got to her car, Kim was shaking so violently she could barely call Clare, but she finally managed to bring up Clare's name.

'Clare, it's Jo who's been attacked,' Kim said. 'We've got to go to the LGI.'

'I'll be waiting outside the house,' Clare said. She had just seen Jo's name on social media.

They didn't talk much on the drive into Leeds. Kim was having to concentrate too hard to control her shaking.

'I wish I could drive for you,' Clare said, but her foot remained in plaster.

They drove past the main road leading into Birstall. It was sealed off; a scene of chaos.

Kim kept driving, totally focused, gripping the wheel hard.

Clare tried to boost Kim. 'She's going to be all right.'

Kim put her hand on Clare's leg. 'Clare,' she said quietly, 'it's not going to be all right.'

Kim knew. She said the words again. 'It's not going to be all right.'

They abandoned the car on a grass verge and gave the keys to an armed police officer as they hurried inside.

Gordon and Jean waited in a small room. They felt bereft. Kim and Jo's cousin, Richard Smith, was also with them. In an ironic twist of fate, Richard, a policeman, was on duty when the call came in to confirm that an MP had been shot.

'Who is it?' Richard asked. 'A man or a woman?'

'It's a man I think,' the officer told him. 'It's Jo someone . . .'

Richard had his own premonition. 'Jo Cox?'

'That's it,' the other policeman said. 'Do you know him?'

'She's my cousin.'

Richard could not take the case because he was family but he wanted to be with his aunt and uncle, and with Kim.

They stood around waiting. Eventually the inspector who had driven them to hospital opened the door.

He looked at them and shook his head. 'You know what I'm going to say . . .'

Clare and Kim walked into the room just moments later. Kim reached out to hug both her mum and her dad. They were all crying.

The inspector said how sorry he felt for them. Jo had died before she even reached the LGI.

Rachel Reeves, the MP for Leeds West and another friend of Jo's, ran down the corridor. 'How is she? Is Jo okay?'

They told Rachel. The inspector then took Kim to one side. Could she call all the next of kin? The news would soon get out. It would be best if close family heard it from her.

Kim nodded. She knew I was waiting to hear from her. She slipped out of the room.

Standing in an empty hospital corridor, Kim took out her phone. It was the hardest phone call of her life.

The train from King's Cross to Leeds sped through the English countryside. I sat in numbed silence, staring out of the window. The world had become a green blur.

My phone lit up again. I looked at the screen. *Kim.*

There was a pause, and then I heard Kim's familiar voice. 'I'm sorry, Brendan. She's not made it . . .'

Jo's many friends heard the news in different ways. Louise Woodall, a fervent Huddersfield Town fan, was at her brother's house to watch the football. Five minutes before kick-off, Clare called. At that point, while the football played out in silence on the screen, and Louise paced around her brother's house, there was still hope.

That hope died when Kim called. The old Heckmondwike Grammar gang had shattered.

Louise drove to Heidi's house. They opened a bottle of wine, for Jo, and drank a couple of glasses in memory of her. Jo was all over the news. Heidi and Louise stared at their friend on the television screen. Jo, as always, was smiling.

Suzy Sumner, one of Jo's many great friends from Brussels, was back in England on a brief work trip. She was in an office in Manchester when her colleague looked up from his laptop and said, 'An MP has been shot and stabbed.'

'Oh no,' Suzy exclaimed. 'Who?'

The man looked at his screen. 'Jo Cox.'

Suzy held on to the desk.

'Jo Cox?' she repeated. 'Jo's my friend.'

The man opposite her was mortified. Suzy looked down. Her phone was vibrating.

'Eloise?'

Eloise Todd had just spoken to me.

People crowded around laptops as they waited. They tried to comfort Suzy, who kept hoping.

The news finally broke on television. *Jo Cox, the Labour MP, is dead.*

Suzy walked outside, just as the heavens opened above

Manchester. It rained heavily for forty minutes. To Suzy, it felt apocalyptic. This was the world without Jo.

In Geneva, Sonia Vila-Hopkins, who had started up Oxfam International's office with Jo, was about to finish work at Unicef. She had been offline all afternoon, so was shocked when she turned on her Facebook page. A good friend of her and Jo lived in Cambodia and had posted a photograph of Jo, alongside a report of the attack.

'Sonia,' she wrote, 'have you seen this terrible news?'

Sonia stared at the screen in horror. She and her family had not been back in Europe for long, after living in Egypt, Indonesia and Morocco for the previous ten years. Sonia had been shocked by how much Europe had changed. People seemed more pessimistic and angry. Now her vision of Europe had been shaken for ever.

Jo's Cambridge gang, her Social and Political Science friends from Pembroke College, met up at the Corinthia Hotel, Whitehall Place, London, in the hours following her death. Sarah Hamilton, Jo's best friend, joined Steve Morris, Josh Blackburn (Jo's partner in her most serious relationship in the years before she met me) and Robin Lawrence, who had lived with her in London.

In shock and disbelief they shared heartfelt memories of Jo while they had a few drinks in her honour. It was difficult to get everyone together as often as they wanted to, so it would have been a great evening – had they not been totally grief-stricken. Sarah was devastated as Jo had meant so much to her.

Eventually, Sarah and Steve climbed into the back of a

black taxi after they had hugged Josh and Robin. The cab rumbled along Whitehall towards Parliament Square. They stared out of the window and saw how, earlier, people had gathered together spontaneously in a candle-lit vigil.

'Can you see?' Steve said to Sarah.

A large picture of Jo had been placed on the grass facing the House of Commons. Surrounded by candles, Jo's face smiled out at them.

The taxi drove on, with Jo's friends lost in their memories and, also, in wonder at how she had affected people so deeply. Jo had become more than just their friend. She now belonged, in death, to the whole world.

24
Love

Our boat is like a steel cradle that rocks from side to side with the changing tide. Sometimes, when a larger boat cruises down the river, the water rises more dramatically. It makes my mum and a few friends feel queasy. *Ederlezi* is rarely still. Like the river, like all our lives, she keeps moving, usually gently but, occasionally, with tumult and upset.

Cuillin, Lejla and I still love living here, even though their bedroom is so tiny it actually resembles a medium-sized cupboard. Cuillin said to me the other day that he would quite like a bedroom in which he can stand up. I agreed. I told him his mum and I had always known that the time would come for us to live on a bigger boat, one where he and Lejla could each have a cabin of their own.

A few days ago I sat them down at the table. It's the same wooden table where Jo and I spent numerous days and nights planning our next series of adventures and challenges. I told Cuillin and Lejla it was time for one of our family meetings; they've always loved a family

321

meeting. When we spent a lot of time in Gordon and Jean's bungalow while Jo was chasing her selection and eventual election as the MP for Batley, we amused the grandparents with the regularity of these meetings.

'So, kids,' I said, 'should we think about getting a new boat now? A bigger one?'

'No,' Lejla said firmly.

'No,' Cuillin agreed. 'Not yet.'

An idea that had sounded exciting a few days before suddenly seemed unattractive.

'Are you sure?' I asked. 'It would be nice to stand up in your bedroom, wouldn't it?'

'Yeah,' Cuillin said. 'But I don't want to leave her yet.'

'We want to sleep next to each other,' Lejla said, carrying the vote.

I looked at them, my two children aged six and four, and nodded. Wherever we look, beyond all the kids' toys and books, and my work, we see Jo, their mum, etched into every inch of our home. Jo turned this boat into our refuge; it still comforts us. The day will come when the needs of the kids demand the move that Jo and I were already planning, but not quite yet.

Nine months have passed since Jo's death. I still feel like a walking wound. The pain is deep and gaping. I remind myself that it's normal for me to feel this way. It's natural – or at least as natural as life can feel when your wife, and the mother of your children, has been murdered. I am allowed to feel utterly bereft.

I haven't stopped since Jo died, which is why I feel shattered. It also explains why my family and friends worry that I am doing too much. Alongside looking after the kids and writing this book, I have been working to contribute to the fight against xenophobia and hatred that seem to be rearing their ugly heads in a way that hasn't been seen since the 1930s. Jo was always at the centre of my thinking on how we might bring communities back together again, in the face of such divisive forces; we tested every idea and insight on each other. Every mountain we walked down, we would debate what was really going on. Most evenings, we would talk about fresh approaches. Jo is still at the forefront of all that, but now she is a silent inspiration.

And I know that her example motivates others too. Those who work on the Loneliness Commission in her name or the initiative that urges Britain to stand up for civilians threatened by war.

By the time this book is published, I hope millions of people in Britain will have marked the first anniversary of Jo's death with the Great Get Together, a series of street parties, bake-offs, barbecues, picnics and 100,000 other planned events all over the country.

For me, the weekend will be an opportunity to remember Jo in the style in which she lived: full of fun and with a zest for life. But for the country, I hope that it will mark a coming together again. The prevailing media narrative in recent years has been one of division and discord but I don't think that is the reality for most people. Brexit, the referendum on Scottish independence, elections – they all divide us, but for most of us they don't dominate who we are and they don't stop us from coming together to form a wonderful country full of kind and compassionate people. It was Jo's sense of community that drove her into politics, and I know she would love it if her death helped in some small way to bring communities back together again. I think we're at a moment where the country is crying out for a sense of togetherness; we're sick of division.

That sense of togetherness is what gets us all through difficult times. When I saw the news of the Westminster attack on 22 March, it immediately brought back the day of Jo's death. The same unanswered questions, the same frenetic media buzz and social media speculation. I felt ill. I felt for the families who were about to get a phone call that would shatter their lives for ever. I felt lost, in my own grief and in anticipation of theirs. I wanted to do something but felt helpless. I saw the media feeding frenzy and the sick voices out to exploit tragedy for their own ends. I felt compelled to say something.

When I spoke to the BBC the following morning, what I wanted more than anything was to encourage the media to keep the focus on the victims and the heroes of that day, not the man who had committed this vile act. I knew that the families waking up that day – if they were anything like me – couldn't care less about the man who killed their relative. Their thoughts would be filled with their loved ones: PC Keith Palmer, Aysha Frade, Kurt Cochran, Leslie Rhodes (and later Andreea Cristea) – and I wanted ours to be with them.

I also wanted us to deny notoriety to the person who did it. We know that one of the reasons extremists commit these acts is to try to gain fame, and I think we have a duty not to give it to them.

Finally, I wanted to encourage us to fight terrorism together. I made the point that the attacker was no more representative of British Muslims than the man who killed Jo was representative of people from Yorkshire. He was an extremist and should be condemned as such. It is my belief that the only way that terrorists can win is by turning us against ourselves, and the only way that we will defeat them is if we act together.

Afterwards, I was amazed most by how united the country felt in the face of these attempts to divide us. The British public have wised up to the terrorists' tactics, and they have no time for far-right extremists, either. They mourned the victims but refused to show fear. They were angry but remained united. They were committed to fighting terrorism but refused to blame any particular community. I was immensely proud of our capital and of our country, while devastated for the families involved.

Jo's spirit and her sheer joy are everywhere I look, whether it's here on *Ederlezi*, at the cottage or, most of all, in the characters and faces of Cuillin and Lejla. It is also here, with the kids, that I feel her absence most acutely.

Every Thursday morning on the boat, when Cuillin bursts into my bedroom at 5 a.m., I think of Jo. The bed is empty and I miss the way her leg would have crossed mine as she groaned at being woken so early. But Jo would have loved the fact that Cuillin is excited at five o'clock on a Thursday morning – it's only twelve hours until Beavers starts and he wants to run through which badges he might go for next.

I gaze at Lejla, too, and I see a tiny Jo. She looks so like her mum that, at the celebration of Jo's life in 2016, Lejla asked me why I'd pasted a photograph of her on a wall of remembrance.

'That's not you, Ledgie,' I explained. 'That's Mummy . . . when she was a little girl.'

Gordon and Jean see Lejla's likeness to Jo even more than I do. It helps them, in their searing pain, to sense Jo in their grandchildren. To witness the death of your own child is awful, but Gordon and Jean have been remarkably brave and positive. They love looking after Cuillin and Lejla; and, with Kim and Clare, they are deeply involved in the Great Get Together and More In Common initiatives in Yorkshire.

Life has buffeted them, though. The morning after the trial verdict, Jean woke up to find that she had lost the sight in one eye. Even today her vision in that eye is badly blurred. It is a consequence of all the stress they have suffered.

The Tuesday after the trial, between Jean's doctor and hospital appointments, they were driving at a steady 25 mph when a car came out of a side street and smashed straight into them. On a bright sunny day the woman who had driven into them had been temporarily blinded.

Gordon and Jean's car was a write-off but, miraculously, they were shaken rather than hurt.

The woman who had hit them kept saying, 'I'm sorry, I'm sorry.'

Jean eventually put her hand on the woman's arm. 'Don't worry. Worse things have happened. We're Jo Cox's parents.'

The woman felt even more upset, but Gordon and Jean reassured her. 'It really is all right,' Gordon said. 'After the last few months this is nothing.'

When Cuillin and Lejla stay with their grandparents now, Gordon and Jean sleep upstairs, to be close to the children. Jo's parents find it very difficult to lie in their daughter's old bed, knowing that she should be in their place. But they are also consoled and strengthened by the fact that Jo has left them with two wonderful grandchildren who give them so much pleasure and love.

My parents, Gordon and Sheila, feel Jo's death as deeply as if she had been their own daughter. They come to London once a week to look after Cuillin and Lejla and visit us often at the cottage, as do Stacia and Andrew and their three kids. It's a great comfort for me to have them around.

The cottage is also visited by our many friends who have supported me and the kids with enormous love and generosity. We all feel Jo's presence especially strongly at the cottage because, as she told us, it was here that she spent the happiest days of her life.

There is pain, too, in my certainty that even happier

days awaited Jo, and us, had her life not been ended by savagery. We had so much to look forward to as a family while, in her work as an MP, she had just begun to bloom.

At least she died doing the work that she loved. As the Member of Parliament for Batley and Spen, she felt fulfilled and driven.

Jo's younger sister, Kim, has done a huge amount over the last nine months. From speaking at the commemoration in Batley, on what was meant to have been her sister's forty-second birthday, to helping Labour's Rachel Reeves and the Conservatives' Seema Kennedy launch the Loneliness Commission, Kim has spoken beautifully about the empathy, inclusivity, kindness and tolerance that defined Jo. She has become an increasingly assured leader of all we are trying to do with Jo's work in Yorkshire. I went to speak at an event that Kim had organised in Batley recently, and it was one of the hardest events I have done yet. I was totally overwhelmed by the love of Jo's community and by how proud Jo would have been of Kim.

Cuillin, Lejla and I talk about Jo every day. At night I tell them another Mummy story, or I relive one of the adventures Jo and I had in Cuba or Romania, Vietnam or Bosnia.

It's hard for me when their tiny room is dark. I sit alone here at the table, writing or working. I wish I could push the laptop aside and see a laughing Jo as I tell her that Cuillin and Lejla started hip-hop dance classes last month. Jo would have loved hearing about them doing their very amusing robot dance – and she would have loved being there as a mum.

I want to tell Jo about progress on the project I continue to work on with determination, to tackle xenophobia in Europe and the US. This is work she was integral to when I started it months before she died. It sometimes feels like a heavy burden, doing all this on top of everything else we are trying to create in Jo's name. But it feels more important and more relevant than ever.

I am still in the very early stages of my own grief. I don't like to talk to people about it too much; I feel self-conscious, and it feels unfair and pointless to burden others with my own pain. Even with counsellors, I would rather focus on the kids. Instead, I try to deal with it by writing about Jo and by talking about her with the kids. I cry with them and I cry alone in the days when I am on the boat by myself. I cry so much that the skin around my eyes has become sore and cracked. At night I try to think of other things in order to sleep – exhaustion and wine help. But when the kids wake me in the night, I feel the void and my mind whirls with loss. In the early days the shock, practicalities and desire to protect my children put me on autopilot. As the months have passed, I have found it harder. The permanence of Jo's absence I still find hard to comprehend, and grief hits me in vicious waves when I least expect it. But I am also defiant. My kids will still live extraordinary lives full of love and adventure as Jo would have wanted. We will be a close and loving family full of joy and fun. I will not let her voice be silenced.

In the immediate aftermath of Jo's death, even in the first dizzying and sickening hours of trying to understand what had happened, I made a promise. It was a vow to myself, and to Jo, that I would take on the hatred that killed her – and I will channel my pain into fighting it and building closer communities. I always want to honour Jo's memory by striving to find ways that accentuate, as she said, that we have far more in common than anything that might otherwise divide us. We have begun that process; and we will always try to maintain and deepen its impact.

Cuillin, Lejla and I have not started climbing any Munros together but we will one day; and at every summit we will bring out their mum's mountain-climbing hat and wave it in celebration. I will, I hope, many years from now, climb my 282nd and last Munro. The memory of Jo will rise up yet again, no matter how old I might be by then.

There is some comfort to my family and friends in the way that an act driven by hatred unleashed an outpouring of love around the world. A murder that was meant to cause nothing but devastation and division has led to compassion and unity. A woman so loved by those of us who knew her well is now valued by millions who had not even heard of her a year ago. A lost and lone man wanted to silence Jo Cox for ever. He took her from us but, in so doing, he ensured that Jo's voice, in the wake of her death, has been heard more clearly than ever before.

It's quiet on the boat now. Even if I have not yet reached peace with my grief and loss, I feel calm.

On the table in front of me there are many books of

condolence, one heartfelt letter following another, as close friends and even people who had never met Jo wrote to me, Cuillin and Lejla about how she had touched them. I am struck again by how, rather than lingering over the cruelty of her death or our sadness, people found the right note. They have written about how Jo made them laugh or, sometimes, drove them mad and, more often, thrilled and inspired them.

That love shines out of Jo as I move from the letters to the photographs of her. In practically every picture she is smiling, often laughing, as if to remind me how lucky I was to spend the last ten years of Jo's life at her side. Jo didn't quite get to spend a full forty-two years on earth. But in her 41 years and 360 days she loved so deeply, so intensely and happily, that she crammed more into her life than anyone I've ever met.

Now, in the months and the years that will follow her death, it seems fitting that her memory remains vivid. It will keep flowing, ebbing and rising at different times, like the waters of this mighty old river on which Jo and I spent so many years together. Jo's memory, and the meaning of her beautiful life, will be sustained by hope and, most of all, by love.

At the age of thirty-eight I have finally learned to drive. I managed to pass my test at the first attempt in December 2016. Jo would have been proud of me, but she would also have said, 'It's about bloody time, Coxy!'

My driving licence had been one of the staple features

on the hundreds of 'To Do' lists Jo and I wrote over the years. Coxy learning to drive is up there with the recurring ambitions of recent years – alongside having fun with Cuillin and Lejla, Jo helping the people of Batley and Spen, doing work on the cottage, tackling Bashar al-Assad and Vladmir Putin over Syria and making gooseberry jam and elderflower champagne. Assad and Putin escaped Jo. But she achieved so much of what she aimed to do in life. And, at last, I've got a driving licence. It's off the list.

I now regularly pile the kids into the back of the car and drive to the cottage. The first time, my best friend Will joined us. I had never driven on a motorway and he was there to watch over me, and also to entertain the kids as I concentrated hard.

Driving is much easier now. Real life is still hard. But it always helps Cuillin, Lejla and me to come down to the cottage. We feel closer to Jo as soon as we reach the valley. I still experience pain as we walk down the hill, without Jo, but the view is so breathtaking that our spirits are always raised.

Each time we arrive during this first spring of our lives without their mum, the kids crane their necks eagerly to see which new flowers of Jo's might have grown since we were last there. The garden outside Beater's Barn becomes prettier and filled with more colourful life every time. Around her grave sit hyacinths, daffodils and – somewhat incongruously – wild garlic. The kids go down to talk to their mum and tell her how much they love her. They know that although she is not with us, she is for ever in their hearts and their heads, hardwired into the very essence of who they are.

In April, during the Easter holidays, I am taking the children to Kenya to see some old friends. They will look after the kids on the couple of days when I have to work; but the rest of the two weeks will see Cuillin, Lejla and me together on holiday in a glorious country. This will be their first trip to Africa. How Jo would have loved to have been with us on this adventure – but, as Cuillin promises in his song for Jo, 'we'll carry her in our hearts' and 'we will not leave her behind'.

The kids are incredibly excited and, sometimes, I have to remind them that Africa is more about the people than the wild animals we will also see. They listen seriously and they nod. I know they understand. But I, too, am excited at the prospect of going out into the bush with them and seeing an African elephant or a lion, a cheetah or a puff adder. It will be special to be back in Africa again, a continent that meant so much to Jo.

I must be feeling stronger because, at the cottage, I found myself writing a 'To Do' list. Jo and I would have compiled dozens over the last nine months had she still been alive; but at least I have started again. My list is very boring compared to those written by Cuillin and Lejla. Jo would have rolled her eyes at its tedium. A list containing 'Find an accountant', 'MOT', 'Supermarket' and 'Insurance' has no zing of adventure.

Lejla wrote her much more impressive list with my help as her writing and spelling are still a little wonky:

1) *Go to cottage*
2) *Play with Cuillin*
3) *Swimming*
4) *Treehouse*
5) *Eat pancakes*
6) *Kenya*
7) *Go to different countries*
8) *Thinking of Mummy*

Cuillin wrote his own 'To Do' list without any help:

1) *Beavers*
2) *Keny*
3) *Tree Hows*
4) *Bosnia*
5) *School*
6) *Cotagge*
7) *Bom fire*
8) *Sum party*
9) *Meet Bear Grils – scout man*
10) *Remebring Mummy*

His spelling, I think, is pretty good for a six-year-old, and his writing is already clearer than mine. More importantly, Cuillin and Lejla's lists lift me. They echo with the spirit of Jo and our family. I am looking forward to writing a proper 'To Do' list soon. I will draw up one with the kids. But, for now, it's enough just to be here with them at the cottage and to look at their own aims, hopes and promises. They make me smile and they fill me up, all over again, with pride, hope and love.

334

The Jo Cox Foundation

After the shock of Jo's murder, her friends and family were determined that her values and the causes she championed should live on. And so, the Jo Cox Foundation was born. Inspired by Jo, it set out to work for a kinder, more compassionate society where every individual has a sense of belonging and where stronger communities help push all forms of extremism to the margins. Jo's words in her maiden speech provide the guiding principle – that we are "far more united and have far more in common than that which divides us".

In an effort to capture her spirit and energy, JCF took up her challenge that nobody in this country should live a lonely life forgotten by the rest of us. The Jo Cox Loneliness Commission, chaired by two MPs, one Labour and one Conservative, Rachel Reeves and Seema Kennedy, produced its ground-breaking report at the end of 2017. Its recommendations resulted in the UK Government appointing the world's first Minister for Loneliness, publishing the first cross-Government strategy and a significant investment of £20 million into the issue.

The Foundation went on to establish three core ambitions: building strong communities, a better public life and a fairer world.

The flagship campaign, The Great Get Together, was launched in 2017. A year to the day since Jo was killed, people came together across the nation to embrace Jo's 'more in common' message and celebrate their local communities. The Great Get Together now takes place annually in June over Jo's birthday weekend. Millions of people have taken part, bringing people together, uniting communities and tackling loneliness.

Since 2020, The Jo Cox Foundation has been developing this powerful annual 'moment' into a year-round 'movement' of community action. Modelled on the very successful 'More in Common Batley & Spen' in Jo's hometown, this growing network consists of regional More in Common groups of volunteers across the UK, working hard to bring people together, tackle community issues and promote Jo's powerful humanitarian message of unity.

The Foundation has always worked closely with other organisations that share its aims and values. In response to the Covid-19 pandemic, the Connection Coalition was set up. In the space of a year, the Coalition welcomed 900 member organisations working with a diverse range of communities in the UK. All are united by their commitment to bring people together, promote the power of human connection and tackle loneliness.

The second stream of work, building 'a better public life', focuses on reducing abuse and intimidation and facilitating political participation, particularly of women and those from minority backgrounds at increased risk of abuse. Abuse knows no political boundaries and tackling intimidation is a cross party issue. Working closely with the Committee on Standards in Public Life, JCF helped draw up a Joint Statement on the conduct of party members. This is an ongoing piece of work, but so far almost all political parties have signed up to the standard.

The fairer world workstream builds on Jo's extensive career as a humanitarian in the aid sector and her advocacy efforts on the Responsibility to Protect. The Foreign, Commonwealth & Development Office (formerly the Department for International Development) agreed to fund the Jo Cox Memorial Grants in 2018. As a result, £10 million of UK Aid is currently providing support to 19 international projects themed on two areas Jo felt passionately about: women's empowerment and building resilient communities to combat identity-based violence. The Foundation believes that even at a time of straitened public finances this work deserves to be continued.

Acknowledgements

The acknowledgments have always been one of my favourite sections of a book. I guess because they let you see under the hood and get a sense of the dynamics that led to the writing.

I've also been looking forward to writing this bit because there are so many thank yous I want to put on record. I've tried to keep them relevant, but for a book like this the line is very fluid and I hope you'll forgive me where I overstep it.

First, of course, to Cuillin and Lejla. Our brave, loving and kind children. Without them I wouldn't have been able to write the book because I wouldn't have seen the point. Throughout the last year Cuillin and Lejla have kept me sane, given me strength and reciprocated unconditional love. They have also kept me very busy. We have protected each other, held each other and found a new level of love. The times I struggle most are when I'm not with them. They embody so much of their mum's character: her fearlessness, joy in living life, love and kindness. They have helped choose the stories that went into the book and, of

339

course, they created most of our best memories. I love you both infinitely.

Also to my wider family: my mum and dad, Sheila and Gordon, who have always been such loving parents and who adopted Jo as their own. They have changed their lives in the last year to help us continue to live ours, another act of supreme generosity in two lives defined by service, compassion and love. To my sister Stacia and her husband Andrew who were Jo's and my role models as parents, and whose example we constantly tried to emulate. They too – together with their glorious children Joseph, Lucas and Henry – have been there when we needed them most, with love, reassurance and practical support.

And, of course, to Jo's parents, Gordon and Jean, for raising an outstanding human being. Thank you both, and also to Kim and Clare, for your love for me, Cuillin and Lejla and all that you have done since Jo's death to take forward her values. She would be incredibly proud of you and thankful for the ongoing role that you will play as Cuillin and Lejla grow up.

Thank you to all those who contributed to the writing process in different ways, from dragging up old documents to reviewing various drafts: Mum, Dad, Stacia, Andrew, Gordon, Jean, Kim, Clare, Heidi, Louise, Nick, Mabel, Gemma, Ben, Sandra, Fazila, Tim, Eloise, Kirsty, Anthony, Iona, Steve, Sarah, Will, Lance, Dan, Sonia and Jane. If there are any remaining mistakes, I can probably find one of them to blame. On a more serious note, your improvements, ideas and insights are the best bits of the book. Thank you.

More professionally, thank you again to Don McRae, without whom I couldn't have written this. Or if I had done, it would have been unreadable. You helped work miracles and pull something together that I hope does Jo some justice. Thank you to the team at Two Roads, Nick Davies, Emma Knight, Helen Coyle, Amanda Jones, Alasdair Oliver, Caroline Westmore and Kim Whyte, but especially to Lisa Highton, our editor, who worked patiently, diligently and calmly despite the brutal timeline we were signed up to. Right from the start Lisa was hugely professional but also personally committed to the mission of the book. Thank you, too, to Karolina Sutton who guided me in the process and helped find a publisher who would do justice to Jo's story; thank you for your advice and guidance throughout.

I also want to place on record my thanks to the wider British public, and especially to our communities in Batley and Spen and on the mooring. The compassion, kindness and generosity of the public and our own neighbours has left our faith in human nature strengthened, not weakened, despite all that has happened in the last year.

Finally, thank you to Jo. The love of my life. The only person I ever met who I wanted to spend the rest of my life with. Thank you for giving me the best of times and for inspiring all of us with who you were. I miss your energy, love and enthusiasm every day – but I am so thankful to have had you in my life. I will fight for what you stood for every day of my life and I will love our children with every breath in my body.

Illustration Credits

Most of the photographs are reproduced courtesy of Jo Cox's family. Additional sources: Alamy: 6 below/Stefan Wermuth/REUTERS. Getty Images: 6 above/Kate Green/ Anadolu Agency, 7 above/Christopher Furlong, 7 centre/ Justin Tallis/AFP, 7 below/Jack Taylor. Mirrorpix: 5 below. Courtesy Barack Obama Presidential Library: 8 below right. Raworth and Raworth Photography: 3 below left and right.

Every reasonable effort has been made to trace copyright holders, but if there are any errors or omissions, Two Roads will be pleased to insert the appropriate acknowledgement in any subsequent printings or editions.

The Jo Cox Foundation

Building a positive legacy for Jo Cox MP
@Jo Cox Foundation

On the fifth anniversary of Jo's murder, the Foundation continues to look to the future – just as Jo would have done. Despite the many challenges our society faces, we remain optimistic, inspired by the many examples of people across the country showing the best of humanity on a daily basis. But our work wouldn't be possible without your support and dedication.

To find out more and offer your support, please visit our website: www.jocoxfoundation.org.

JCF is on social media: @jocoxfoundation, and if you'd like to find out more or get involved in creating your own More in Common group, please visit www.jocoxfoundation.org/moreincommon.